CROP TO CUP

Conversations over Coffee

By
Jonathan Kingsman

© 2020 Jonathan Kingsman
All rights reserved.
ISBN: 9798565777093

'It is doubtful if in all nature there is a more cunningly devised food package than the fruit of the coffee tree. It seems as if Good Mother Nature had said, 'This gift of Heaven is too precious to put up in any ordinary parcel. I shall design for it a casket worthy of its divine origin. And the casket shall have an inner seal that shall safeguard it from enemies, and that shall preserve its goodness until the day when, transported over the deserts and across the seas, it shall be broken open to be transmuted by the fires of friendship, and made to yield up its aromatic nectar in the Great Drink of Democracy.'

- William Ukers – All About Coffee, 1922

Contents

Preface 1

Introduction 3

Chapter 1: A Brief History of Coffee 5
   A Conversation with Andrea Illy 16

Chapter 2: How Coffee Conquered the World 27
   A conversation with Jan Lühmann 36

Chapter 3: From Crop to Cup 48
   A conversation with Teddy Esteve 59

Chapter 4: Commodity Coffee 69
   A conversation with Steve Wateridge 79

Chapter 5: Markets & Merchants 89
   A Conversation with Nicolas Tamari 99

Chapter 6: Market Intervention 110
   A conversation with Shirin Moayyad 119

Chapter 7: Merchant Traders 131
   A Conversation with Ben Clarkson 142

Chapter 8: Roasters 153
   A conversation with Martin Löfberg 164

Chapter 9: Speciality Coffee 175
   A conversation with Ric Rhinehart 182

Chapter 10: Café Culture 193
   A Conversation with Chris von Zastrow 204

Chapter 11: Economic Sustainability 215
   A Conversation with Daniel Watson 223

Chapter 12: Social sustainability..235
    A conversation with Jorge Cárdenas Gutiérrez.........................239
    A Conversation with Ricardo Arenas..243
Chapter 13: Environmental Sustainability..................................251
    A conversation with Bridget Carrington......................................259
Chapter 14: Certification..270
    A Conversation with Michelle Deugd..279
Chapter 15: Coffee & Health...289
    A Conversation with David Griswold..300
Chapter 16: Take-aways...310

Bibliography...319
Acknowledgements..323
About the Author...324

Preface

With coffee representing about one per cent of our GDP – and with Switzerland one of the largest trading platforms for green coffee – it is a pleasure to write these lines as President of the Swiss Coffee Trade Association (SCTA). Our 44 active members represent a volume of more than 50 per cent of global coffee exports. Our members are mainly Swiss-based trading and industrial companies. However, we also welcome non-Swiss based companies actively engaged in coffee trading, processing/roasting, or as service providers to our industry, for example, warehouse keepers, financial institutions and insurance companies.

The SCTA is globally and nationally well connected to other associations and institutions. We have strong links to the STSA - the Swiss Trading and Shipping Association - with whom we discuss common topics at government level. In this way, the SCTA helps its members to address regulatory and legislative questions.

The SCTA endorses the UN Guiding Principles for Human Rights and encourages its members to implement those. Sustainability is the number one topic for all of us. We are investing in a hands-on approach as well as in cooperation with the various initiatives. Climate change, together with social and economic factors, are immensely challenging issues, and I am proud of the membership in its willingness to face up to the situation. Sustainability is in our DNA, and we owe it to future generations to act; mindful of this, we have set up the SCTA NextGen.

Every October we organise a conference and a gala dinner, which attracts about 800 people. It has become the main coffee event in Europe and one of the leading coffee events in the world.

I suggested to Jonathan that he write this book after reading his previous work New Merchants of Grain; I felt that the coffee family would benefit from something similar. Although many books have been written about coffee, none have looked at our supply chain, nor at the critical role coffee merchants play – and the value they add - in the journey from Crop to Cup.

I was delighted when Jonathan accepted the challenge and even more delighted when he asked me to present the SCTA in a preface. He tells me that he has thoroughly enjoyed writing the book, and I am sure that you will get equal enjoyment in reading it.

But before you begin, may I suggest that you first make yourself a delicious cup of coffee!

Stay Safe & Healthy
Nicolas A Tamari

Introduction

'I never drink coffee at lunch. I find it keeps me awake for the afternoon.'

- Former US President Ronald Reagan

I trust you are following Nicolas' advice and reading this with a cup of coffee in your hand. If you are, then you are in good company. Coffee is arguably the world's favourite hot beverage with over 2.25 billion cups drunk every day.

As I write this, I am gently sipping on a cup of Lingtong Raja Toba from the tropical highlands on the Indonesian island of Sumatra.

I have been on a world tour since I started writing this book. My adventure began gently with Huehuetenango from Guatemala, with its notes of chocolate and fruit. I then travelled on through Colombia, Brazil, Kenya, Ethiopia, Uganda, Zimbabwe, and then back to Asia with a coffee from the Sigri Plantation in Papua New Guinea.

Coffee is an unusual commodity in that it is produced in developing countries and consumed in rich countries. Coffee and cocoa are the only agricultural commodities that directly connect consumers to third world producers. As people usually consume cocoa as chocolate, coffee has more of a direct connection. When you grind your coffee beans at home (as I have now learned to do), you are touching the same beans that the farmer picked on his farm.

Coffee not only connects the two hemispheres; it also connects the wealthy with the less affluent. With that comes enormous responsibility. We, as consumers, are directly responsible for the well-being of millions of coffee farmers around the world.

As well as being more connected, coffee is also more complex than other crops. Like most commodities, coffee trades on specifications stipulated in a contract, but it also trades on taste. Coffee traders need to be able 'cup' coffee – to differentiate it by taste. And its flavour, like fine wine, depends on its terroir - a mixture of climate, soil and altitude. It also depends on the skill of the millers who process it and of the roasters who roast it.

Switzerland, where I live, is the centre for the world coffee trade, accounting for more than 60 per cent of global transactions. Geneva and Zurich are important hubs, but the Olympic city of Lausanne is equally important. Starbucks' international trading office, which purchases the coffee for the chain's more than 30,000 coffee shops around the world, is situated in the centre of town.

Lausanne is also the headquarters of Nespresso, while Nestlé is in Vevey, just a short bicycle ride along Lake Leman. Not wanting to miss out, Keurig Green Mountain (now Keurig Dr Pepper) moved their coffee trading operations to Lausanne in 2015.

I live in Pully, a suburb of Lausanne. My home is less than two kilometres from the headquarters of ECOM, the world's second-largest coffee trader. And sometimes, when the wind is blowing from the north, I can smell coffee being roasted in Nestlé's factory in Orbe, 30 km away.

Without previously thinking about it, I live and – literally -- breath coffee.

I wanted to write this book to tell you the story of coffee and to introduce you to some of the people who bring you your morning 'cuppa'.

I hope you enjoy reading this book as much as I have enjoyed writing it.

Chapter 1:
A Brief History of Coffee

No matter what historians claimed, BC really stood for 'Before Coffee'.

— Cherise Sinclair

According to legend, coffee was first discovered when an Abyssinian goatherder called Kaldi noticed that his goats started dancing after eating the red berries from a coffee tree. Kaldi tried the berries himself and then gave some to his imam. The imam wasn't impressed and threw the beans into the fire in disgust, only to be surprised by the powerful aroma that the beans gave off. He retrieved the roasted beans, ground them up, and made a drink that kept him awake all night. He then got hold of some more beans, roasted them, and distributed them among his followers, called 'dervishes', to help keep them awake at night, during his long - and possibly rather tedious - sermons.

In his book Food of the Gods, Terence McKenna outlines the 'stoned ape' theory of human evolution, that human development – particularly language - began when apes came down from trees and ate psychedelic 'magic' mushrooms. It is perhaps lucky for us that coffee berries are a stimulant and not a psychedelic drug. Otherwise, goats, rather than humans, might have ended up ruling the world. (But then, mobile phones would have had to be considerably larger to account for goats' cloven hooves.)

The oft-repeated legend of Kaldi might make for good marketing, but it is almost certainly untrue. Coffee did originate in Abyssinia, and there are still an estimated 3-4,000 different varieties of coffee trees growing wild in present-day Ethiopia. The early Ethiopians, however, made their coffee from the leaves rather than the beans of the coffee tree. One theory is that those Abyssinian goats preferred the leaves to the berries, but a tea trader tells me that goats won't eat tea leaves because of the caffeine they contain. In that case, I don't see why goats would eat coffee leaves either.

Ethiopians in rural areas still drink coffee made from the roasted leaves of the coffee tree. They call it Kati or Kotea. There is an earlier version of the drink, now mostly extinct, called Amertassa, where the fresh-picked leaves are not roasted but instead left to dry in the shade for a few days.

The Oromo tribe from south-eastern Ethiopia is known to have made Kati and combined it with cow's milk to produce a more nourishing drink, Hoja. They also fried the coffee cherries in butter and salt, eating them as an energy-rich snack. The Oromo believe that the first coffee tree grew from the tears of the sky god as the god's tears fell on the body of a dead wizard.

The Ethiopians invaded and ruled Yemen for some 50 years in the 6th century, and they may have planted coffee trees while they were there. They still made their drinks from the coffee leaves, but they also chewed the beans.

Some 600 years later, a Sufi holy man by the name of Ali Ibn Omar al-Shadhili – later known as the 'Monk of Mokha' - is credited with making a drink from the beans, although with green, rather than roasted, beans. The Shadhilis are a Sufi sect, and they used coffee as a religious drink. By the end of the 15th century, Shadhili dervishes had spread coffee deep into the Arabian Peninsula and throughout North Africa. You can still order a coffee in Algeria by asking for a cup of 'al-Shadhili.'

The first reference to coffee as we know it today was in the early 15th century when the Arab mystic al-Dhabhani saw Ethiopians drinking 'qahwa', now the Arab word for coffee. The Ethiopians, however, call coffee 'buna', which also means bean.

As coffee gained popularity throughout the Arab world, it began to be used less as a religious drink and more as a social stimulant. In 1511, Khair-Beg, the governor of Mecca, ruled that coffee was like wine and hence banned by the Koran. He ordered the city's coffee houses to be closed, only to have the ban overturned by his boss, the Sultan of Cairo.

Despite its growing popularity, coffee production was slow to pick up; it was only after the Ottomans occupied Yemen in 1536 that they began to extensively cultivate the crop in the country. The Ottomans exported the coffee from the port of Mocha, and it became known as 'mocha'.

When the first English sailor reached the port in 1606, he wrote that there were over thirty-five merchant ships, some from as far away as India, waiting to load the precious green beans.

Some of the coffee was shipped to Alexandria in Egypt and then on to Venice. Still, mostly it stayed within the Ottoman empire, reaching Damascus and Istanbul by the middle of the century. By then, coffee was no longer considered just a religious drink, but also a social one. By the end of the 16th century, there were over 600 coffee shops operating in Istanbul.

The way of brewing coffee changed as it travelled. Arabic coffee (qahwa) is a light-coloured liquid made by lightly toasting the beans, crushing them with various spices such as cardamom, and then boiling them in water. Turkish coffee (kahve) is made with more darkly roasted beans and brought to the boil at least twice but without spices.

For a time, the Ottomans successfully prevented coffee cultivation from spreading outside the area of Mocha; they refused to let berries leave the country unless they were first boiled in water to prevent their germination. However, exports had grown to such a level that it was impossible to stop some un-boiled beans from getting through. As Muslim pilgrims returned to their homes, they took coffee beans with them.

One such pilgrim, Buba Budan, is credited in 1600 with smuggling out some beans by taping seven of them to his stomach. He took them back to India and planted the beans next to his hut at Chickmaglur in the mountains of Mysore. Buba Budan is now (rightly) revered as a saint, but it was not until 1840 that the English began the commercial cultivation of coffee in India; the plantations extend now from the extreme north of Mysore down to Tuticorin.

In 1614, Dutch traders brought a coffee plant from Mocha to Amsterdam, and by mid-century, they had taken plants to Ceylon (now Sri Lanka) and Dutch Malaba (now Cochin), where they started small plantations. From there, in 1696, the Dutch took cuttings from the plants to their colonial island of Java. A flood washed away the early seedlings, but the Dutch tried again three years later, this time successfully. In 1706, the first Java coffee had reached Amsterdam; some coffee plants were grown successfully in Amsterdam's botanical gardens.

During the 17th century, 'Mocha' and 'Java' became synonyms for coffee; they are still so today. The port of Mocha went of business with the opening of the Suez Canal in 1869. Coffee continues to be grown on the Indonesian island of Java. Still, the early arabica plantations were devastated by coffee rust (Hemileia vastatrix) in the 1700s and gradually replaced with lower quality robusta.

In 1714, the mayor of Amsterdam gave a coffee tree to King Louis XIV; he had his gardeners plant it in the Jardin des Plantes in Paris. The tree may have been the progenitor of most of the coffees in the French colonies and throughout the Americas, but only due to the stubbornness of a certain Gabriel Mathieu de Clieu, an aristocratic French naval officer based in Martinique.

The dashing Mr de Clieu obtained several of the plants from the French court through a French 'lady of quality' with whom he had a romantic liaison. (Mr de Clieu was married four times during his lifetime, the last time at the age of 83.)

He took one of the plants with him back to Martinique, embarking at Nantes in 1723. The merchant ship was attacked by pirates, hit by a violent storm, and then becalmed for a month. De Clieu shared his precious water ration with his coffee plant. They both survived the voyage, and De Clieu harvested the first coffee beans in Martinique in 1726. Descendants of that one plant may have spread through the West Indies and Central America, reaching Guatemala in 1750-1760.

The oft-repeated story of Mr de Clieu is a romantic one; it may even be partially correct. When Mr de Clieu arrived in Martinique in 1723, coffee had been growing in Saint-Domingue since 1715, and in Surinam since 1718. This coffee may have made its way to South America via the Isle de Bourbon, today's Reunion, hence giving the variety its name of Bourbon. The plants from Martinique may have replaced these earlier coffee plants in those regions, but it is not clear. In any case, the romantic and dashing Mr de Clieu remains a hero in the small world of French coffee historians.

The equally romantic and dashing Mr Francisco de Melo Palheta is a hero among Portuguese coffee historians, credited with successfully introducing coffee into Brazil in either 1723 or 1727 (depending on which version of the story you believe).

Mr Palheta, a Portuguese diplomat, was sent to Guiana where he had an affair with the wife of the colony's French governor. As he was leaving to return to Brazil, his lover gave him a bouquet of flowers; hidden inside were coffee seeds. Once home in Para, he planted the seeds and began, with limited success, the first commercial production of coffee in Brazil.

It was only in 1760 that a certain Joao Alberto Castello Branco brought a coffee tree to Rio de Janeiro from Goa, Portuguese India. The trees thrived on the region's well-drained red soil. In 1774, a Belgian monk presented some coffee seeds to the Capuchin monastery in Rio in 1774. (It may not be a coincidence if the coffee in your hand is a cappuccino!) Later, the bishop of Rio, Joachim Bruno, encouraged the propagation of the plant in Rio, Minas, Espirito Santo, and Sao Paulo.

Elsewhere, the Spanish voyager Don Francisco Navarro introduced coffee into Costa Rica from Cuba in 1779. A priest, José Antonio Mohedano, brought some Martinique coffee seeds to Venezuela in 1784. Coffee cultivation was first cultivated in Mexico in 1790 and was widespread in the State of Vera Cruz by 1817. By 1825, farmers had planted seeds from Rio de Janeiro in the Hawaiian Islands.

In 1878, the British planted coffee for the first time in British Central Africa – and by 1901, they had introduced it into British East Africa, with seeds from Reunion. In 1897, the French introduced the crop into their colonies in Indochina. The British introduced it into Queensland, Australia in 1896.

Coffee is a labour-intensive crop to grow, to tend, and to harvest. To meet the demand for labour, European colonialists imported slaves from Africa to work on the plantations. Coffee followed on the heels of sugar in a triangular trade that depended on the prevailing winds in the Atlantic: manufactured goods sailed to Africa to buy slaves; slaves sailed to the Americas to purchase coffee; coffee sailed to Europe to buy goods for Africa.

By 1788, French-occupied Haiti was supplying half of the world's coffee. Conditions in the plantations were atrocious, with slaves routinely beaten, tortured, and killed by their European masters. In 1791, the slaves revolted, burning the farms to the ground and killing the plantation owners. The revolt was successful, but coffee production collapsed. Napoleon tried to regain the island in 1801, but by 1803, he had admitted defeat. Famously, he exclaimed: 'Damn coffee! Damn colonies!' Today, Haiti produces very little coffee.

Brazilian coffee plantations also relied on slave labour. Over history, Brazil has imported more slaves than any other country in the world - an estimated four million of them. The British abolished slavery in the British Empire in 1833, and Brazil banned the import of slaves in 1850. However, Brazil's coffee growers still needed labour; they found it in 'indentured' workers, a system where (mostly young) people paid for their passage to the New World by working for an employer for a certain number of years, usually five or seven. After they had completed their indenture, they were free to go off on their own.

Once at their destination, employers had little interest in looking after their indentured workers. Indeed, they looked after their slaves better; they owned a slave for life while they only had the indentured worked for five or seven years. Plantation owners worked their indentured workers harder than their slaves; they also gave them worse housing and fed them less. In 1856, Swiss and German indentured workers in Brazil revolted over their conditions.

In 1884 the Brazilian government changed strategy and agreed to pay the cost of transporting foreign workers to the country; by 1914, more than one million immigrants had arrived to work on the coffee farms.

In 1776, Adam Smith criticised slavery in his book The Wealth of Nations: 'The experience of all ages and nations, I believe, demonstrates that the work done by slaves, though it appears to cost only their maintenance, is, in the end, the dearest of many.' Unfortunately, it took Brazil's plantation owners over a century to come to the same conclusion. In 1888, the Brazilian government passed the 'Golden Law', freeing the remaining three-quarters of a million slaves still in the country.

In many parts of Latin America, the coffee industry, rather than importing slaves from Africa, depended on the semi-slave labour of the indigenous populations. In his book Coffeeland, Augustine Sedgewick describes how El Salvador's plantation owners forced native inhabitants off their land, preventing them from growing their food and giving them no choice but to work in the coffee fields.

Native workers were paid partly in cash but mainly in tortilla and beans. Plantation owners uprooted any food crops that sprung up accidentally among their coffee trees to ensure that if the population wanted to eat, they had no choice but to work in the coffee plantations. Their choice was to work or starve.

When coffee prices collapsed during the Great Depression, local protest labour movements turned into a full-blown revolution. For the rest of the 20th century, El Salvador teetered between dictatorship and rebellion, culminating in the terrible Salvadorian civil war of the 1980s.

The collapse in coffee production in Haiti in the early 1800s prompted the Dutch to encourage production in their colony of Java. In his novel, Max Havelaar, a Dutch civil servant by the name of Eduard Douwes Dekker described how Dutch landowners forced Javanese natives to harvest coffee for a pittance. Dekker noted that whole villages died of starvation as a result.

As I wrote above, there are between three and four thousand different varietals of coffee native to Ethiopia – and they still grow there. However, only two varietals, Typicia and Bourbon, spread around the world, forming the basis of modern arabica coffee cultivation.

In 1898, a certain Emil Laurent discovered a species of coffee growing wild in the Belgian Congo. He, as was the custom of the time, named it after himself: Coffea Laurentii. It later became known as Coffea robusta. The world had been searching for new coffee varietals after rust disease had first appeared in Sri Lanka in 1869. Within a few years, it had wiped out most of the coffee plantations throughout Asia.

Hopes had been high when a new variety of arabica coffee, Coffea libericia, had been discovered growing wild in Liberia, but that too was susceptible to rust. Coffea robusta, was, well, more robust. It was also higher-yielding and thrived at lower altitudes than its arabica cousin.

The only problem was that it tasted harsher than arabica. (It also contains more caffeine.) In 1912, the New York Coffee Exchange concluded that robusta was 'a practically worthless bean' and banned it from the Exchange. It is still banned today. (The London Exchange accepts robusta.)

The Dutch began replacing their disease-stricken arabica plants with the hardier disease-resistant robusta, growing it among the rubber trees in Java and Sumatra. By 1920, 80 per cent of the coffee produced on Java was robusta.

The French introduced robusta into their colonies in Indochina (Vietnam is now the world's largest producer of robusta coffee), and the British did the same in India and in East Africa, where it grew particularly well in what is now Uganda. The Brazilians at first tried to ban it, but then later rescinded the ban. Brazilian robusta, or conilon, accounts for about 30 per cent of the country's total coffee consumption.

Sometime during the 1940s, Bourbon arabica varietals bred with robusta to produce Timor Hybrid. It combined the rust-disease resistance and higher yield of robusta with some of the flavour characteristics of arabica. It quickly spread to the Americas where it crossbred with Caturra in Brazil to produce an even higher-yielding varietal by the name of Catimor. Unfortunately, it tasted even worse than the original Caturra.

Robusta coffee did, however, find a welcoming home in instant (soluble) coffee. In 1906, a Belgium with the unlikely name of George Washington came up with the idea of producing crystals from brewed coffee. In 1910, he left Guatemala where he had been living, and moved to New York where he started G. Washington's Refined Coffee.

His coffee found a ready market with the US Army during the First World War; soldiers could quickly prepare it in the trenches. Demand was so great that other roasters jumped on the bandwagon but, when the war ended, the market dried up.

In 1929, the Brazilian government was desperately looking for new outlets for their over-production; they asked Nestlé if they could develop a coffee stock cube. At that time, Brazil was carrying so many stocks that they used coffee to fuel railway locomotives; they even burned it in giant bonfires.

It took Nestlé a few years to come up with a product that met their standards. They launched Nescafé, a spray-dried product, in 1938. It was just in time for World War II and another spike in demand from soldiers on the front lines. Along with Nescafé and G Washington, ten other companies sold soluble coffees during the war, and the US Army requisitioned their entire production. Instant coffee became so crucial to military morale among the GI Joes that it soon earned the nickname of a Cuppa Joe.

By the mid-1950s, instant coffee accounted for nearly 20 per cent of the coffee consumed in the USA. In the UK, coffee consumption doubled during the 1950s, coinciding with the launch of advertising breaks on commercial television in 1955. Viewers had time to make a cup of instant coffee during the commercials, but not to brew a pot of tea. (Tea producers fought back with the invention of the teabag.) By the 1990s, 90 per cent of the coffee sold in the UK was instant.

But robusta was not only used in instant coffee. Its availability and cheapness led to strong demand in Europe. By 1960, it accounted for 75 per cent of French consumption. Dutch and Belgian consumers also developed a taste for the harsher, darker coffee, while Portuguese consumers preferred their espressos, called bica, made with robusta from their colony Angola. In Italy, roasters also began to favour robusta for their espresso blends because of its thicker crema.

And talking of espressos and Italy, let me introduce you to Andrea Illy, the King of Italian espresso coffee!

A Conversation with Andrea Illy

Good morning, Andrea. Could you tell me a little about your company's heritage?

It is the Italian and Austrian heritage that has made coffee great. We have the good fortune to share both heritages.

My grandfather was Hungarian, but at the time of the Austro-Hungarian empire. He lived most of his youth in Vienna; this is where he fell in love with coffee and decided that coffee was what he wanted to do in his life. When he came to Trieste, the city was still part of the Austro-Hungarian Empire. He started his coffee business with a Viennese heritage.

Trieste and my family share the same heritage: both started as Austro-Hungarian, but both became over the decades very much Italian. We nurture both. Our Italian heritage is about coffee and particularly espresso coffee. Our Austrian heritage is more about coffee as a hot drink: filter or café latté. We respect them both!

Why does illycaffè produce blended rather than single-origin coffee?

Blending gives you the richness and the complexity of the aroma spectrum. If you listen to a single violinist, you can discern specific notes. However, if you listen to a symphony orchestra, you get the richness and the complexity of the composition – the full spectrum of sounds. Blending is to coffee what a symphony orchestra is to music.

Blending gives you balance in the coffee. It enables you to compensate for the disparities of different origins. For example, Brazil is famous for its chocolatey aroma, whereas Central America is famous for its flowery or fruity fragrance. You can also compensate acidity with the bitterness, say, of a sun-dried coffee.

Blending gives you consistency. We want a product which is always of precisely the same quality.

You can only obtain these three fundamental attributes by blending. I don't believe in pure origin. Pure origins are suitable as a kind of a tasting at a coffee experience, but if you are seeking the best possible quality, then it has to be a blend.

Our blend consists of nine origins. Of course, the better the quality at the source, the better the blend.

How do you control quality at the origin?

We work hand-in-hand with our coffee growers to improve their agronomical practices and produce a coffee that is better from the taste profile, better from the nutritional profile and better from the sustainability profile. We want to have everything controlled, including social sustainability. Workers on a coffee estate can only produce an ultimate coffee quality if they are well looked after and well educated. They also have to be loyal.

We want to have total respect for the environment. We don't want the indiscriminate usage of chemicals: fertilisers and pesticides. It is all about applying agronomical practices which are superior to market standards. We want to elevate these quality standards that are unique to illycaffè. The coffees that we buy are superior to the best market standards.

You mentioned loyalty.

We want to perpetuate our supply chain year after year, forever. To do this, we need loyalty. We want the same growers to sell us their coffee every year, and every year to make their coffee a little bit better. This requires us to build a long-term relationship, a community.

Our community is called 'Circolo Illy'. We get a unique product in a reliable, fully traceable, fully sustainable supply chain.

Do you purchase your coffee on a flat price, or do you buy it on a premium against the futures market?

We buy more and more now on long-term contacts. It gives the growers the certainty they need to make the necessary investments in their farms and their trees to improve their practices and their quality. It gives them a predetermined profit of around 30 per cent on average, no matter what the crazy world price does!

A flat price long-term contract is our preferred method, although we still buy some of our coffee on a differential against the futures.

Can sustainability certification schemes, along with Fairtrade, raise grower incomes if they don't first improve quality?

The current certification systems are based on solidarity, which means that consumers pay a premium price no matter the quality differentiation. This is a significant first step toward sustainability. Still, it would be better and more sustainable if consumers paid a premium price not just for solidarity, but also for better quality.

I define 'sustainability' in terms of quality. I wish that the certification systems would gradually upgrade their protocols towards sustainability, not only solidarity. This is important because solidarity has reached a limit. Many consumers don't receive better quality when they purchase certified coffee. They buy it occasionally just to feel good.

On the other side, the system has created an oversupply of certified coffee. As a consequence, many growers have to sell their certified coffee at the same price as their non-certified coffee. In that sense, the system is a little bit broken. However, certification has been positive for the industry because it has created a lot of awareness. The growers themselves have benefitted because the certification companies have helped them to manage their farms better.

So, I remain positive about certification. I think it is part of the fundamental long-term trend of coffee de-commoditisation.

Could you tell me about your University of Coffee?

We have organised our University of Coffee into three different departments: one for growers; one for hospitality professionals; and one for coffee connoisseurs. For the last ten years, we have run a master's degree in coffee. We take twenty students from all over the world; they stay with us for six months.

As a company, we serve nearly 9 million cups of coffee per day. To make sure that each cup is as good as the last, we have to educate our farmers, and we have to educate our baristas. But we also want to educate our consumers to appreciate coffee.

Coffee still has a long way to go to reach the same level of sophistication that exists in the wine industry. By that, I mean sophistication in terms of product expertise: how you produce your wine and how you drink it.

I also mean sophistication in terms of narrative. A glass of wine in a restaurant will cost you a minimum of 6-8 euros, while a cup of coffee will cost you 2-3 euros. Coffee is as good as wine, and it should be as expensive as wine.

It is not healthy to drink too much wine. But coffee makes you live better and longer. Coffee is a beverage of success: socially and professionally, and for your health.

My dream is to bring coffee culture to the same level of nobleness as premium wines. This means approaching coffee in a sophisticated way, and this is what we teach our students.

When you joined illycaffè in 1990, you introduced something called the 'Total Quality Programme'.

When the third generation of the family gradually took over the business, we first reorganised the commercial department and started our marketing department. My brother Riccardo, who now takes care of all the non-coffee businesses, introduced a powerful brand value proposition which substantially accelerated sales.

However, we still organised production in a way which could not sustain this growth. We had no process automation. Our paradigm shift was to introduce Total Quality in the Japanese way – the Toyota model - with standardised processes and controls while delegating all the quality control and assurance to the production people. We introduced automation that allowed us to achieve almost zero defects in our beans.

Is it the quality that enabled you to build the brand?

Yes, to build a successful brand, you must have a narrative, an image, and a product. The question is: Which comes first? Do you start with an incredible product that you narrate to the consumer, or do you start with a beautiful narrative around which you then build the product? We were in the first case: we had this unique product; we started narrating the coffee culture, and we created our image, our point of difference and our philosophy around it.

illycaffè has been called 'the Armani of coffee'. Is illycaffè a luxury brand?

It's not a luxury brand. It is a high-end brand, what we call 'altagamma'. Luxury is more inaccessible and exclusive. Coffee is by its very nature inclusive. I'm proud to say that unwealthy people with a good palate can enjoy our coffee even though they pay a premium price for it.

Our coffee has all the paradigms of luxury: the superior quality and the savoir-faire in both production and consumption. It has a beautiful image. It has everything that a luxury brand has except the exclusiveness. It is an inclusive product.

Are you afraid that if you stretch the brand too much, it will lose its high-end appeal?

Yes, this is one of the reasons why we don't want to sell illycaffè. We want to limit its size. We have already made a long-term decision as a family that when illycaffè becomes so big that it starts to lose its brand equity, then we will do other businesses. With this strategic goal in mind, we have begun chocolate and other non-coffee activities, but of course, with the same philosophy of making only the best.

We don't want to be a giant in coffee nor to stretch our brand in a way that it becomes a multi-billion mass-market premium, rather than a high-end, product.

There is another reason we don't want to grow our coffee business too much, and that is our supply chain. We can buy now maybe 0.6 per cent of world production of coffee with our standards. If we do an excellent job over the next few decades, we will be able to reach one per cent of total world production, but no more. One per cent would be now 1.5 million bags, which is a small brand in the Top Ten.

How do you maintain quality across your stores?

There are three aspects to running a café: coffee; food and beverage; and service.

As far as coffee is concerned, we control quality at the point of sale in the same way we do with all our customers throughout our 140 countries. We created the University of Coffee to transfer and share knowledge with the barista at the point of sale – to make the perfect espresso and the perfect cappuccino.

We also control quality by using the best technology - not only choosing the best machines but retrofitting them for the exact illy parameters. We have developed our preparation technology and digitalised it so that we can control the process remotely.

It's a mix of knowledge and technology. We still have a long way to go because not all of our cafés are 100 per cent perfect, particularly when you consider the most sophisticated and demanding coffee, the Italian espresso.

As far as service is concerned in our mono-brand illycaffè, we created a specific department for food service management, led by one of the best professionals in the industry; she has been in coffee shop management for over 30 years. It is, of course, all about management systems; it's an entire division of the company dedicated to service.

As far as food is concerned, it is about defining high standards in terms of recipes. Some of our cafés have kitchens, but most of the time, we work with premium food commissaries that we control thoroughly for the quality of the product.

But still, it's a nightmare! I don't wish anybody to complicate their business model with such a problematic industry like running a café. It is very detail-oriented and requires a specific skill set.

Could you tell me a little about your positioning in the single-serve – or capsule – market?

Our goal was to make single-serve machines better than barista machines, but they are different technologies. Our single-serve *Iperespresso* capsules involve a two-stage process of hyper-infusion and emulsion that produces more aroma, more flavour, and more crema; it gives a better mouthfeel. It is a different product than an espresso.

I understand that illycaffè pioneered the single-serve system, but from your earlier comments, I appreciate that you went for the quality rather than the market share. Is that correct?

Illycaffè pioneered single portion coffee. We did not pioneer capsules. My father did not want to do capsules for environmental reasons; he was ahead of his time in that respect. Our original single-serve system is a paper one, fully compostable and environmentally friendly. This system still exists. It is called 'easy serving espresso'.

When other companies started doing capsules, we stayed with our paper pods for nearly twenty years. Eventually, when it became clear that the market was shifting strongly towards capsules, we realised that we had also to do capsules.

With paper pods, you need secondary packaging to keep the paper pods fresh. You also need an extraction system in your machine. Capsules are self-preserving, and the devices don't need an extraction unit in themselves. They are also more consistent in terms of quality.

We decided to do capsules, but we also decided we wanted to do the highest performing capsule ever done. It was our goal when we developed *Iperespresso*.

We also decided not to try to capture the dominant position in the market. It would have been unrealistic considering our limited means and the unlimited means of our competitor. We decided to stay prudent, to follow our strategy and course, and not be distracted by this dominant player.

Competition is not only negative; it is also positive. The competition helped to create a market which otherwise would not have been possible. We would not have had such a considerable coffee capsule market without such a massive investment by such a gigantic company.

Do you see ready-to-drink – RTD - coffee as a significant trend for the future?

Yes and no. It is the best alternative when you are on the go. It is also better than lousy freshly brewed coffee made by a terrible machine. But freshly brewed coffee is still perceived to be superior. It is challenging to make RTD coffee better than a fresh brew. In terms of value, freshly brewed is cheaper than ready-to-drink.

There is the issue of stabilisation. Freshly brewed coffee is not stable; it oxidises. To produce RTD coffee, you have to stabilise it, and this modifies the aroma profile. It is why the milk based RTD coffees are more successful than black ones. It is a chemical limitation.

What has been driving the recent consolidation in the coffee sector?

Profit. Investors discovered that coffee is a sustainable, profitable and anti-cyclical business. Previously, except for the top three guys, it was quite fragmented. In that sense, the coffee sector is rather like the beer industry, which has seen similar consolidation. JAB has been driving the consolidation in coffee, and they are now challenging the leader, Nestlé. I think in volume terms they have passed Nestlé, but not in revenues.

I don't know if JAB has completely recovered their investment; they have invested a lot of money to acquiring so many brands, but it makes sense from a strategic point of view.

I'm sure potential buyers have approached you.

Our strength is in our heritage and our uniqueness. This heritage is entirely based on being family-owned - the thought leadership in the industry, and governance that never compromises. Our dream is to regenerate the same model generation after generation, to grow illycaffè sustainably, and to transfer it to the next generation in a way that we can perpetuate the family brand.

Our strategy is to be a leader in quality, not in volumes. I believe that in business you either lead quality or you lead quantity, but not both. Ours is a niche business. Our product is unique and recognised to be superior by tens of millions of consumers around the world. We can command a premium price which allows us to protect our niche.

Our business model is unique, starting from the way we source our coffee. We pioneered direct sourcing in the industry beginning in 1991, and we now buy 100 per cent of our beans directly from our growers. They produce coffee precisely according to our standards, which enables us to control our quality from plant to cup.

Why change it? We have plans to grow in the next decade, strategies that allow us to develop autonomously. We are not a greedy family. We're not looking at cashing out; we reinvest all our profits back into the company to continue to grow.

As a family, we have been educated to be at the service of the company, and not vice versa.

Your company motto is 'Live Happily'. Could you please tell me a little about that?

Happiness has two philosophical definitions: one from Aristotle and one by Epicure. For Aristotle, happiness is living in a world of virtue, combining altruism, knowledge and wisdom – living for the greater good.

The Epicurean definition is about hedonism. It is about the three pleasures in life: the 'natural necessary'; the 'natural unnecessary'; and the 'unnatural unnecessary'. Epicure says that you should forget about the 'unnatural unnecessary'; it will destroy you. You should be moderate with the 'natural unnecessary', but you should take full advantage of the natural, necessary pleasure.

I consider coffee a 'natural unnecessary' pleasure for the 1.5 billion coffee drinkers around the world - in terms of joy, in terms of energy, in terms of health, in terms of social life, in terms of mood.

And each cup that you drink helps the at least 25 million people in the coffee supply chains – people who depend on coffee for their human development and their quality of life. Most of these people live in developing countries, and they have no alternative to coffee. By taking your little treasure every day, several times a day, each time you know that you are helping a family in Ethiopia, or Guatemala or wherever.

It is the dream of coffee.

Thank you, Andrea, for your time and input!

Chapter 2:
How Coffee Conquered the World

Coffee is the common man's gold, and like gold, it brings every person the feeling of luxury and nobility.

- Sheik-Abd-al-Kadir, In Praise of Coffee, 1587

When in 1511, Kair Bey, the governor of Mecca, ordered the city's coffee shops to be closed and the coffee in the city's warehouses burnt, he didn't expect his coffee-loving boss, the Sultan of Egypt, to override the proclamation. Nor did he expect to be later tortured to death for extortion and public theft – perhaps partially in revenge for his earlier ban on coffee-drinking.

In 1524, his successor once again closed Mecca's coffee shops, but wisely still allowed coffee to be drunk at home. He later allowed coffee shops to reopen, even if the government continued to view them as hotbeds of revolutionary ideas. Coffee, even back then, made people think; it made them question authority, and it arguably kept them from their mosques.

In 1534, a preacher in one of Cairo's mosques had had enough. He claimed that coffee drinkers were not 'true believers', and he encouraged his congregation to attack the city's coffee shops and beat up their customers. The town became divided between pro-coffee and anti-coffee groups, and it took the intervention of the city's chief justice to calm things down.

When the Ottomans introduced coffee into Constantinople from Egypt in 1517, it caused similar disturbances, and it wasn't until 1554 that the city dared open its first coffee shop. The peace was short-lived; in 1570, preachers ruled that it was a greater sin to enter a coffee house than it was to enter a tavern. The coffee houses were once again closed, but coffee 'speak-easies' sprung up: they continued to sell coffee, but behind closed doors.

These places for illicit coffee-drinking continued to operate until the Grand Vizier Kuprili clamped down on them during the Cretan War of 1645 – 1649. He feared that they had once again become hotbeds of sedition. Anyone found selling coffee was beaten; second offenders were sewn into a leather bag and thrown into the Bosporus. The Grand Vizier did, however, allow the taverns to stay open; he saw alcohol drinkers as less of a threat to his regime than coffee drinkers. The Grand Vizier ended the ban once the war had ended, and coffee has been freely sold in Constantinople (Istanbul) ever since.

Coffee became so indispensable for the Ottomans that it was a legitimate cause of divorce if a man refused or neglected to give coffee to his wife. (Maybe it still should be.)

Venetian merchants introduced coffee to Europe towards the end of the 16th century, at about the same time as Dutch merchants introduced tea – but about a century after the Spanish conquistadors introduced cocoa.

Coffee proved no less controversial in Europe than it had been in Arabia. A group of Catholic priests asked Pope Clement VIII to ban it, claiming it was an invention of Satan. The Pope sampled a cup and exclaimed: 'Why, this Satan's drink is so delicious that it would be a pity to let the infidels have exclusive use of it. We shall fool Satan by baptising it and making it a truly Christian beverage.' Even with the Pope's blessing, consumers used it initially for medicinal purposes; it wasn't until 1645 that Venice saw its first coffee shop open.

Coffee made it to France during the middle of the 17th century, introduced by Marseilles merchants. The first coffee house opened in Marseilles in 1671. Physicians were against its use as a drink, arguing that, 'it burned up the blood and induced palsies, impotence, and leanness, from all of which we must necessarily conclude that coffee is hurtful to the greater part of the inhabitants of Marseilles.'

Meanwhile, in 1669, Soliman Aga, the Turkish ambassador, arrived in Paris with a large sack of coffee beans. He stayed in Paris for less than a year, but by the time he had left the city, coffee had become all the rage among the fashionable classes. In 1672, an Armenian by the name of Pascal opened Paris's first coffee shop in Saint Germain. By 1720, there were around 280 cafés in the city; by 1750 there were a thousand; by 1790 there were 1,800.

In 1637, Nathaniel Conopios, a Greek student at Balliol College, Oxford, is credited with being the first person to drink coffee in England. He was undoubtedly the first western student to use coffee to help him revise for his exams. Coffee was so popular among the students that they encouraged a certain Arthur Tillyard, 'apothecary and Royalist', to sell 'coffee publicly in his house against All Soules College'. Royalist students continued to meet at Tillyard's, eventually forming the Royal Society, now the world's oldest independent scientific academy.

A manservant by the name of Jacob opened the UK's first coffee house in 1650 in Oxford, but he possibly only made the drink for his master and his friends. Pasqua Rosee, an Armenian from Smyrna, is credited with opening the first coffee house in London in 1652; within ten years, 82 licenced coffee shops were operating in the capital.

Pasqua Rosee published a handbill to promote his new business, claiming. 'It will prevent drowsiness and make one fit for business.' Indeed, it did, and the city's business community migrated from the taverns to the coffee shops to conduct their affairs. The most famous coffee shop, Lloyds, was opened in 1688.

Coffee was first mentioned in English law in 1660 when the government imposed a duty of four pence on every gallon of coffee sold.

English women were far from enthusiastic about the growing habit of coffee consumption. In 1674, they published a pamphlet, the Women's Petition against Coffee, that complained that coffee led their men to 'trifle away their time, scald their chops, and spend their money, all for a base, black, thick, nasty bitter stinking, nauseous puddle water'.'

King Charles didn't like coffee either, but not for the same reason. He was worried that the coffee houses were becoming centres of sedition against his reign. On 23rd December 1675, he issued a proclamation closing all of the nation's coffee houses, claiming that they were the 'great resort of idle and disaffected persons (who) misspend much of their time, which might and probably would be employed in and about their lawful calling and affairs'.

He claimed the coffee houses were places where 'divers false, malicious and scandalous reports are devised and spread abroad to the defamation of His Majesty's Government, and the disturbance of the peace and the quiet of the realm'.

The proclamation was to prove to be one of the UK's shortest-lived laws. The public outcry was such that the King, fearing a genuine rebellion, suspended the law two weeks later, on 8th January 1676, two days before it was due to go into force.

As often happens, he needn't have worried. Having lost control of the coffee trade to the Dutch and the French, the British East India Company was more interested in promoting tea rather than coffee among the British. The company launched a campaign that described tea as 'the cup that cheers'; by the middle of the 1700s, tea had taken over from coffee as the nation's favoured drink.

Coffee arrived in Germany in the late 17th century and began to find favour among the fashionable classes. It was so pervasive in society that, in 1732, Johann Sebastian Bach wrote his Coffee Cantata in which a young lady begs her father to let her drink coffee. She describes the drink as 'lovelier than a thousand kisses'. Without it, she says, she becomes 'like a dried-up piece of goat'.

Coffee was as controversial in Germany as it was elsewhere. In 1777, Frederick the Great wrote: 'It is disgusting to notice the increase in the quantity of coffee used by my subjects and the like amount of money that goes out of the country in consequence. My people must drink beer. His Majesty was brought up on beer, and so were his ancestors.'

The King tried to limit coffee consumption but failed. Ludwig van Beethoven was obsessed with the drink, apparently counting out precisely 60 beans to make every cup.

The Ottoman Empire's siege of Vienna was a turning point in European history. The Turks attacked the city on 7th July 1683, cutting it off from the world. The Austrian Emperor Leopold escaped the city and joined up with Austrian and Polish forces waiting to launch a counterattack. They asked for a volunteer to pass messages through enemy lines to those trapped in the city. They found one in a Polish soldier by the name of Franz Georg Kolschitzky, who had previously worked as an interpreter for the Turkish army. He made several trips back and forth behind enemy lines and is considered a hero to this day.

The Austrians finally defeated the Turks on 12th September 1683. The Turkish army fled, leaving behind their supplies, including 500 bags of coffee. The Viennese didn't know what to do with the coffee and began to burn it. Kolschitzky recognised the smell from his time in Constantinople and rushed to its rescue. He said that if no one else wanted the stuff, he would willingly take it.

No one objected, and he began selling coffee from house to house, serving it in little cups from a wooden platter. To make it more palatable to the Viennese, he filtered out the grounds and added milk, something that the Ottomans had never done. To thank him for his bravery Vienna's Municipal Council gave him a house at 30 Haidgasse, where he opened the Blue Bottle coffee house, arguably the first coffee shop in Vienna.

Napoleon Bonaparte was a lover of coffee and once said: 'Strong coffee, and plenty awakens me. It gives me warmth, an unusual force, a pain that is not without pleasure. I would rather suffer than be senseless.' However, during the Continental Blockade, when the British prevented ships from entering or leaving French territories, Napoleon had little choice but to seek a coffee substitute. He found it in home-grown chicory. The blockade was imposed in 1808 and lifted in 1814, but to this day many French people still drink a chicory-coffee mix.

Chicory also found its way into Germany where Frederick the Great encouraged its consumption to reduce the amount spent on coffee imports. The Germans were unimpressed, and Otto von Bismarck, who lived from 1815 until 1898, detested the mix. One day, while with the Prussian army in France, he entered a country inn and asked the owner to bring him all the chicory that he had in the house. The man obeyed and handed Bismarck a can of the stuff.

'Are you sure this is all you have?' asked Bismarck.

'Yes, my lord,' the innkeeper replied. 'Every grain.'

'Then,' replied Bismarck, firmly holding on to the can. 'Go and make me a pot of coffee!'

Chicory made a reappearance during the American Civil War when, in 1861, naval blockades cut off the port of New Orleans, at the time one of the US's largest coffee ports. Louisianans began mixing chicory with coffee and acquired a taste for it, continuing to drink it even after coffee became readily available again.

Coffee was probably first bought to North America by Captain John Smith, who founded the Colony of Virginia at Jamestown in 1607. He is said to have acquired the coffee habit during his previous travels in Turkey. There is no record of coffee amongst the cargo of the Mayflower in 1620, although the early settlers are believed to have used a wooden mortar and pestle to grind coffee.

The Dutch may have bought coffee into New York when it was New Amsterdam (from 1624 to 1664), but the first official record of coffee in North America was in 1670 in the colony of New England. In 1683, William Penn bought coffee for his settlement on the River Delaware, paying 18 shillings and nine pence a pound in the New York market, the equivalent in today's money of over $135 per pound, a price that current day growers can only dream about!

Just as they had done in the UK, the British East India Company tried to convert their North American colonies to tea rather than coffee. Their plans hit a brick wall when in 1865 the British King George imposed duties on imports into the US of paint, oil, lead, glass and tea. The colonists resisted with the now-famous cry of 'no taxation without representation', and the British Parliament repealed all the duties except for tea. On 16th December 1773, a group of colonists staged the Boston Tea Party, dressing up as indigenous Indians and throwing some newly arrived chests of tea into the harbour.

From that moment on, drinking coffee rather than tea became a patriotic duty for all Americans. In 1774, John Adams, one of the Founding Fathers and the second President of the US, wrote: 'Tea must be universally renounced, and I must be weaned, and the sooner, the better.'

When the Industrial Revolution began in the middle of the 18th century, coffee played a role in the US that tea played in the UK. The British had tea breaks while the Americans had coffee breaks. Workers added sugar to the hot drinks, providing them with the quick energy boost they needed during their long working days.

There is an argument to be made that the Industrial Revolution would not have been possible if it were not for tea in the UK and coffee in the US.

Coffee also helped win wars. During the US Civil War, while Confederate soldiers diluted their coffee with chicory, Union soldiers were given a whopping daily allowance of one-tenth of a pound of green beans, enough to make ten cups per day. The army even issued some rifles that had a coffee grinder in the stock of the gun.

Generals realised the importance of coffee as a stimulant, and they made sure that soldiers drank plenty of it before going into battle. In September 1862, at Antietam, Sergeant William McKinley – who later became a US President – came under heavy fire while he served coffee to the frontline troops. His commanding officer later wrote that giving a coffee to the troops was 'like putting a new regiment in the fight'.

But it wasn't just soldiers who got a boost from coffee. Coffee breaks introduced into US munition factories during the Second World War increased efficiency. By the mid-1950s, most US companies had coffee breaks as a standard part of the working day. In an advertising campaign, the Pan-American Coffee Bureau advocated: 'Give yourself a coffee break – and get what coffee gives you.' The Bureau also campaigned for coffee breaks on the road, arguing that coffee kept drivers alert.

Coffee first arrived in Japan in the late 17th century, introduced by the Dutch East India Company. Japan was at that time a closed country under the Tokugawa shogunate. The government forbade all contact with Westerners except for the Dutch. The Dutch were only permitted to interact with Japanese merchants and prostitutes on the small artificial island off Nagasaki. The island's prostitutes prized coffee for helping keep them awake during their work! It was only in the late 19th century that coffee entered mainstream Japanese society.

The first coffee house was opened in Japan in 1888, while the first chain – Café Paulista – got up and running in the early 1900s. The

Japanese government restricted the amount of coffee that could enter the country, only lifting the limits in 1960. Many of the coffee shops – or kissaten – developed their own way of brewing coffee, and a whole culture has grown around its preparation and consumption. Japan is now the third-largest importer of coffee in the world.

Coffee was first introduced into China by a French missionary in 1892. The story goes that he carried some coffee seeds over the border from Vietnam into Yunnan and planted them next to his church in the village of Zhukula. Yunnan is famous for its tea, and no one was particularly interested in either drinking or growing a competitive product. This has now begun to change, and China is now the fastest-growing coffee market in the world, admittedly from a low base. The country now has more Starbucks cafés than any other country outside the US.

Even so, it is refreshing for me to discover a commodity market where China is not the most critical player. It may become so in future years, but it could take a generation or so for the population to be weaned off tea, their traditional drink.

In any case, for much of its history, coffee has been a delivery mechanism for caffeine for soldiers on the battlefield, workers in a factory, drivers on the road, and office workers sitting through internal (infernal?) company meetings. But as it conquered the world, coffee also transformed it, creating not only new markets and new money flows, but also new social habits and new organisational arrangements.

A conversation with Jan Lühmann

Jan Lühmann was previously Global Head of Procurement for Jacobs Douwe Egberts and is now an independent consultant.

Good morning Jan, how did you start in coffee?

I am from Hamburg, Germany. It is a merchant city, connected to the world through its harbour, so when I was young, I had dreamt of travelling the world—and ideally getting paid for it!

I completed a two-year apprenticeship in green coffee buying with Tchibo in their quality department. The company is a significant roaster in Germany, as well as in other European countries. I then worked as an assistant to the assistant buyer for another year.

On the off chance, I replied to an advertisement in The Herald Tribune for a coffee trader position in France. I was excited when they accepted me. The company was only a start-up when I joined, but four or five years later, it ended up being the most significant coffee and cocoa trader in France. I learned a lot about trading while I was there. We were mainly involved in West African coffee and cocoa, but we also originated coffee from Central America – mostly from El Salvador. That was the late 1980s when El Salvador was in the middle of a civil war.

In 1994, when Volcafe offered me a position to lead their business in Papa New Guinea, I thought they were out of their minds. I was 28, and of course, that did not stop me. I went for it. I stayed in Papua New Guinea for four years. It was one of the most enriching experiences in my life from every angle: personal, cultural, business, and coffee. But mostly from the cultural side.

From there, I went with Volcafe to Kenya to join Taylor Winch, a premium quality coffee company they own. I then spent two years in Uganda – still for Volcafe. Uganda was a turnaround situation at the time. It was a massive challenge.

You were a merchant in the old-fashioned romantic sense, travelling the world to trade coffee.

That was my motivation at the time. The travelling and the romance have increasingly taken a backseat to my genuine enthusiasm for other aspects of coffee, especially for the people in the business.

The coffee business is a community. It is always personal. People know that there's a company backing you up, but they trade with you as a person. As such, your reputation and integrity are essential.

And coffee is a small community where your competitor can become your customer, or your employee, or your boss. I love meeting people again in different roles.

Did you return to Europe from Africa?

I decided that I didn't want to have an ex-pat career, so I returned to Europe to Volcafe's head office in Switzerland. I stayed with them for another seven years, firstly as a senior trader, and then as managing director of their Swiss trading operation. In total, I was with Volcafe for 15 years.

I then joined Sucafina in Geneva, where I spent four years as head of trading and operations. Towards the end of those four years, Sucafina gave me the opportunity of a lifetime to start the Kahawatu Foundation.

Could you tell me a little about Kahawatu?

We founded Kahawatu intending to improve productivity among smallholder farmers in Burundi. My time there was a deep dive into the NGO and development world: fundraising, working with donors and implementing acceptable agricultural practices. It gave me a real insight into the developmental challenges in East Africa. It also fundamentally changed the way I look at the coffee business.

My experience with Kahawatu and Burundi helped me enormously when I went on to join Jacobs Douwe Egberts as their coffee buyer. As a roaster, I understood that we had a responsibility to move beyond certification.

Sucafina is a commercial operation. Why do they think they founded a philanthropic organization?

Sucafina and the Tamari family care deeply about coffee farming and farmers' welfare, especially in East Africa. But there was also a business angle to it. We knew that if we were going to have any hope of running a successful coffee business in Burundi - and even in the broader regional area that includes Rwanda and Uganda - we had to be part of the solution to make the whole industry sustainable.

In coffee, we have productivity champions like Brazil, where industrial agriculture is being developed very smartly, in a very modern way - getting costs down and yields up.

But there are also smaller countries that produce differentiated coffees, countries that haven't yet found the tools to get the yields they need. A multitude of societal issues holds them back. These smaller producers often get higher prices for their coffee because it tastes better. It's more delicate. It has a complex identity. However, these premiums, although real, are not enough. The smaller producing countries need help, or I fear they will diminish or even disappear.

It is in the interest of the trading companies to leverage their penetration into these supply chains and to do this in a pre-competitive way with public-private partnerships. Sucafina and many other people in the business believe in this, and so do I. It is the only way to make these smallholder farmers sustainable.

Coffee-trading companies need to be part of that solution, but they shouldn't be shouldering it all by themselves. It's simply too much.

Why did you focus on Burundi?

Sucafina had an existing operation in Burundi, and the civil war had just ended. However, we focused on Burundi mostly because coffee represents more than 70 per cent of the country's export revenues. We were able to quickly get traction politically because coffee is at the core of the country's economic activity. It also makes the donor discussion more relevant; more doable. Go to an NGO and ask for funds for a sustainability project in Brazil. Hard. In Burundi, the willingness to engage is there because the need and the potential impact on that nation are massive.

There seems to be a difference in the market now between a coffee trader and a coffee merchant.

The speciality coffee sector doesn't have a trader's skills or mindset and doesn't want to be associated with either. 'Trader' is considered a dirty word these days.

However, I believe you cannot be successful at scale in the green coffee business without an understanding and appreciation of trading. Trading is just as much a reality of the coffee business as is the quality of the coffee. Similarly, you cannot be a successful coffee trader in the long run if you cannot 'cup' the coffee - if you have no notion of its quality or identity.

Companies will put a different emphasis on their businesses, but you need both trading and merchanting mindsets and skills, and frankly, those terms overlap.

From Sucafina you went on to be head of coffee buying with Jacobs Douwe Egberts, part of the JAB group. How does JDE rank up in terms of the pecking order for roasters?

Jacobs Douwe Egberts was founded in 1753 in Friesland, the Netherlands, and now employs over 14,000 people in 44 countries. It is by far the largest entity in the JAB group when it comes to green coffee buying. JAB also owns Caribou, Keurig Dr Pepper, Peets, Intelligentsia, Espresso House, Krispy Kreme, Pret à Manger, and many smaller entities. JAB buys roughly the same volume of green coffee as does Nestlé.

JAB merged JDE with Peets and took the combined company public in May 2020.

You're one of the few people I've come across who moved from a merchandising to a purchasing role. What's the main difference between merchants and roasters?

Technology, brand building and process are more important for a roaster than for a trader or merchant. Roasters focus a lot on technology, be it single-serve, instant coffee or other proprietary USP's (Unique Selling Points). The roasting industry also has a strong emphasis on process, while the trading mindset is nimbler and more reactive as it needs to adapt to market situations and shifting client needs quickly.

There seems to be a connection that consumers have with coffee and coffee farmers that doesn't exist in other commodities. How do you explain that?

There are two angles to this.

The first has to do with the product itself. You're consuming a product that has tremendous diversity and distinctiveness, and people will drink the coffee that they like. It becomes quite personal; consumers develop opinions around that. You tend not to establish those opinions around many other products. Maybe chocolate is similar to coffee, but sugar tastes the same regardless from where it comes.

The second angle has to do with coffee farming and sustainability. In many consuming countries, there is a consumer sensitivity around the living and the social conditions of coffee farming. Those consumers don't want to support something of which they disapprove.

Many people have strong opinions around coffee, for those two reasons. But not everyone does. I may not like it, but for many consumers, coffee is just another product. It is both a considerable challenge and opportunity for this industry.

Is there a dichotomy, a divergence, between a roaster's commercial department and its sustainability department? The sustainability people want to make sure that farmers stay in business, but the commercial people just want the lowest price possible.

The people in both the sustainability and commercial departments of roasters have specific targets to achieve. Yes, there is the commercial drive to buy cheap, but it's for management to pull those contradictions together and align them into a coherent brand strategy.

Many roasters struggle with this, but that is what is so interesting about the coffee business in general. It is complex. It is changing. It has tensions. These tensions will be resolved, sometimes with more of an emphasis on the commercial aspect, and sometimes with more of a focus on the sustainability aspect.

In the long run, the consumer is the ultimate arbiter on those choices.

Many roasters only buy certified coffee. There seems to be a lot of certification systems: are there too many; and are they effective?

It's too easy to be critical of certification.

My view is not that there are too many certifiers or that they do a lousy job. I firmly believe that the people in the certification business are good people who mean well and who do make a positive difference.

However, it is imperfect. And whatever positive impact one has in coffee-producing countries the situation will remain flawed. We are thus certifying imperfection.

There is a risk that you're over-promising. Even though the legal wording in the documents is smart enough so that the occasional unacceptable incident will not compromise a roaster's legal position, consumers will nevertheless expect perfection.

Also, the desire by roasters to portray perfection can lead to a misallocation of resources. How much of the global sustainability spend reaches farmers and makes a real difference, and how much serves to prove perfection in a roaster's supply chain? As a coffee industry, I believe we should be moving towards a mindset of transparency.

Acknowledge the imperfections and then focus on mitigation and continuous improvement.

At JDE, I was proud to be part of the group's effort to think differently - to move from a mindset focused on certification to one where you acknowledge the imperfections in the supply chains, and then be a part of remedying them, ideally in a pre-competitive way.

So, you are saying that certification is part of the solution, but it's not sufficient?

Yes. Also, let's not forget that the traders are doing what the roasters are asking of them. The trade is a service provider to the industry. The buck stops with the roaster.

What is the solution?

People are very fast with quick answers, quick conclusions and one-liners, but coffee is complex. There are a lot of tensions around development and sustainability, but you can't limit the discussion to agriculture when many of the challenges are social.

The economic challenges in coffee-producing countries aren't always rooted in the price and productivity of coffee alone; societal issues often drive them. Many of the good NGOs are working on that.

The realities of coffee are just as varied and diverse as the different tastes of coffee: complex, contradictory, fascinating and not easy to resolve. But many very positive and engaging discussions are on-going.

How is Fairtrade viewed within the sector?

Fairtrade is a good thing: a good and imperfect approach, just as all approaches are imperfect. It is focusing on one aspect of the ills of the industry, but I think we all need to recognize that no one has a silver bullet.

But what in particular can be done to help the farmer?

People often talk about small coffee farmers when, in fact, these people are not coffee farmers. They often don't even see themselves as coffee farmers. They are subsistence farmers who happen to have coffee trees. If you want to address their issues, you cannot just address their coffee trees. You also have to manage their bananas, their sweet potatoes and their livestock, and often the social and legal context as well. Well-meaning parties should stop focusing on one aspect of what they do (coffee) and look at all their challenges holistically.

It is not the roaster or the trader that is the enemy of the poor coffee farmer. The enemy of the poor farmer is the wealthy farmer in a different producing country – these are the people who are driving productivity gains, driving down costs and consequently driving down prices.

The coffee business over the past forty years has been a battle between differentiation and productivity. In the mainstream segment, productivity champions are winning.

You need to approach the challenges of poor subsistence farmers with a holistic approach – and to do so pre-competitively in public/private partnerships.

A lot of the roasters seem to be more brand managers than coffee companies. Is that your experience?

There are two main aspects to a roaster.

The first is brand management, and this is where sustainability and certification come in. The brand is the roaster's biggest asset.

The second is technology. The coffee business is driven by technology on the industry side. The technology of roasting is not that hard. What is problematic are single-serve solutions. Included in that is the quest for more sustainable solutions, especially with a focus on packaging materials. This area is where roasters have a considerable challenge to be more sustainable. Technology is also crucial with instant coffee.

In the past, I understand that some roasters set up trading departments, but they have since closed them. Is that correct?

There have been waves of this. Both roasters and farmers are easily attracted to the idea of going direct, to cut out the middleman - the evil trader. And on the surface, many will agree that this makes sense. However, they quickly find out that traders have many real and vital service functions. Roasters also found that trading is counter to their industrial DNA.

I don't think it is possible to run a real trading functionality within an industrial company.

Do traders still have a role to play?

Yes, but I believe the service provider aspect is gaining importance, and classical trading is losing relevance. The industry will be rewarded for the services that they bring in the supply chain: quality, finance and sustainability. Earning a living out of an intelligent market view is getting much harder these days.

Also, it has become clear that a trader who focuses on the trading element and views service as a necessary evil will, at times, trade against his customer and thus fail in the long run.

One of the interesting questions is when will a platform emerge that allows roasters and farmers to connect and bundle together the various trade functionalities. I see two such platforms emerging today, one being a blockchain-driven traceability tool and one a powerful and highly efficient supply chain platform. Both are Swiss, so Switzerland is likely to remain a key player!

Merchants are increasingly under pressure to prove that they can continue to add value. I believe that they do, but their margins have been squeezed to virtually zero, and they continually have to reinvent themselves.

You have to ask, how much of the disruption seen today in trading is due to smart, well-funded and highly respected growers, coops and farmers in producing countries? You also have to ask, why has the global coffee trade not participated in the growth of global production? The top five traders move the same volume today as they did twenty years ago. The traders have lost market share. To whom? Local competitors in producing countries!

Even so, would you recommend a young person to join the coffee business? And if so, what advice would you give them?

Yes, there is so much variety, so much to do. Learn, be curious and then do your thing. The coffee business is always changing. Be part of that change.

What's the most significant challenge that the coffee industry faces at the moment?

To protect and promote the diversity that we have in coffee, be it the number of origins or the complexity of qualities within those origins.

Are you a coffee addict?

Yes, I love this business. You can touch it, feel it, smell it. It's tangible. I like the physicality of coffee: the beans and the beverage.

I like the social aspect of coffee: it's a people business in trading and sustainability with the farmer and the consumers.

What's your favourite coffee? And how do you prepare it?

I was lucky to have lived in my favourite producing countries: Kenya and Papua New Guinea. I use an Aeropress.

Thank you, Jan, for your time and input.

Chapter 3:
From Crop to Cup

Coffee should be black as hell, strong as death and sweet as love.

- Turkish Proverb

Coffee grows in tropical regions between the tropics of Cancer and Capricorn in what is known as the 'bean belt'. Arabica generally likes higher altitudes of 550 to 1,950 metres (1,800 to 6,300 feet); anything above 1200 metres is ideal. Coffee grown below about 1,000 metres may be of inferior quality, although Hawaii is an exception. Robusta varieties prefer a lower elevation of 180 to 750 metres (600 to 2,400 feet) with warmer temperatures. Within those ranges, the altitude profoundly impacts the coffee. High elevation coffee will produce more acidic, aromatic and flavourful coffee; lower elevation coffee tends to have less acidity and a more muted character.

Coffee plants are evergreen shrubs that can grow up to 4-6 metres tall with broad, glossy leaves and white flowers. Older varietals take 3 to 4 years to bear fruit while recent varietals will bear their first crop two years after being planted out.

The fruit, the coffee cherry, ripens around eight months after the emergence of the flower. The cherries are harvested once they have changed colour from green to deep red. In most coffee-growing countries, there is one major harvest a year. A few countries, including Colombia, have a primary and secondary crop: the main harvest is from April to June and the smaller one from November to December.

Just as there are two main kinds of coffee, arabica and robusta, there are two main methods of coffee cultivation: sun-grown and shade-grown. Shade-grown coffee is the more traditional approach that mimics the natural way coffee trees grow in the wild, underneath a forest canopy. Farmers, particularly in Brazil, began growing coffee in full sun in the 1970s to increase yields and production.

Coffee trees growing in the shade of a forest maintain the forest's biodiversity, particularly its wildlife, and shade-grown coffee often trades at a premium to full-sun coffee. However, the thick forest cover - combined with the steep mountain slopes where coffee grows - makes harvesting more difficult and costlier. It is much cheaper to produce coffee on open flat land, especially if it is mechanically harvested.

There are different degrees of shade-grown coffee production. Rustic shade-grown coffee is where the trees are planted in an existing forest with only the lowest levels of the original forest removed. Once planted, the coffee trees require little care and often no pesticides or herbicides. It is the least capital-intensive method of coffee production. It suffers from a low yield and is quite rare except in India and some of the western coffee areas of Ethiopia.

Traditional polyculture involves planting other (usually food-bearing) trees alongside the coffee trees under a natural forest's canopy. Commercial polyculture consists of removing or pruning much of the native forest trees to allow sunlight to pass and to give space for the coffee and other crops to grow. The shaded monoculture system is where farmers plant and then prune a single species of tree to provide shade for the coffee trees, allowing them to be grown more densely.

Over the past half-century, growers have developed new sun-tolerant coffee trees and shrubs to combat disease (particularly rust-leaf disease) and provide higher yields. As a result, the percentage of coffee that is shade-grown has been steadily falling. The increase in global production over the past twenty years has almost all been full-sun coffee. Shade-grown coffee fell from 43 per cent of the total cultivated area in 1996 to 24 per cent in 2014. It has almost certainly continued to fall since then.

Coffee is picked by hand in most countries. In Brazil, where the landscape is relatively flat and the coffee fields immense, the process has been mechanised. Mechanical harvesters strip-pick all the cherries from the trees in one go, whether they are unripe (green), ripe (red) or overripe (purple/black). Mechanical harvesting can stress and damage the trees, reducing the yield the following year.

Coffee is sometimes also strip-picked by hand, particularly the lower quality arabica or robusta varieties. Better quality coffees tend to be selectively picked by hand. The pickers rotate among the trees every eight to ten days, choosing only the cherries which are at the peak of ripeness.

Selective hand picking is more labour intensive and more costly; it is used primarily to harvest the higher quality arabica beans. Red berries, with their higher aromatic oil and lower organic acid content, are more fragrant, smooth and mellow. As such, coffee picking is one of the most critical stages of coffee production.

Once picked, millers or farmers have to remove four layers from the coffee cherry before they get to the bean. They remove the first three during processing and the fourth during roasting.

The first layer is a cherry-like skin, called the fruit, flesh, or pulp. The second layer is a sticky, gluey substance called mucilage or honey (because it is sweet.) The third layer is called parchment, a thin layer of cellulose that protects each of the coffee seeds. When dried, this layer looks and feels like parchment paper, hence the name. (Coffee beans can sometimes be sold locally in parchment form, but not internationally.) The fourth layer is called the silver skin, which usually comes off during roasting; at this point, it is commonly known as chaff.

About 95 per cent of coffee cherries contain two beans. The remaining have only one seed, called a peaberry.

There are four principal ways of processing coffee; they differ in the number of layers that are removed before drying. In the natural method, no layers are removed before the beans are dried. In the washed process, the skin, pulp, and mucilage are removed using water and fermentation. In the pulped natural method, the pulp is removed mechanically without fermentation. In the honey method, growers remove the skins and the pulp, although some or all of the mucilage (honey) may remain.

But before we go into details, a word of warning: there are many variations on the four principal ways of processing coffee beans – and they are often called differently in different countries.

The natural method is the oldest and original form of coffee processing. The harvested cherries are first sorted and cleaned to separate the unripe, overripe and damaged cherries and to remove dirt, soil, twigs and leaves. This can be done by winnowing, which is commonly done by hand, using a large sieve. Any unwanted cherries or other material not winnowed away can be picked out from the top of the sieve. The ripe cherries can also be separated by flotation in washing channels close to the drying areas: insect or disease damaged cherries will float, while healthy cherries will sink.

The whole coffee cherries are then laid out in the sun to dry. On a commercial scale, this is usually done on brick or concrete areas, but the cherries can also be left to dry on the bare ground. Doing this can impact the taste of the coffee, giving it an intense and earthy flavour. To avoid it, many producers place their cherries in thin layers on raised beds, turning them regularly to reduce the risk of mould. Even so, some fermentation can occur.

Depending on the weather, it may take up to four weeks before the cherries are dry. On larger plantations, the cherries are sometimes machine-dried to speed up the process after the coffee has been pre-dried in the sun for a few days. Once the cherries have dried, the coffee is hulled either mechanically or by hand, to remove the outer layers.

The washed method is the most commonly used coffee processing method. The growers send the whole cherries to a wet mill where they are first sorted by immersion in water: rotten or unripe fruit floats while the ripe fruit sinks. The ripe cherries then pass through a de-pulping machine that removes their first layer of cherry or fruit pulp. After this initial processing, the beans will be fermented in water to remove the mucilage.

The beans can remain in their fermentation tank for 12 to 24 hours, depending on the temperature of the water. The longer the beans ferment, the more they absorb sugar from the mucilage, making a sweeter coffee. If they ferment for too long, they can develop a vinegar-like quality. The end of the fermentation is traditionally assessed by feel, as the parchment surrounding the beans loses its slimy texture and acquires a rougher pebbly feel.

After fermentation, the beans are removed and washed in a tank or channels of clean water. They can then be dried mechanically or laid out in the sun on drying tables or patios. If the latter, the process can take between 10 and 22 days, depending on the weather. To ensure that they do not grow mould, they have to be regularly turned and covered in the case of rain. Generally speaking, the slower the drying time, the better the balance and complexity of the bean – and the better the final beverage. Mechanical drying will typically take around three days and can produce excellent results.

The drying operation is the most critical stage of the process. If you over-dry coffee it will become brittle and produce too many broken (defective) beans during hulling. If you under-dry it, the beans will be too moist and prone to rapid deterioration if attacked by fungi and bacteria. Once the moisture content of the beans is down to around 12 per cent, the parchment layer is removed by rubbing the beans together mechanically in a hulling machine.

Pulped Natural is the standard processing method in Brazil where dry conditions mean a minimal risk of mould. The beans are pulped and laid out to dry on patios with varying degrees of the mucilage left on them. It is similar to the washed process except that the mucilage is removed using a pressure washer, skipping the fermentation process altogether. It uses less water than the washed process, so it is sometimes called Semi-Dry. Since there is no fermentation, there is little risk of over- or under-fermentation, thus increasing overall consistency. Without fermentation, the flavour can be consistent, but it can also be bland.

The honey method is a hybrid process that varies from country to country, or from region to region within a country. It requires less water than the washed process, and the beans are less susceptible to the defects of the natural process. It is sometimes called the wet-hulled or semi-washed process. It begins in the same way as the washed process with the harvested cherries pulped. The beans are then partially sun-dried until 30 to 35 per cent of the moisture in the bean remains. The beans are hulled and returned to the patio until the drying process is complete and the beans turn a dark bluish-green colour. Growers in Indonesia often use this method.

Coffee beans have to be processed through the washed method to be deliverable against the New York futures markets. Most of the coffee in Brazil is unwashed and cannot be delivered. By removing the pulp and the mucilage before drying, washed coffee does not absorb any of the flavours that might be absorbed during the other methods of processing. Many people prefer washed coffee, arguing that the process highlights the real character of the bean and lets you taste you what's on the inside of the bean, not the outside.

Natural or honey-processed coffee acquires flavour from the fruit pulp and mucilage around the bean. Washed coffees depend almost entirely on the bean having absorbed enough natural sugars and nutrients during its growing cycle rather than during processing.

Washing is primarily done in arabica-producing countries; robusta is rarely washed. Speciality coffee is almost always washed to maintain consistency. The natural process can lead to inconsistent flavours as a result of unripe fruit drying and turning brown alongside ripe fruit. However, some enthusiasts are now turning towards natural coffees because of their sometimes more exciting flavours.

Producing countries tend to favour one particular process. Most of Eastern Africa, except for Ethiopia, and most of Central America historically used the washed process, while as much as 90 per cent of the coffee grown in Brazil is processed with the dry method; as is most of the coffee grown in Paraguay, India and Ecuador. Almost all robusta coffees are also processed using the dry method.

The wet method requires the use of specific equipment and substantial quantities of water. Wet processing produces wastewater which can be a pollutant. Ecologically sensitive farms reprocess the wastewater and compost the shell and mucilage to make fertiliser.

Honey processing bridges the gap between washed and natural coffees as it generally possesses some of the body and sweetness of a natural coffee while retaining some of the acidity of a washed coffee. Honey coffees often have a syrupy body with enhanced sweetness and earthy undertones.

Once dried, the cherries are sent to a dry mill where hulling, sorting, grading and bagging take place. The beans are sometimes polished to remove any silver skin that remains on the beans after hulling.

The coffee is then sorted by density and bean size while removing any miscellaneous debris. Sorting can be done by hand or by machine. If the latter, the beans are blown into the air; those that fall into bins closest to the air source are heaviest; the lightest (and likely defective) beans, plus chaff, are blown in the farthest compartment. Other machines shake the beans through a series of sieves, sorting them by size and density.

The final step in the sorting process is where defective beans are removed, usually by hand. Machines sometimes do the job, with the beans falling past sensors that identify defective beans and remove them with a puff of air.

Once cleaned and sorted, the coffee is then graded according to various criteria. These criteria include the size of the bean, where it was grown, and how it was processed and picked. Coffees are also graded by taste ('cup quality') and by the number of imperfections (broken, under-ripe, or otherwise defective beans; pebbles; sticks; etc.) per sample.

In the early 1960s, the International Coffee Organization (ICO) instituted an identification code for coffee exports to enable it to apply the export quota system that existed at that time. This coding system continues to be used today. For example, in code 002 – 1961 – 0978, the first group of numbers identifies the country of origin, the second the exporter, the third the individual shipment.

Green coffee is usually packed and stored in jute or woven poly bags. While green coffee may be usable for several years, it is usually best within 12 to 18 months.

Green coffee is now almost always exported in containers, sometimes in bags, but increasingly in bulk, in a box fitted with an inner plastic liner. Recent years have seen a substantial increase in the movement of coffee in bulk containers. A container can hold about 21 tonnes of coffee in bulk, compared to only about 18 tonnes in bags. It represents a freight saving of about 15 per cent per container.

Unless packed in sealed vacuum packs, the coffee loses its natural oils and flavours relatively quickly after it is roasted. Traditionally, therefore, green beans are traded and shipped and then roasted locally – as close to the consumer as possible. Additionally, importing countries often insist that roasters mark their packs with a sell-by or use-by date. It puts an exporter at a disadvantage compared to a local roaster.

Coffee roasting fits in with the colonialist model where poor southern hemisphere countries ship a low-value commodity to rich northern hemisphere countries to be processed into a high-value consumer product. As we will see later, most, if not all, of the value within the coffee chain is added in the developed world.

Many books describe how to roast coffee, but in brief, there are three main stages: the drying stage, the browning stage and the development or roasting stage.

A green coffee bean has a humidity of 8–12 per cent and must be dried before it is roasted. The stage typically lasts 4–8 minutes in a traditional drum roaster. The temperature at the end of the drying stage is generally 160 °C. Above that temperature, the browning stage begins, where sugars and amino acids react (the Maillard reaction), making hundreds of different aroma and colour compounds known as melanoids.

During the drying and browning stages, the beans collect energy in an endothermic reaction that makes them expand. The beans release that energy in an exothermic reaction at the beginning of what is called the development stage. The noise the beans make when this happens is known as the first crack. It is similar to the sound made by cooking popcorn.

If you continue to roast the beans, the coffee will go through a second crack where it releases further energy and produces a very dark-roast coffee. Most roasters will try to aim for a roasting time between the first and second crack.

Once roasted, the beans can be sold as whole beans or ground coffee. They can also be made into soluble (instant) coffee.

When you make soluble coffee, you heat water under pressure to around 200°C and pass it through roasted, ground coffee. The concentration is then centrifuged to remove non-soluble particles. It is then evaporated to a coffee content of 50 per cent when it is introduced under pressure into the top of a large cylindrical tower and spray-dried with a jet of hot air. The droplets dry into a fine powder; these can be agglomerated into granules by wetting them in low-pressure steam. The wet granules dry as they descend through a second tower and are sifted to provide a uniform final granule size.

Freeze-drying consists of freezing the coffee liquor into a 6 mm thick cake on a moving conveyor at a temperature of minus 45° C. The frozen cake is then broken into small particles, and the ice crystals removed by a process known as sublimation. Freeze-drying is more energy expensive, but it is gentler on the product as less heat is applied to evaporate the water content. Consequently, the finer and more costly blends of instant coffee tend to be freeze-dried.

What about decaffeinated coffee?

Caffeine is a natural substance found in the leaves, seeds or fruits of more than 60 plant species worldwide; it acts as natural protection against insects. Arabica coffee beans contain 1–1.5 per cent caffeine, whereas robusta beans contain more than 2 per cent. In the European Union, the caffeine content of decaffeinated coffee may not exceed 0.1 per cent in roasted coffee or 0.3 per cent in soluble coffee. In the US, decaffeinated coffee is coffee whose caffeine content is less than 3 per cent of the original content.

Coffee is decaffeinated at the green bean stage. The process is the same for both soluble and roasted coffee. The beans are mixed with water or steam, and the caffeine is then extracted with water, a solvent or activated carbon. The decaffeinated coffee beans are then hydrated back to their correct moisture level. Besides water, the solvents typically used during decaffeination are ethyl acetate, methylene chloride, or supercritical CO_2.

The Swiss Water decaffeinating method uses only water to wash out the caffeine, trapping the larger caffeine molecules in a carbon filter and returning the natural oils (and flavours) to the beans. The process is more natural than using a solvent and is gaining popularity.

Apart from the Swiss Water Process, the other methods collect the caffeine and sell it on to the pharmaceutical and soft drink industries. Although this helps the economics of the process, decaffeinated coffee still costs more to produce than ordinary coffee. Even so, it is often sold for the same price as caffeinated coffee.

Decaffeinated coffee is estimated to account for around 10 per cent of all coffee sales, but it is losing market share.

A conversation with Teddy Esteve

Good morning, Teddy. How did you end up living and working in Mexico?

I grew up in Lausanne, and after attending the HEC, I got a job in the Philippines. I was following a girlfriend, but my family said: 'Hey, nobody goes to the Philippines in this family!' They wanted me to go to Mexico instead, and I said: 'Okay, I'll do it for six months if that is good for you.' That was 38 years ago.

Did you meet a Mexican lady and fall in love?

Yes, I did. That was ten years later.

What relationship are you to the founders of ECOM?

ECOM is a seventh-generation business that started in cotton in Barcelona, Spain, and I'm part of that seventh generation. There are still quite a few of us from that seventh generation involved in the business, from three branches of the family. My father had three brothers. The four brothers together had I don't know how many children, but many of those work today in the company. I also have cousins from other branches of the family who work in the company, especially in Brazil.

But you know that in the commodity business every generation has to reinvent itself. Commodities trading is not something that you inherit. That's what I tell my three kids at least. I have two sons and one daughter.

Will your children join you the business?

I would love them to join me, but there will be close to 100 cousins in the next generation of the family, and they can't all join the company.

Does ECOM have any shareholders other than the family?

Some of our managers own shares.

You mentioned that you went to Mexico for six months but stayed there ever since. How did you end up on in the coffee side of the business?

When I arrived in Mexico, I was going to work for a bank, but when the government nationalised it, my uncle Jorge asked me to join the family firm.

Cotton has always been the company's main focus, but he said: 'Hey, what do you want to do? Do you want to work in cotton, or do you prefer coffee?' Cotton was the company's main business, but except for Brazil, we only had one coffee mill - in Mexico. We were also doing some tolling in Guatemala.

When you are 22 or 23, as I was at that time, you're not interested in business; you are more interested in having a good time. I had never drunk coffee. I came from Switzerland; I had grown up on hot milky chocolate rather than coffee. But I told my uncle I preferred to join the coffee side of the business.

I started drinking coffee, and I went to work in the coffee business. It has been fantastic, and I have never regretted my decision. You know, it was an adventure.

I see from your website that ECOM is the number one coffee miller and the number two coffee trader in the world.

Our company started in coffee in 1953 in Brazil. Brazil has always been our origin coffee, and when we started in Mexico, we had a different shareholder structure than the one in Brazil. Our guys in Brazil were worried that our new operation would tarnish their reputation. When you start a business, you make a lot of mistakes, and the Brazilian team was afraid that we would not live up to their excellent reputation.

Today we are one group under united management with an excellent understanding of each other, so we work very well together. Those early days are long gone.

How did your business develop in Central America?

The operation in Mexico had started a few years before I arrived.

ED&F Man had come to us and said: 'Hey, you guys know Mexico, and we know coffee, so let's start a joint venture coffee operation in Mexico.' We set up Omnicafé, a 50-50 joint venture, and we lost a bundle in the first year. It was tough in Mexico in those days because the government controlled everything. At the end of the first year, we went to EDF Man and said: 'Listen, you guys know coffee, you keep this.' But they said: 'No, no, you know Mexico, you keep the company.' We were fighting because nobody wanted the coffee business in Mexico, and in the end, we lost the fight and kept it! That was in 1981.

It was a tiny business, but big enough to lose maybe a million dollars a year, which in those days was a lot of money. We were doing 50,000 bags a year, and my uncle said to me: 'Hey, aren't you guys planning on growing?' So, we constructed another warehouse 40 km from the first one and then another one a hundred kilometres from there.

We built the business from the ground up. We grew by knowing the industry inside out. It's a huge advantage when you don't inherit a business. It's much easier to start a business, to build it from the ground up and to run it, rather than it is just to show up and say: 'Hey, you're now the manager of a company that does all these millions of bags.' You don't know the essence of a business unless you build it.

What's the most important thing you learned?

Countries like Honduras, Guatemala and Mexico are geographically close, but the way they do business is entirely different. We often said: 'Hey, why don't we just centralise everything?' But in this business, it's not possible. Every country has its way of doing business.

Did the acquisition of Cargill Coffee in 2000 boost your business?

Anyone that buys something from Cargill, well it's a real wow!

We bought Cargill's coffee operation after Neumann, Volcafe, and probably others turned it down. Cargill was keen to sell it, so we bought it on good terms. The purchase was an important one for us. They had a lot of inventory, and Cargill is, without doubt, the best school there is for commodity trading. We still have excellent ex-Cargill colleagues working with us.

Our purchase of Cargill was well received by the US coffee sector. They said: 'These guys are buying Cargill; they must be serious.' We had the opposite reaction in Europe where some roasters were afraid to do business with us; they were worried that we were overreaching.

Buying Cargill Coffee gave us a lot of exposure and a good platform for future growth. Cargill is an example of how to run a commodity business. We learned a lot from them, but we still maintained our own style, and things worked out very well.

In 2013, you took over Armajaro's coffee operations. Was that also a boost to your business?

We bought Armajaro for their cocoa business, and it has been the best thing that could ever have happened to our cocoa business. It was an excellent deal.

For coffee, it was right in the sense that the purchase included Dorman's in East Africa. Dorman has an excellent operation in Kenya, Tanzania and Rwanda. Armajaro also had some outstanding contracts on their books with roasters.

Do you spend a lot of your time travelling?

I travel a lot – probably six months of the year.

We have offices in the main producing countries, with a significant presence in Brazil, Vietnam and Columbia. We have a smaller presence in producing countries such as Indonesia. Ethiopia and Tanzania. We have distribution offices in Japan, Singapore, China, Australia, and of course throughout Europe. Our head office is in Switzerland, and we have two offices in the US.

About eight operations report to me in Latin America.

Our Brazilian operations are mostly autonomous. Our people there are excellent, and they know their job better than anyone. They have been in this business forever, and they just get on with it. I try to go to Brazil every year, but it works out more like once every two years, or once every year and a half.

ECOM is a low-profile company. Do you see that changing in the future?

I want to be high profile with my roasters and my farmers, but outside of that, I don't see any need to increase the company's public profile. It's all about what is best for the company. In many countries in which we operate, the least they know about you the better.

What is your trading style?

We are very different from our competitors. We are the least trader of the traders, and we are the most merchants of the merchants. If you have a scale with a wine merchant at one end and a soybean trader at the other end, I see myself more as a wine merchant than as a soybean trader.

Our growth has been driven not by aggressiveness, but by strategy. We are devoted to farmers - we have over a thousand agronomists working for the company – and if our farmers thrive, so do we!

We are also devoted to our roasters. At ECOM, we want to help the roaster sell their coffee more expensively. That's what we do.

People ask me how they can make more money: by buying cheaper coffee? No, by selling more expensive coffee, not by buying cheaper!

You buy expensive coffee because you expect more, and we expect more, and we want our customers to expect more as well. Why do we sell so much coffee? It's because we buy a lot of expensive coffee.

Is all coffee traded basis the futures on a differential basis?

The is a growing trend to buy coffee on long term flat price contracts independent of the futures price.

If you look at your screen today, you will see New York is trading at $1.1895 per pound. The buying power is with the roasters, but they know that if they try to buy coffee at the New York price then pretty soon there won't be any coffee left to buy!

Except for low grades, the average price of my trading book is easily $1.80 per pound. Our clients know that if they want to continue to receive Mexican coffee, they have to pay that price. If you look at Costa Rica, nobody sells below $2 - it's the new Hawaii. Guatemala is the same.

Colombia is a different story because their production has gone up a lot, but good roasters know what it takes to build a supply chain and to keep that supply chain throughout the year.

Why is the price of coffee so low – is it because Brazil and Vietnam are so efficient?

Brazil sets the price of robusta. Today if you take delivery of the futures market in London you will get only conilon – Brazilian robusta. Few people want conilon. So, if you have conilon, the easiest place to go with it is the futures market. That's why the differentials for Vietnam are so high. Today, you have to pay 200 points over the futures for a decent Vietnam coffee. So, although Vietnam produces more robusta than Brazil, it is Brazil that sets the futures price because the London Exchange represents Brazils.

Brazil also sets the price of arabica. Brazil produces a lot of coffee at a low cost, so if a country wants to compete with Brazil, they have to compete on something else other than price. They have to compete on quality. In the long run, nobody can compete with Brazil just on price. You need something else.

I always say that there's the Wolf of Wall Street and there's the coffee merchant. The Wolf of Wall Street is currently taking all the conilon from Brazil to England where there is no demand for it. That depresses the market. Prices are low because the Wolf of Wall

Street has found a way to push the market down. That's the game they play. They are making money, okay, but it's depressing prices. It's not our game.

How do you hedge the differentials?

That's a tough question. When the price of New York increases to a level where farmers are making a living, the differentials for high grades get squashed. Similarly, low-grade coffees are currently worth 60 cents/lb, but if the futures market rallies one hundred cents, then those low grades might be worth 70 cents.

That's why I say we are not soybean traders. The basis in coffee is almost more volatile than the flat price. Any market move is a basis move and, depending on the quality, it is complicated to hedge. It's a question of experience, everything that we have learned.

Is the world of coffee pricing broken?

There are currently too many producers who can't make a living out of coffee. However, there are also a lot of people who should not be in coffee because, even if the price were to triple, they would still not be able to make a living. So, yes, in that sense coffee pricing is broken; it has been broken for a while.

There are a lot of companies who pay farmers correctly. Just the other day I had a customer who said: 'Hey, Teddy. I went to buy coffee from that farm.' When I asked them how much he wanted to pay, he asked me to send him over the farmer's cost of production, and he would pay him more. I have many customers like that, and they are not small companies. These are people who know that you cannot live by taking advantage of others.

But it's challenging to help a disorganised country, and where the quality is not there. It's tough to pay a price that would allow farmers to live. Unfortunately, there are too many places where that is the case.

Will ECOM join one of the coffee sector's blockchain initiatives?

Within ECOM we have a company called SMS, Sustainable Management Services, which has all the data and all the information that would make up a blockchain. It's not called a blockchain. It's called SMS Integrity.

Creating traceability in our business is essential, but we have our initiatives. One day I would like blockchain to be the vector of my endeavours, but for the moment it's competing with SMS.

Is there much government intervention to help growers in coffee?

None – well, virtually none.

Colombia is maybe the country where producers get the most support from the government. They get seedlings; they get financing. The (Coffee Producers) Federation has been building roads; they cover particular needs. I would say that the Federation has been an asset for the farmers, but it has been a liability for the country because it has cost a lot of money. Maybe they could have spent some of that money better.

What are the main environmental sustainability issues in coffee?

Water treatment in the wet milling process is the biggest issue in coffee sustainability. At ECOM, we follow the strictest covenants as far as water treatment is concerned. I don't know who else in the world treats water as efficiently as we do!

Deforestation is an issue; shaded coffee needs forest cover; it preserves biodiversity.

What about social sustainability, particularly child labour?

Nobody wants children to work on farms. It is the worst thing in terms of running an ethical business. It's also the worst thing for the reputation of our customers. We have to protect the brands of our customers.

The lives of these kids are more important than the brands, but it's everything combined. It's an absolute 'No, no'.

We make no distinction between kids helping their family with the harvest during the school holidays and kids that are working full time. We want children to be in school during term time and not working during the vacation.

What is your favourite coffee? And what's your favourite brewing method?

My favourite coffee is Dorman's from Kenya. Once you drink it, you can't drink anything else. It's like Petrus. Once you drink Petrus, you can't drink anything else. That's why I haven't started drinking Petrus.

I use a French press.

Thank you, Teddy, for your time and input.

Chapter 4: Commodity Coffee

At the first glance, a commodity seems a commonplace sort of thing, one easily understood, (but) analysis shows that it is a very queer thing indeed, full of metaphysical subtleties and theological whimsies.

- Karl Marx

There are two main types of coffee: arabica and robusta. The former accounts for around 60 per cent of world production, while the latter makes up the remaining 40 per cent. There are a few thousand varietals within the arabica species, but the most common are Typica, Bourbon and Catura.

Robusta is grown in West and Central Africa, Southeast Asia, and in South America including Brazil, where it is known as conilon. It has a relatively high tolerance to leaf rust pathogen, white stem borer and nematode invasion, and has the potential to give consistent yields. Robusta is hardier than arabica and grows well at low altitudes in open humid conditions. It is cheaper to produce than arabica.

In some countries (Uganda and India, for example) robusta is also cultivated at reasonably high altitudes (above 1,200 m) and under shade, producing better-quality robusta beans for speciality blends. Robusta has a coarser taste than arabica and is mainly used to make instant (soluble) coffee. You also find it in most espresso blends, where it is responsible for the espresso's crema. Arabica has a more delicate taste.

Coffee provides livelihoods for an estimated 25 million farming families across some 70 producing countries. An additional one million families worldwide depend on coffee for their living, whether transporting, roasting or retailing it.

The world's coffee farmers currently produce around 175 million 60 kg bags of coffee per year; that's just under 10 million tonnes of green coffee. Vietnam is the world's largest producer of robusta coffee, while Brazil is the world's largest producer of arabica coffee. Colombia is the world's third-largest coffee producer, followed by Indonesia, Honduras, Ethiopia, India, Uganda, Mexico and Guatemala.

The top five coffee-producing countries account for more than 70 per cent of global output, with Brazil (at 65 million bags) and Vietnam (at 30 million bags) accounting for around 55 per cent of the total. Brazil produces both robusta and arabica coffee, while Vietnam's output is 95 per cent robusta. Colombia, the third-biggest coffee-growing country at 14 million bags, is 100 per cent arabica.

Yields vary enormously across the globe. Vietnam produces nearly 40 bags (of 60 kg each) per hectare whilst Brazil produces just under 25 bags per hectare. Colombia, Guatemala, Honduras and Nicaragua produce an average of 15 bags per hectare. India produces an average of around 14, Ethiopia 11, Indonesia 8, and Mexico 5 bags per hectare. As a result of this disparity in yields, Mexico has nearly as many hectares under coffee as Colombia even though it produces far less overall.

Out of the world production of 175 million bags, only about 35 million are consumed in the producing countries themselves, leaving 140 million for export. Unsurprisingly, the top producers are also the top exporters. When you include roasted and soluble coffee, Brazil exports on average around 40 million bags per year, Vietnam 27 million, Colombia 13 million, Indonesia 6-7 million, Honduras 6 million, India 5-6 million, Uganda 4.5 million, Ethiopia 4 million, Peru 4.5 million, Guatemala 3.5 million, Mexico 3 million, and Nicaragua 2.5 million.

Some producing countries are more dependent on coffee exports than others. In value terms, coffee makes up only 3 per cent of Brazil's merchandise exports and only 2 per cent of Vietnam's exports. In some medium-sized producers, such as Honduras and Ethiopia, coffee's share of exports exceeds 20 per cent, while in other smaller producers, such as Uganda, the percentage is even higher. Rwanda and Burundi export between them less than 5 million bags, but coffee is the biggest export earner in both countries.

Less than 10 per cent of all coffee exports from producing countries are in processed (non-green bean) form. Almost all of those non-green bean exports are in the form of instant coffee; roasted coffee exports have never exceeded 0.3 per cent of total coffee exports from producing countries.

It is often reported that in value terms coffee is the second most important internationally traded commodity after crude oil. That may have been true for a short time in the 1970s when coffee prices were trading at over $3 per pound, but it is no longer the case. In the international trade of agricultural commodities, coffee comes third after soybeans and wheat by value.

Nearly all coffee, both commodity and speciality, is priced against the futures markets. The London market trades robusta, while New York trades arabica.

The New York Coffee Exchange was founded on 7th December 1881, partly as a result of the bankruptcy one year earlier of B. G. Arnold & Co, one of the biggest coffee trading companies at the time. Somewhat surprisingly, Benjamin Arnold became the Exchange's first president. Somewhat unsurprisingly, few people believed that the Exchange would be a success. Eventually, however, confidence grew, and business gradually took off.

The Exchange created standards for coffee grades, established an arbitration procedure to deal with disputes, and allowed buyers and sellers to hedge the risks associated with market volatility.

Robusta coffee futures first started trading in 1958 on the London Commodity Exchange; prices were quoted in pounds sterling until 1992 when they switched to US dollars.

Both the London and New York markets are now owned and run by ICE – The Intercontinental Exchange.

The 'C-Contract' in New York is the world benchmark for arabica. The contract prices physical delivery of exchange-grade green beans, from twenty countries of origin, in a licensed warehouse in several ports in the US and Europe, with stated premiums or discounts for ports and growths. The contract size is 37,500 pounds and prices are quoted in US dollar cents per pound up to one-hundredth of a cent. The Exchange trades electronically: open outcry trading ended in 2008.

Before delivery, a Notice of Certification is issued based on the grade and cup quality of the beans. The Exchange uses certain coffees to establish the basis. Coffees judged better than the basis are delivered at a premium, while those deemed as inferior are at a discount. At the time of writing, Mexico, Salvador, Guatemala, Costa Rica, Nicaragua, Kenya, Papua New Guinea, Panama, Tanzania, Uganda, Honduras, and Peru have no discount or premium. Colombia trades at a 400-point premium. Burundi, Rwanda, Venezuela and India trade at a 100-point discount; the Dominican Republic and Ecuador at a 400-point discount; and Brazil at a 600-point discount.

Delivery can be made to Exchange licensed warehouses in the Ports of New York District, Virginia, New Orleans, Houston, Miami, Bremen/Hamburg, Antwerp and Barcelona.

The New York and Virginia delivery points are at par with the futures price; the New Orleans, Miami and Houston delivery points are at a discount of 0.50 cents/lb; the Bremen/Hamburg, Antwerp and Barcelona delivery points are at a discount of 1.25 cents/lb.

The London contract is based on Class 1 robusta coffee with other qualities deliverable at set premiums and discounts. The contract size is ten tonnes, with prices quoted in US dollars per tonne. As with the New York C-Contract, you can deliver to Exchange-nominated warehouses in London and the UK home counties, as well as in a nominated warehouse in Amsterdam, Antwerp, Barcelona, Bremen, Felixstowe, Genoa-Savona, Hamburg, Le Havre, Marseilles- Fos, New Orleans, New York, Rotterdam and Trieste.

Coffee is a somewhat unique commodity in that it is produced in the developing world and consumed in the developed world – a striking north/south split. The EU consumes around 46 million bags of coffee each year, the US 28 million, Japan 7.5 million, Russia 4.5 million and Canada 4 million.

Other consuming countries are catching up fast. Coffee consumption in the Asia Pacific (APAC) region has been growing at around seven per cent per year for the past ten years. Consumption has been growing at four per cent per year in the Middle East North Africa (MENA) region, while consumption in Latin America has been growing at three per cent. Consumption in Europe and North America has been growing at around one per cent per year.

For the past decade or so, global coffee consumption has been growing at 2.2 per cent per year.

There is a good correlation between coffee consumption and income, both on an individual or family basis and a country basis. As real incomes rise, as measured by GDP, coffee consumption increases by a similar amount. Nordic countries have the highest per capita consumption at around 10 kg per person per year. Germany, Switzerland, the Netherlands and Austria also have a history of drinking coffee and also enjoy relatively high personal incomes. Per capita, coffee consumption is less in less wealthy countries

Coffee has two distinct market segments: home consumption and out-of-home consumption. It varies from country to country, but retail sales for in-home consumption generally account for 70-80 per cent of the overall market.

Although most coffee is still consumed at home, consumption shifts from home to out-of-home as real incomes rise. The type of food consumed in restaurants also plays a role in coffee consumption: you are more likely to drink a coffee if you are eating a doughnut than if you are eating a curry or a chow mein.

While incomes play a significant role in determining the demand for coffee, other factors such as health issues and competition from alternative beverages also play a role.

Forty years ago, when I first started to drink coffee, people tended to smoke a cigarette with their morning cuppa; it was a reflex. Several studies at that time concluded that coffee might give you cancer, but scientists now know that it was the cigarettes that were the real culprit. I will discuss the health aspects of coffee in a later chapter, but coffee is currently generally perceived as beneficial for your health.

Meanwhile, decaffeinated coffee is now widely available, allowing consumers to drink more coffee (without getting jittery), as well as to not just think of coffee as a morning or after-lunch drink.

Against that, coffee has faced competition from fizzy soft drinks, particularly among younger people. The coffee sector has responded by introducing a wide range of Ready-To-Drink (RTD) coffees that compete alongside the soft drinks on the supermarket shelves. There has been a big jump in the last few years in the consumption of RTD products, especially among the young generation, and particularly in Asia where they are mainly sold in vending machines.

RTD coffee products account for an increasing share of total coffee consumption in Asia, and they are slowly gaining market share in the EU and the US. As Andrea Illy explained earlier in this book, black coffee oxidises, and it is easier to make and market RTD coffee as a milk-based drink.

Soluble coffee consumption is also growing, although it is not growing at the expense of fresh brew. Globally, Nestlé and JDE dominate the world market in soluble coffee, although production is increasing sharply in Asia. In the UK, soluble coffee accounts for almost 80 per cent of total consumption.

Traditional soda beverage producers such as Coca Cola are moving into coffee; they see the health benefits of coffee compared with the health hazards associated with sugar-sweetened soda. You can now buy Coca-Cola flavoured coffee at some Costa Coffee outlets, as well as coffee-flavoured Coca Cola in many supermarkets.

Organic coffee is also gaining market share, but mainly in the EU and the US where consumers are willing to pay a little more for a product that they perceive to be better for their health and the health of the planet.

These trends, together with the demand for better quality speciality coffees in developed countries and increased demand in Asia, is prompting some analysts to predict a global consumption growth of as much as 5 per cent per year over the next five to ten years. Whether that pans out remains to be seen.

Vietnam and Brazil have, between them, met the increase in global consumption over the past 25 years. Between 1995 and 2017, Brazil increased its coffee production by a third while Vietnam doubled theirs. The two countries have achieved this through increases in yield and productivity through better agronomic practices, training, infrastructure, and the broader availability of financing. Yields in other producing countries have tended to be flat by comparison.

Brazil's coffee sector is diverse, ranging from large-scale mechanised farms to family-run farms that rely on hand-picking. It is the largest farms that have seen the most significant productivity increases.

According to the Brazilian Institute of Geography and Statistics' (IBGE) last agricultural census, Brazil has approximately 264,000 coffee farms, of which 72 per cent are under 20 hectares, 16 per cent are between 20 and 50 and hectares, and 12 per cent are over 50 hectares. Separate estimates suggest that approximately 70 per cent of the coffee harvested in Brazil is picked by hand, generating about 2 million seasonal jobs during the harvest.

Vietnam became the world's largest producer of robusta in 1997-98, displacing Indonesia, and the country was the second-biggest producer for all types of coffee by 1999-2000.

In Vietnam, the coffee sector is almost entirely composed of smallholder farmers. Their productivity has risen sharply as a result of investments in irrigation, chemical fertilisers and improved varieties. Nestlé has played a significant role as a big buyer of Vietnamese coffee for their soluble coffee factories. Vietnam's government has also played a critical supporting role with its Sustainable Coffee Development plan introduced in 2014.

Coffee growers in Brazil, and to a lesser extent, Colombia and Vietnam, have received a huge helping hand from their weak currencies. From 2010 to 2020, the Brazilian Real fell from 1.5 to 5.5 to the US Dollar; the Colombian Peso fell from 1.7 to 3.7 to the US Dollar. Over the past 25 years, the Vietnamese Dong has fallen from around 11,000 to the US Dollar to more than 23,000 today.

Even though world coffee prices (in terms of the NY futures market) have fallen from a high of $3 per pound in 2011 to a little over $1 per pound at the time of writing, producers in Brazil, Vietnam and Colombia are still making money in local currency terms.

Other producers are having a more challenging time covering their costs. Some producers, such as Kenya, have shifted to more profitable export crops such as fruit and vegetables, as well as cut flowers, for the European market.

Some producers are increasing their revenues by improving the quality of the coffee that they produce. Consumers in developing countries have got used to paying more for better quality speciality coffees, and these now capture premiums over and above the prices trading in the futures markets.

Even though most of the books on coffee focus on the speciality sector, it accounts for only 5-10 per cent of global coffee production and consumption. The overwhelming majority of coffee is commodity coffee.

There have been various attempts at the international level to fix coffee prices at levels that provide an adequate income to producers. On a smaller scale, the Fairtrade initiative aims to give growers more equitable - and more stable - prices. I will cover both topics in later chapters, but in the meantime, coffee professionals the world over are asking how the Coronavirus will affect their industry.

The initial concern in the early stages of the pandemic was that production would be affected. People asked whether lockdowns and travel restrictions would prevent migrant workers from travelling to the coffee-growing areas, particularly in Central and South America. In these areas, the harvest depends on migrant labour with pickers often living in temporary shared accommodation. No one was sure that farmers would be able to get and house their pickers.

As the harvest progressed, however, it became clear that these concerns were unfounded, especially in Brazil where the country finished the year with record production. Attention has since focused on the effect that the virus is having on the currencies of the three largest exporting countries; all three weakened significantly against the US dollar, effectively increasing the price of coffee in local currency terms. It will probably result in increased plantings and an increase in production in three or four years: greater supply and possible lower prices.

It slowly became clear that the virus would have a more immediate and dramatic effect on consumption with many workplaces, coffee shops and restaurants forced to close. At the time of writing – a few months into the pandemic – analysts are marking down their coffee consumption estimates for the year. Before the virus, most analysts had pencilled in the usual 2.2 per cent increase in annual demand, but they now believe that total global consumption for 2020 could fall by 1 per cent. Although that may not sound much, it is effectively a 3.2 per cent difference from what analysts had earlier predicted.

The virus has also changed the way that people consume their coffee. Even before the pandemic, Starbucks had already begun to focus less on their traditional cafés, and more on counters. Some customers prefer to order via an app, and then either pick up their coffee or have it delivered. The pandemic could accelerate this trend.

It is unsurprising that as a result of the pandemic, coffee drinkers increasingly prepare their coffee at home. Soluble coffee sales have increased in Asia, as have the sales of roasted beans in the West where there has been a corresponding surge in the sales of coffee grinders. There has also been a significant increase in the sale of coffee capsules over the internet. Not everyone wants to go through the bother of grinding their beans; capsule coffee offers a convenient alternative.

As a result, consumers are learning that they can make excellent coffee at home – and that they don't need to go to a specialised coffee shop. The industry is asking itself whether this trend will continue once the virus is under control (through mass vaccination), or whether people will put their grinders back in the cupboard. The future of hundreds of thousands of coffee shops depends on the answer to that question.

A conversation with Steve Wateridge

Good morning, Steve. Could you please tell me a little about yourself?

After studying Economics at the London School of Oriental and African Studies, I joined Rowntree's as an economist in their buying office. In 1988, I moved to ED&F Man to become head of cocoa research. Three years later, they merged cocoa and coffee, and I took over as head of both. When ED&F Man bought Volcafe in 2004, I became head of coffee research for Volcafe.

In 2006, I moved to the US to join the Ospraie hedge fund. I worked there for four years before coming back to the UK to co-found Tropical Research Services. The company advises clients on the coffee, sugar and cocoa markets.

What is the most significant change you've seen in the coffee market over your career?

I think the biggest has been the growing dominance of Brazil and Vietnam. In 2002 Brazil and Vietnam accounted for 43 per cent of global production. This year they account for 55 per cent. Brazil and Vietnam have accounted for 80 per cent of the increase in production since 2002.

Both countries are low-cost producers, and the cost of production is critical in commodity markets. When you have oversupply, the high-cost producers are the first to drop out. When you are in deficit, it is the low-cost producers that are the first to fill the gap.

What role does currency play?

The coffee price is closely correlated with the Brazilian Real. At the moment, for instance, we have a developing shortage of arabica, but in domestic currency terms, Brazilian farmers are receiving record prices. The markets are not moving much in dollar terms because the Brazilian Real is doing the job for you. Over the past seven or eight years, the Real has gone from about 1.80 to 5.80.

When you do your analysis of the underlying supply and demand in coffee, you also have to have a view on what impact a move in the Real may have.

Where does Vietnam fit into this?

Robusta has a problem at the moment. London previously represented Vietnam as most of the Brazilian robusta crop was consumed internally; the country's growers exported very little. Over the past few years, Brazil has produced a surplus of robusta – conilons. This surplus has been shipped and is now sitting in Europe. Most of the demand for this stuff is in emerging markets, in the US, in Mexico and Russia. There is very little demand for it in Europe.

The conilons have what we call a 'hard cup profile'. Roasters don't like it, and consumers don't like it. What should happen is that the price differentials between Brazil conilons and Vietnam robustas become so large that roasters start blending in a few conilons and see what they can get away with.

There is, however, a problem in that the EU has just tightened up the rules on pesticide and herbicide residues, particularly glyphosate, in food. Brazilian growers use more glyphosate nearer the harvest than in other producing countries.

A lot of the conilons already in Europe no longer meet the tightened EU restrictions, and no one in Europe wants the conilons. No one wants to take delivery of London. The calendar spreads are weak, and the coffee continues to get carried forward. Meanwhile, the funds stay short, picking up the roll yield each time they roll. The contract is broken.

What's going to happen to those conilons?

Maybe they will be shipped to Russia, the US or Mexico. Robusta certified stocks have been coming down, so the market is slowly finding a solution.

On a more general topic, how do you structure your S&D balance sheet?

We look at the global annual balance sheet. There is a two-year on-off cycle. A bumper cherry crop one year inevitably means less branch growth, and hence a smaller crop the following year. The smaller crop will allow the tree to grow its branches, but these have to be pruned. It effectively means that you lose about one-sixth of the harvest each year.

Why do you have to prune the trees?

Two reasons: first, because it makes the tree more comfortable to pick; second because smaller trees give a higher yield. It is easier for the nutrients to reach the extremities and to produce the cherries if the tree is smaller.

Growers prune fifteen per cent of their trees every year; over six years, the farmer completely renovates his trees.

Doesn't this complicate the analysis?

You have to look at the balance sheet over two years.

What should happen is that on-cycle years produce a surplus that is then whittled down in the off-cycle year. If an off-cycle year is in excess, then you know that the surplus is structural; it will be even bigger the following year.

If an on-cycle year is in deficit, you know that you will get a more significant deficit in the off-cycle. That's when you need to incentivise production to encourage farmers to apply more fertiliser and plant more to expand production.

What is the swing factor between the Brazilian on and off years?

It is more than 10 per cent. Over the past ten years – that's five cycles – four of those years have been affected by drought and are not representative of the cycle.

So, the weather is critical?

Coffee has always been a weather crop, but now it's the weather events in Brazil and Vietnam that are critical. You can have a significant weather event in Indonesia and only lose a couple of million bags. If you have a significant weather event in Vietnam, you can lose 5-7 million bags; in Brazil, you can lose 10 million bags.

By weather events do you mean frosts or droughts?

These days the problem is mainly drought.

Frosts were a big problem in Brazil in the 1970s when coffee was mainly grown in Parana, in the south of the country. Since then, production has slowly moved north, reducing the risk of frost, but not eliminating it. We have had two frost events in the past five years in Minas Gerais, but they were confined to the valleys, so the loss of coffee production was relatively small. It didn't get cold enough to wipe out a significant part of the crop; we were 1-2°C away from a problem.

Global warming is also a factor. Average temperatures in Minas Gerais are higher now than they were twenty years ago. It's not unreasonable to believe that the frost risk is lower.

The risk in coffee these days tends to be drought. We have had two significant droughts in the last six or seven years. In 2014-15, we had a 1-in-70-year drought in Minas Gerais that wiped out a considerable part of the arabica crop. Then in 2016/17, we had a 1-in-70-year drought in Espirito Santo that wiped out a large part of the conilon crop.

Is coffee irrigated in Brazil?

Most of the conilon crop is irrigated, as is a significant acreage of the arabica crop.

Is harvesting mechanised in Brazil?

Not everywhere. Some parts are heavily mechanised, while in other parts it is all picked by hand. The hilly areas tend to be small family-owned farms that require more labour. Espirito Santo is mixed: some harvesting is mechanised.

As an analyst, you must have a lot of people in the fields looking at the way the crop is developing.

That's how we get our edge.

To give you an example, we currently have a team doing a crop survey In Vietnam, visiting - at random – hundreds of farms over a 3-4-week period. Our teams visually assess the expected yield of individual trees on each farm. We look at the yield in terms of litres per tree – the number of one-litre Coke bottles that could be filled by the tree's cherries. It can be anywhere between 2 and 10 litres per tree, although some trees will produce as much as 18 litres. The teams also measure the distance between the trees to calculate the yield per hectare.

We've got guys who have been doing this for 20 years; they are very experienced. Once they have collected the data, we can crunch the numbers and come out with a reasonably good estimate of production. It helps us stay ahead of the game in predicting exports up to two years in advance.

In Brazil, we start with a flowering survey. Then in December / January, we will go out for a five-week tour. The cherries are tiny at that time, so it is quite tricky for the forecasters to predict yields - you need a lot of experience to look at the small pinpricks of cherries and try and visualise what they will be like when they are full grown. This survey gives us an early estimate for production.

Just before the harvest, in May, when the cherries are full, we go back again to check that there haven't been any significant changes.

We did a flowering survey in Vietnam in January this year, and it looked like it was going to be a record crop. Since then, the dry season has been severe, and prices are now below the cost of production. The farmers are telling us that they may reduce the amount of fertiliser they use and that they may have to irrigate if the rains don't return on time. However, they might not have either the water or the cash to irrigate. It could be a game-changer. The first indicator of that will be in the next two or three weeks during the survey we have just started.

Several companies do these macro-surveys, but we are one of a few analytical companies that also do what we call a micro-survey.

Every six weeks in Brazil we go around to 50 individual farms in the south of Minas and another 50 in Espirito Santo where we count the number of cherries on separate branches that we mark – with the agreement of the farmers, of course. This method is not as reliable as the macro-forecast, but it is useful for three reasons.

First, if the two forecasts concord, it gives us more confidence in our production number. Second, if there is a difference, we know the direction of a likely error. Third, it allows us the opportunity to get to know individual farmers. It helps us to what we call 'soft information' on things like cost of production, or how they would respond to a labour shortage, or high fertiliser prices, or even to higher or lower coffee prices.

In addition to our crop surveys, we do a stock survey every June in Brazil, and one every month in Vietnam. Farmers in Vietnam can hold a lot of stocks. If prices are low, they may hold back coffee over the crop year and release it the following year when prices recover. You need an idea of stocks at the farm level, as well as at the ports.

It takes 2 to 5 years for a coffee tree to be productive: does that mean that supply responds only very slowly?

It is where the art rather than the science comes in. If there is a global shortage, you need prices to go up so that some people consume less; that's pretty straightforward. And, at the margin, it will encourage better fertiliser use and better farm care. You might get more supply in a relatively short time. It may bring out stocks you didn't know were there. There's often a bit lying around.

Coffee demand is relatively price inelastic. When you pay $3 for a coffee in a coffee shop, the actual price of coffee is relatively small, maybe as little as 3-5 cents. A 20 per cent increase in the price of coffee beans at the origin isn't going to stop you from picking up a coffee from a coffee shop on your way to work.

Some markets are more price-sensitive: Mexico, Russia, Indonesia are examples. There you can see changes in the outright price affecting overall consumption. You can also see changes in relative prices, leading to changes in the blends. They are not as fussy as maybe some more mature markets.

How do you measure consumption?

Consumption is the hardest thing to measure. We have good production and stock data, but consumption data is an absolute nightmare. It is challenging to combine the published sales for coffee shops with those from the supermarkets. All we can look at is the stock figures at the end of the year to see whether the stocks tie in with our expectations based on our supply and demand estimates; we then adjust consumption accordingly.

You can't even start doing that until June-July because you're looking at stock numbers to the end of September, and they are so variable during the year. Looking at March stock data tells you nothing about what it's going to be like in September.

Do you do your statistics on a calendar year basis?

The coffee-year runs from October to September. Brazil's crop-year runs from July to June; Indonesia's runs from April to March and Peru's runs from May to late April. Every other country runs from October to September. We have to allow for that and adjust our figures accordingly. As such, I do two balance sheets – one on a crop-year basis and the other on a coffee-year basis.

The coffee-year smooths out the on-off cycle in Brazil and is useful for looking at long term trends, but for the short term, I focus on the crop-year balance sheet.

What drives coffee demand?

The growth in both population and GDP. There is a strong correlation between GDP growth and the increase in coffee consumption.

Soluble coffee is driving demand in Asia, while speciality coffee is driving the market in North America.

How is the cake divided up between robusta and arabica?

Last year it was 59 per cent arabica and 41 per cent robusta. If I go back 20 years to 2001 it was nearer it was 64 per cent arabica and 36 per cent robusta. The robusta is mainly used for soluble (instant) coffees. Arabica is less water-soluble and tends to be uneconomic unless prices are really low.

What other changes have you seen over your career?

One of the most significant changes that I have seen in the market over the past twenty years has been the increasing involvement of hedge funds. Over the past five years, there has been a distinct shift from funds managed and traded by humans to funds traded by computers – algorithmic funds. Far more money is now with the algo-type – the AI (Artificial Intelligence) – funds than with the fundamental funds.

Whether that will change again depends on whether the algos make money or not. If the algos perform well, they will receive further fund inflows. If they don't perform, then you may see a shift back towards what I would call the traditional managed funds.

Do hedge funds carry stocks? Do they take delivery and deliver?

They have done so in the past, but less so now. Machines don't take or make delivery.

Does hedge fund activity make your life as an analyst easier or harder?

My view of funds – an idea that isn't shared by many people in the trade - is that funds make the market more efficient. Markets were less efficient before the funds got involved. I will give you one example.

In 1977, there were crop problems in cocoa which led to a massive bull market; prices went to their highest level ever: $5,200 per tonne. People picked up on it late, and we ran out of physical stock. Chocolate makers were bidding against each other just to get enough cocoa to keep their factories running. That was a time when there was no hedge fund involvement.

Since then, we have had several occasions where the balance sheet was similarly tight. Just five years ago, we had a strong El Nino weather pattern, and there was a real risk of a severe shortage of cocoa. Instead, the funds piled in on the long side and pushed prices higher, rationing demand early and encouraging marginal supply before the shortage developed. The result was no shortage. The market, with the help of the hedge funds, solved the problem before it happened.

We see that on the downside as well. Funds get accused of pushing prices too low, but the sooner the market reacts to a surplus, the quicker the balance sheet can adjust.

What are the other significant changes you have seen over your career in coffee?

Sustainability has become a big issue for both roasters and merchants. When I started in coffee, the roasters traded significant positions on the market. They now trade much less. Their primary concern now is to ensure that their supply chain is sustainable, environmentally and socially.

Thank you, Steve, for your time and input.

Chapter 5:
Markets & Merchants

It is not from the benevolence of the butcher, the brewer, or the baker that we expect our dinner, but from their regard to their own interest. We address ourselves, not to their humanity but to their self-love, and never talk to them of our own necessities but of their advantages.

- Adam Smith, The Wealth of Nations, 1776.

Swiss supermarkets are small compared to American and French ones, but the amount of stuff in this one was overwhelming. Even though it wasn't on my shopping list, I knew that we needed some capsules for our coffee machine. There were shelves of them, different types for different devices. Within each class, there were different categories: caffeinated, decaffeinated, short, long, espresso, americano, as well as various origins. Did I want coffee from Ethiopia, Vietnam or Columbia – or did I want a blend? I didn't know.

'How does the supermarket owner know what coffee his clients want to buy?' I asked myself. 'All these people producing things, and these people consuming things; how does it all work out?'

For an answer to that question, we should go back to 1759 when the Scottish philosopher Adam Smith introduced, in a book entitled The Theory of Moral Sentiments, the concept that an 'invisible hand' ensures that the supply of a particular product matches the demand for it. He realised that in a free market, it is the price that balances supply and demand. If demand increases or supply falls, prices rise to encourage supply while at the same time reducing demand. If supply increases or demand drops, then prices fall, sending a signal to producers to reduce output or to consumers to increase demand.

He developed the idea further in 1776 when he published *The Wealth of Nations*. He argued that an economy works best in a free-market scenario where everyone operates for his or her self-interest – and where the government leaves people to buy and sell freely among themselves. Adam Smith argued that when an individual pursues his self-interest, he unintentionally promotes the good of society: self-interested competition benefits the community by keeping prices low while still building in an incentive for a wide variety of goods and services to be produced.

There was certainly plenty of variety among the different types of coffee in the supermarket. What I saw lined up in front of me was the results of thousands, or millions, of individual decisions taken all along the coffee supply chain, in every corner of the planet.

'Should I pull up my coffee trees and plant orange trees?'

'Should I ship my beans to Japan, Europe or the USA?'

'Should I put the coffee into capsules or sell it as ground?'

'Should I make more decaffeinated coffee this year than last year?'

When a market is working well, price should answer all of these questions. If coffee pays better than orange juice, a farmer will leave my coffee trees in the ground. If shoppers in Japan value coffee more than shoppers in Europe then, providing the difference covers the extra cost of shipping, growers will sell their coffee in Japan, not Europe.

If consumers like the convenience of coffee in capsules – and if they are willing to pay enough of a premium to cover the cost of the capsules packaging – then roasters will sell their coffee in capsules. The same applies to decaffeinating the coffee; if consumers are willing to pay enough of a premium, then roasters will produce it. If not, they won't.

Why are there so many different varieties of coffee in the supermarkets? The answer is that we are not all the same; we like and value different things. My wife prefers a decaffeinated coffee. My son likes espresso, and I like americano. Producers try to meet these varied demands.

Price is the invisible hand that matches supply and demand. If coffee production is low and the cost of coffee increases, then consumers might switch to tea instead, reducing coffee demand to a level where it matches supply. Alternatively, producers might respond to higher coffee prices and produce more. If the price of decaffeinated coffee increases relative to the cost of ordinary coffee, my wife may switch to drinking regular coffee, and producers may make more decaffeinated coffee.

There is a saying in commodities that 'demand is the backdrop against which changes in supply play out'. Covid aside, the demand for coffee doesn't change suddenly; it moves at a glacial speed following long-term trends. It is supply that drives the price in the short and medium-term. But what drives supply?

The weather is the most critical factor in determining the supply of all agricultural commodities. Demand for a particular commodity could vary by a percentage point from year to another, but a frost or a drought in Brazil could lead to a collapse in production from one year to the next. Market participants spend a considerable amount of their time worrying about the weather.

The second most important factor that affects the supply of an agricultural commodity is the price of that commodity, both in outright terms and in relation to alternative competing crops. It leads to a circular situation where the price of a particular commodity will depend on its supply, while the supply depends, at least partially, on the price. It is a feedback loop with a time lag; the length of that time lag depends on the commodity. The cost of alternative crops can also have a significant impact on production.

As coffee is a tree crop, most growers do not have easy decisions. Imagine a Brazilian coffee producer faced with low coffee prices. His neighbours are pulling up their coffee trees and planting orange trees instead. He is wondering whether to do the same. The problem is that the farmer might know the relative prices of coffee and orange juice today or, by looking at the futures market, the comparable prices in two years. But he won't know the relative prices in three or four years, which is when the first harvests are ready. Too much can happen between then and now.

Unfortunately, markets are imperfect. Winston Churchill once said: 'Democracy is the worst form of government, except for all those other forms that have been tried from time to time.' He could have said the same thing about markets.

Agricultural markets over-react in both directions and can take time to correct. Shortages now usually lead to surpluses in the future. Prices tend to rise too far in times of penury and tend to fall too far in times of plenty. They also tend to stay higher for longer and lower for longer than you would expect.

But why might coffee prices stay low for long periods? Once prices fall below production costs, won't farmers stop tending their trees? Unfortunately, not all of them have a choice. Coffee may be the only cash crop that a smallholder grows; he needs the cash no matter what the coffee price.

Also, once the coffee cherries are on the trees, it doesn't cost that much to pick them. Coffee growers will gather and process their cherries as long as the price at which they can sell them covers what economists call the variable cost of picking and processing them. The price a Brazilian farmer receives for his coffee may not cover his fixed costs, the rent he pays for the land or the interest he has to pay to the bank for any loans he may have taken out. However, he is still better off picking the cherries rather than letting them rot. He will only abandon his trees if the price he receives for the cherries is less than the cost of harvesting and processing them.

Although markets often get a bad rap, remember that commerce has always played a central role in our lives. As Paul Collier and John Kay wrote in their book Greed is Dead: Politics After Individualism:

'When one of us recently asked a taxi driver to take us to the centre of the small capital of his poor country, he deposited us in a busy location and pointed. 'There is the old market, straight ahead,' he said, and 'There is the new market, to the right.' For most of history, and in less-developed countries today, the marketplace was not the enemy of the community; the marketplace was where the community came to life. Indeed, the market is the process that replaces the isolation of self-sufficiency with the communalism of independence. The institution of the market is the essential first step in the journey out of mass poverty.'

Adam Smith was an advocate of free markets, but he was wary of businessmen and warned of their 'conspiracy against the public or in some other contrivance to raise prices'. He wrote of the collusive nature of business interests, in the form of monopolies, fixing the highest price 'which can be squeezed out of the buyers'. He also wrote: 'the interest of manufacturers and merchants is always in some respects different from, and even opposite to, that of the public.'

In practice, markets may not always be efficient, and governments may need to interfere to correct those inefficiencies. It might happen if producers club together into a cartel to raise prices, requiring the government to intervene and break up the cartel. But even without a cartel, a particular producer might be so big in a specific commodity that he becomes a monopoly seller, forcing prices higher.

Besides, markets might not correctly price what economists call 'externalities'. These could be the environmental costs of factory pollution or heavy traffic on the country's roads at harvest time. Nor do markets correctly price 'collective goods'. Individual producers might not value the benefits of research into new crop varieties or of infrastructure investment such as railways or ports. On a broader scale, governments rather than markets may better provide collective goods such as education and health services.

But what role do traders and merchants play in the way markets function?

Coffee traders and merchants move coffee from areas where it grows well (and cheaply) to places where it grows less well, or not at all. They transport coffee from surplus areas to deficit areas. If coffee is worth more money in the US than in Brazil – and if that difference is more than the cost of shipping it (plus a little profit margin to make it worthwhile), then the trader or merchant will make it happen.

Coffee traders do not only move coffee from surplus to deficit areas. They also store and process it. They hold coffee at times when it is not needed (after the harvest) until a time it is needed (throughout the year). Coffee millers process coffee from a form in which it is not wanted into a condition in which it is wanted, transforming cherries into green beans. Roasters transform the green beans into roasted or soluble coffee.

Millers and roasters are, by definition, traders. A miller buys cherries and sells green beans, while a roaster buys green beans and sells roasted beans. Just as a trader may depend for his livelihood on his skill in buying coffee in one country and selling it in another, a roaster depends on his skill in buying coffee in one form and selling it in another. Millers and roasters are traders, and they need trading skills to perform their tasks correctly.

When you think about that a little, it becomes clear that what a trader is most interested in is not the outright price of coffee but the difference in the prices of that coffee in its different geographies, times and forms. It is the price differential that matters, not the outright price. Traders like to limit their exposure to the outright, or flat price, of a commodity. They usually hedge their outright price risk, preferring to make their money on the differentials – the difference between the cost of the futures and the price of their particular coffee.

All traders – and that includes roasters – will try to reduce their risk of future price movements by hedging what they buy, taking an offsetting position for the same quantity in the futures market. Having purchased the physicals, a trader will sell futures as a hedge. When he sells the coffee, the trader will buy back their futures hedge; they no longer need to be protected against a move in the outright price of coffee because they don't own it anymore.

Everyone involved in the coffee supply chain is taking and managing price risk. The farmer is perhaps taking the most significant risk by growing coffee in the first place. He may try to offset some of that risk by selling in advance – selling something that he doesn't (yet) have.

The trader is taking a risk on the quantity that he buys but offsets that risk by hedging in the futures market. The roaster is also taking a risk; he has invested in his roasting machinery and has the risk that coffee prices will be too high to allow him to make a profit when he sells his roasted beans.

When I began my trading career with Cargill in the late 1970s, my first business card gave my title as 'Commodity Merchandiser'. But what is the difference between a trader and a merchandiser? Traders take positions on the markets, betting whether prices – or the differentials between prices – will rise or fall. Merchandisers move commodities along the supply chain, taking a tiny margin at each stage of its journey.

Traditional commodity merchandising has become more challenging and less profitable over time. It has become tough to make a margin just moving coffee along the supply chain.

One of the significant difficulties that merchandisers now face is that information is widely and freely available. It also travels incredibly fast. Technological change has reduced the potential for traders to arbitrage prices between geographical regions.

The other significant change is that governments and government agencies have pretty much left the coffee business. In the past, governments were often responsible for selling their country's production, and this led to opportunities for corruption. Low-paid government officials were easy targets for unscrupulous traders; selling tenders were often rigged in favour of the traders that gave the biggest bribes. The markets have now been privatised, and this no longer happens.

In a world of instant information, it is no longer possible for merchants to take advantage of price differentials in various countries; instead, they now have to anticipate them. It is the point where a merchant becomes a trader. A trader predicts where shortages and surpluses will occur, and he takes a position in the market in anticipation of future price moves. As a result, analysis has become the lifeblood of trading.

It is not unusual for a trading company to employ more analysts than traders. Nor is it uncommon for traders to spend most of their time not on trading, but analysis. It is impossible to succeed in the commodity markets without an experienced group of traders and analysts to interpret and understand the mass of information that needs to be absorbed.

But analysis is not the only thing that you need to succeed in the physical commodity markets: you also need clients. Traders, therefore, have to keep in regular contact with their client networks, and they have to move physical coffee along the supply chain. There is now such an overlap between trading and merchandising that they are pretty much the same thing.

Merchandising coffee allows you to see the trade flows, helps with your analysis, and enables you to anticipate trading opportunities in the coffee market. But the margins on straight merchandising are now so thin – and sometimes even negative -- that it is pretty much impossible for a pure coffee merchandiser to survive. The profits from trading subsidise the lack of profits, or the losses, on merchandising. In that sense, merchandising enables trading, and trading facilitates merchandising. They are mutually dependent.

A market participant who is not a trader/merchandiser is usually and colloquially referred to as a commodity speculator. The US Commodity Futures Trading Commission (CFTC) refers to speculator as 'non-commercials', which is a better descriptive term. A non-commercial is an entity – it could be an individual, a hedge fund, a pension fund or a bank – that is not involved in the physical transformation of the underlying commodity. It is not directly involved in the commercialisation of the commodity on its journey from producer to consumer.

However, a non-commercial is indirectly involved. A non-commercial assumes some of the price risks that commercials have to accept as they move coffee along the supply chain. They are, therefore, an integral part of the supply chain. Without them, merchants and roasters would have to assume more risk.

Non-commercials may like to be involved in the markets for different reasons. Pension funds may want to hold commodities as part of a diversified risk portfolio. Hedge funds and banks may believe that they can beat the market and profit from price movements. Some smaller speculators may just like the thrill of the risk.

Commodity professionals are often frustrated by the way the media portrays non-commercials. People refer to someone who buys shares in Apple Inc - and then sells them out again a week later - as an 'investor'. He is generally seen as contributing to the global good. Someone that buys coffee futures one day and sells them a week later is referred to as a 'speculator' and is generally seen as contributing to global evil.

By assuming some of the price risks in the coffee supply chain, the coffee speculator is contributing more to the global good than the Apple Inc investor.

Finally, non-commercials play a role beyond risk assumption. By buying before a supply deficit, or selling before a supply surplus, a non-commercial helps ensure that price moves before the event occurs. They help supply and demand to balance itself out quicker.

Together, both speculators and traders help to make sure that a market is working efficiently and sending the correct signals to both producers and consumers.

A Conversation with Nicolas Tamari

Good morning, Nicolas. Could you tell me a little about yourself and Sucafina?

My family is originally from Palestine. We are Christian Palestinians from a city called Jaffa to the south of Tel Aviv. My family business started in 1905; we used to export citrus from Jaffa and import food products that we distributed in the Arabic peninsula. By food products, I mean sugar, coffee, tea, maise flour etc. We would import food products because the norm at that time was barter, rather than exporting and getting paid.

As well as exporting our oranges, we also played a role as a cooperative for other citrus producers who couldn't export. As such, we have a long history with the concept of sustainability and working in a cooperative model.

In 1948, with the creation of the state of Israel, Jaffa becoming part of Israel, and my father, his brothers, sister and parents left. My father, at that time, was 26 years old and was already involved in the business. One of his brothers decided to base himself in Amman, while my father based himself in Lebanon. They could no longer export oranges and citrus, but they continued importing food products, distributing them in the Arabic Peninsula.

In 1975, with the war in Lebanon, my father moved to Switzerland and started Sucafina in 1977. At that time Sucafina stood for 'Sugar, Coffee and Finance'. He viewed it as a continuation of his previous business but focusing now only on coffee and sugar. Instead of importing and distributing the Middle East, he started what I would call the international trade.

His brother - my uncle - stayed in Jordan and continued the merchanting business in the Middle East for multi-commodities, but the two firms became separate. One was Sucafina, owned by my father, and the other one became a multi-commodity import business owned by my uncle.

In the early 1980s, my father decided to stop trading sugar. He saw how the sugar market was becoming consolidated, and he decided to focus exclusively on coffee. He saw more opportunities in coffee than in sugar because the fragmentation that he saw in coffee didn't exist in sugar.

The oranges that you exported - were they the famous Jaffa oranges that I grew up with as a child in England?

Exactly! We had about 10 per cent of the export market, but unfortunately, we lost everything and had to restart from scratch.

When did you join the family firm?

When I finished University, I went to work in a bank. I didn't like it; I didn't like the corporate environment. I found that there was no entrepreneurship. So, I decided to join the family business of Sucafina in 1994. At that time, both my brother and my father were working in coffee, so I started a new division, concentrating on instant coffee. It is still running; we call it 'Sucafina Ingredients'. It buys and sells instant coffee.

I ran this business for a little more than ten years. We had a branded product called 'Cafe Ambassador'. We sold the coffee in Russia and the CIS, but we quickly realised that we were competing with our clients, the brand owners. So, we sold the brand to a publicly listed company. It is still alive in Russia and the CIS and is doing quite well.

In the early 2000s, we decided to spin off our asset management and investment business into another company. My brother Wahbe chose to lead that, so that led to me taking over responsibility for Sucafina.

Your father continued to come to the office until he was in his 90s. Was it easy to work with him, or did he second-guess your decisions?

When my father handed over the business, he still followed what was going on in the markets and the company. He would give his opinion, but he would always make sure not to make the decision. He was very encouraging. When I would make a mistake, he never criticised me. Instead, he would be supportive and try to guide me in seeing the issue differently. So, it's been an excellent handover. I think the secret of success is to truly empower the person to whom you hand over the business.

My father is based now in Beirut, Lebanon, but he still comes to the office when he is in Geneva.

Do you have any other brothers or sisters?

Yes, I have a sister, Della, who runs our family foundation, the Tamari Foundation. It focuses principally on education and provides funds and support to students in need. It's a Swiss-based foundation.

Right now, with the economic crisis in Lebanon, we are allocating the majority of our funds to the Middle East, but we are not limited to the Middle East. We give funds to students from developing countries, the Middle East and a little bit Europe.

Why didn't your father change the name of the company when he decided to drop sugar to concentrate on coffee?

When my father founded Sucafina, the name stood for 'Sugar, Coffee, Finance'. My mother chose the name. Today Sucafina stands for Sustainable Coffee Finance.

'Sustainable' because sustainability is our DNA.

'Coffee' because we're a coffee company.

'Finance' because you have to have finance to survive as a merchant.

While many of your competitors have historically sourced supplies from Central America, Sucafina has historically sourced East African coffee into Europe.

We had a revolution in the coffee market in 1989 when the ICA - the International Coffee Agreement – imploded.

The ICA was based on a quota system - a little bit like OPEC - and we would source our coffee at the origin from government-owned institutions. For example, in Uganda, we had to buy from the State Coffee Marketing Board. It was the same for all the buyers.

The world coffee business was effectively privatised after the ICA collapsed. Merchants had no choice but to invest in origin countries to secure a supply of raw material, to run their own mills and domestic supply chains. Previously, government institutions would do that for you.

So, 1989 was a crucial year in the reinvention of coffee merchanting. A lot of old established companies that had depended on political connections – for example, in West Africa - disappeared. We had a rebirth of the coffee trade in the course of the 1990s.

That was when we decided to focus on East Africa. Our peers went to other jurisdictions, but we thought that Africa as a continent had many opportunities. I think it was the right decision because today we are globally recognised as the premier supplier of East African coffee in the world.

But Sucafina is also present in other geographies.

Historically we've been in East Africa and Europe, but in the last decade, we have focused on growing in the Americas. We've strengthened our operations in Brazil and Colombia, and we have opened a multitude of offices in North America.

Our strategy in the next five years is to do the same in Asia. We want to look at Asia first as a sourcing network, for example in Papua New Guinea, East Timor and China, and second as a consumer, for example in China, Korea and Malaysia etc.

A couple of months back, we acquired a speciality coffee merchant based in Hong Kong, Australia and New Zealand. It used to be called MTC, which stood for 'Mountain Top Coffee', but we have since rebranded it as 'Sucafina Speciality'.

What is your global footprint now?

One out of every 20 cups of coffee drunk in the world comes from Sucafina.

That is a significant number, but we look more at profitability rather than volume. Volume does not drive us. We often say: 'Volume is vanity, profit is sanity, and cash flow is reality.' We look to be profitable, not to fight for market share.

Who owns Sucafina today?

The company today is owned by the family and by the management. We believe that commodity trading companies should be owned by the management. It's a people business.

We encourage key people to become shareholders. To become a shareholder, you have to have worked for the company for a minimum number of years, to share our values, and to contribute to the bottom line financially.

I know that you are still young, but do you have a succession plan in place?

We are a meritocracy. I am the only family member working in the company. My successor may be a non-family member, and we're currently grooming several people for that position. I have a number two in place if something were to happen to me tomorrow, but otherwise, we have an exciting programming cycle in the company called 'Sparks'. We're grooming kids between 25 and 35 to be the future of the group.

How many people are there in the company?

We are about one thousand people.

Where exactly do you situate in the supply chain between the farmer and the consumer?

Our vision today is to be the **leading sustainable farm to roaster coffee company in the world**. Let me break that down for you.

We want to lead, meaning we want to innovate in our industry. We'd rather be the Tesla of coffee than the Nissan of coffee.

Regarding **sustainability**, we believe that everybody in the supply chain must make money. We're not shy to say that if you don't have economic sustainability, you can't have social and environmental sustainability.

Farm to roaster defines our position in the supply chain. We are not farmers, but we want to make strategic partnerships with farmers to share market know-how and effective agricultural practices. We want to start at the farm without owning a land bank, and we want to finish at the roaster.

We want to own a roaster, but we don't want to own a brand. We're happy to be a private label roaster, but not a brand owner. If you are a brand owner, you are competing with your customers.

Our goal is to add as much value in the supply chain as possible without competing with our customers. Our primary customers are the big brands who often have roasting facilities of their own.

Coffee Company because we just do coffee.

In the world because, as I said before, we used to be European - East African Centric, but now we are a global player.

Where is the value in the supply chain today?

The principal value is in the brands. The closer you are to the consumer, the more value you add. We are not tempted to develop a brand. We believe that this is a red line that we should not cross because we would be competing with our customers.

Do some of your customers source their coffee directly from the origin?

A lot of companies want to source directly, and we encourage them to do so. We are happy to put in place a transparent model where we show our customer the supply chain, and we agree on a specific margin for us for the logistics and the operational risks we take. It happens more in the speciality segment.

For mainstream coffee, the roasters are looking for the lowest price, and they don't always have secured and recurrent supply chains.

Changing the subject, why are there so many coffee trading companies in Switzerland?

Switzerland has been a hub for commodity merchants for the last fifty to seventy years. Companies originally came to Switzerland for the banking infrastructure - remember, finance is our lifeblood - but now they also come for the talent pool.

As for coffee traders, a lot of the big coffee roasting companies have their procurement headquarters in Switzerland, for example, Starbucks and Keurig in Lausanne and Nestlé in Vevey. Being in Switzerland means that we are close to our customers.

Going back to the coffee market, why are prices so low, and do you see any relief for growers soon?

Prices are currently low because the Brazilian Real is low against the US Dollar. Brazil is the largest producer and exporter of coffee, and a soft Real enables Brazilian producers to obtain a reasonable return.

I do see relief shortly for prices. Even with the Coronavirus, I am confident that coffee consumption will keep growing in the decade to come.

Do the futures markets work well? Are they liquid and do they set prices correctly?

Yes, both are liquid, and they set prices correctly.

Most of the coffee traded against the New York Exchange is not tenderable; it has to be produced using the washed method. The Brazilians can wash less than ten per cent of their arabica coffee. They can only deliver that ten per cent to the Exchange.

Traditionally - for the last hundred years or so - the Brazilians rarely washed their coffee. They do not currently have the infrastructure to wash it, and it would need substantial capital expenditure to build it.

It results in a de-correlation in the differentials between the physical and futures prices in terms of the basis.

Historically, differentials were not particularly volatile, except for Colombia in 2009 when we had a weather problem. Recently, differentials have become more volatile, leading to a total de-correlation between physical and futures.

Right now, we're currently living with a scenario where washed arabica coffee is trading at the massive premium to the underlying futures. There is a shortage of washed arabica coffee, but an excess of natural arabica coffee.

Do you see any room in coffee for trading against reported prices?

The ICO, the International Coffee Organisation, has a lagging physical indicator, but few people use it. I think we need to reinvent the way we price coffee, but we need a shock for that to happen. Our current methodology is, in some cases, not sustainable.

Has the introduction of single-serve capsules led to a fall in demand for coffee?

When you used to make a big pot of coffee and drink two or three cups, you would throw away the rest. We used to say that the sink was the best customer. The sink is now drinking less.

On the other hand, since we launched single-serve capsules, people are enjoying a better cup of coffee, and they are drinking more coffee overall. The better the quality, the more you drink.

I don't buy the theory that demand is lower because the sink is consuming less coffee. I believe that you can offset this by the fact that coffee is getting better, and people want to drink two coffees instead of one.

Changing the subject again, I understand you are a marathon runner.

I have run a marathon every year since 2013. It keeps me fit and helps me with my work-life balance. It also helps me to push my limits. I'm proud to say that at 50 years old I'm running a marathon 20 minutes faster than when I was in my early 40s. Marathon running is a sport where you can keep improving independent of your age.

I ran my last marathon in 3 hours and 42 minutes, raising money for the Kahawatu Foundation, which is involved in helping smallholder coffee growers in East Africa.

I run a different marathon every year. My favourite was Geneva because it was my fastest! The most exciting one was New York because you have thousands of people cheering you on. The hardest one was Athens – the 'authentic' marathon; it is very hilly!

Marathon running has taught me that we set our own limits. You can do things you don't expect you can only by pushing your boundaries. In terms of endurance, I think that both life and coffee trading is a marathon. So, you need always to be ready to hold more pain and to have more oxygen in your lungs. You have to dig deep.

Thank you, Nicolas, for your time and your insights.

Chapter 6: Market Intervention

As long as there was coffee in the world, how bad could things be?

— Cassandra Clare (Author)

It is difficult for anyone who joined the world of coffee after the collapse of the International Coffee Agreement in 1989 to imagine what it was like before that date; there is a pre-1989 and a post-1989 coffee world.

It is just as challenging to understand why well-meaning attempts to support coffee prices to help producers often leads to the opposite result. To understand why, you have to look at the history of coffee market interventions – both on a national and international basis - to see what worked and what didn't. We will start at the turn of the last century.

Thanks to a bumper harvest, Brazil exported more than 10 million bags of coffee in 1901, two-thirds of the total world demand. Their massive crop, along with an aggressive export policy, drove world coffee prices to 6 cents/lb, way below the cost of production at that time.

The following year, Latin American coffee producers met in New York to try to find a way to push prices back up again. The only agreement they reached was to meet the following year – and even then, that didn't happen.

Having failed to win an international agreement, growers in Sao Paulo met with their state government to plead their case. In 1903, the Sao Paulo government imposed a tax of $180 an acre on any new coffee plantations in the state, valid for five years. It effectively put a stop to new plantings, but as it took four or five years for new trees to enter into production, the measure had little effect on output until 1907. In the meantime, Brazilian production continued to grow.

Later in 1903, coffee growers asked the Sao Paulo government to join with growers and merchants to buy up surplus coffee and hold it off the market to raise prices – a so-called 'valorisation' scheme. The state government refused to get involved, arguing that even if the plan were successful, producers elsewhere in the world would take advantage of the higher prices to expand their production and take market share away from Brazil.

Brazilian production continued to expand until 1905 when Sao Paulo's growers agreed on a scheme to buy up the country's surplus coffee and hold it off the market. They asked the government to fund the project, but again the government refused.

In 1906, the growers obtained a bank loan for £1 million to finance the purchase of surplus coffee stocks, but the amount was insufficient to have any meaningful effect. The growers approached other banks without success and eventually turned to one of the leading coffee traders of the day, a certain Hermann Sielcken. He successfully put together a consortium of banks and traders and convinced the Sao Paulo government to join the consortium to the tune of 20 per cent.

The consortium began buying coffee in the export market, paying up to 7 cents a pound and shipping it to warehouses in Europe and the US. By the end of the year, they had bought about 2 million bags, too little compared to the 20 million bags that the country produced each year. The State of Sao Paulo quickly ran out of money and could no longer finance their 20 per cent. Undeterred, the consortium obtained an additional £3 million loan from a syndicate of banks.

By 1908, coffee prices had risen above 7 cents/lb, and the consortium sold off one million bags out of the 8 million that they were by then holding. Rising prices encouraged other banks to join in the syndicate and lend the consortium a further £15 million. As Brazil's production eventually slowed as a result of the tax on new plantings, prices rose further. By 1911, world prices had reached 14 cents/lb. Sielcken said at the time that 'it was the best loan I have ever known'.

In 1912, Sielcken, a US citizen, was called in front of a US congressional committee, accused of manipulating the price of coffee. Even though prices had doubled, the consortium still had 4 million bags in warehouses around the world. The US Attorney General began a legal battle to confiscate the 900,000 bags that they were holding in the US and, when that failed, to force the consortium to sell, something which they did the following year. The consortium sold off the remaining 3.1 million bags that it held in Europe off over the next three years.

After the end of the First World War, the Sao Paulo government conducted further price support – valorisation – schemes. In 1921, they borrowed £9 million to finance 4.5 million bags that they were holding off the market. Coffee prices doubled, and they sold off the coffee, repaying the loan. With some of the profits that they made, the government built bonded warehouses in Brazil to hold future stocks, rather than keeping them overseas.

In 1926, the consortium, now known as the Sao Paulo Coffee Institute, borrowed £4 million to repeat the trick. By the end of the year, they were storing 3.3 million bags in their domestic warehouses. The following year the country produced a bumper crop of 30 million bags, and Sao Paulo asked other states to help the scheme by limiting the quantity of coffee sent to the ports.

Meanwhile, Colombian growers were taking advantage of Brazil's valorisation scheme to increase production. Colombia's coffee production doubled during the 1920s. In 1927, the Colombian coffee industry founded the National Federation of Colombian Coffee Growers to manage the sector in the best interests of its growers. It was funded by a tax on coffee exports.

Back in Brazil, the Coffee Institute had borrowed a further £10 million from banks keen to repeat past successes. Still, with the tax on new plantings now rescinded, Brazil's planted area was growing strongly again. When, in 1929, the consortium sought a new loan for £9 million, the banks turned them down. Rumours began circulating that the consortium would have to sell their entire stocks, estimated at a whopping 10 million bags.

On 11th October 1929 coffee prices began to slip on the floor of the Santos Bolsa, Brazil's local coffee Exchange and word quickly spread that the Institute was bankrupt. World coffee prices collapsed. On 29th October the New York stock market also collapsed, sparking the Great Depression.

Was the coffee price collapse the catalyst for the stock market collapse and the Great Depression that followed? It may have played a part.

By 1931, coffee prices had fallen to 8 cents/lb from their high of 22.5 cents/lb two years earlier. There were 26 million bags of coffee in Brazil's warehouses, a million bags more than the entire world's annual consumption. The only solution was to destroy the coffee. In the first year, the government burned 7 million bags held in warehouses, but it still wasn't enough to cope with the inflow from the new crop. They stepped up the rate of burning with a massive 17.2 million bags burnt in 1937.

As well as burning their excess stocks, the Brazilians looked for other means of deposing of their surplus coffee. As I mentioned earlier, Brazilian growers approached Nestlé in Switzerland to see if they could use some of their stocks to produce instant coffee. Their approach spurred Nestlé into inventing a new process to make instant coffee, but it took them almost ten years to do so.

Brazil also tried to increase the demand for brewed coffee. In 1936, they joined forces with other Latin American producers to form the Pan-American Coffee Bureau to promote consumption.

That same year Brazil entered into a price maintenance scheme with Colombia. It quickly fell apart with the Brazilians accusing the Colombians of taking advantage of the system to increase their market share. The Brazilians had got that right at least. Brazil's attempts to support world coffee prices had allowed other producers to expand production. In 1906, Brazil had grown 20 million bags of coffee while the rest of the world produced 3.6 million. By 1938, Brazil was making 22 million bags and other producers 10.2 million bags.

By 1940, the world's coffee price had fallen to 5.75 cents/lb, a historic low, and the US government was concerned that low coffee prices might push Latin American producers towards either the Nazis or the Communists. In response, the US agreed to increase the quantity of coffee that they imported from the region and allocate imports via quotas.

The Inter-American Coffee Agreement, signed in November 1940, read: 'It is necessary and desirable to take steps to promote the orderly marketing of coffee to assure terms of trade equitable for both producers and consumers by adjusting supply to demand.'

The Agreement gave Brazil about 60 per cent of the US import quota, Colombia 20 per cent and other Latin American producers the rest. By June 1941, the world coffee price had almost doubled from its previous year's lows. It remained strong throughout the war and long afterwards, but whether that was a result of the agreement or increasing demand remains a moot point.

On 4th July 1953, a severe frost in Parana Brazil destroyed the crop, along with many of the trees themselves. For the first time, the price of coffee broke $1 per pound.

By 1959, producers were once again worried about low prices. The problem was the expansion in robusta production in Africa and Asia, as well as in Brazil. Robusta was cheaper and easier to grow than arabica, and the trees produced a crop two years after planting compared to the four years it then took for arabica trees. Besides, instant coffee, made with robusta coffee, was driving the growth in demand.

By 1960, Brazilian stocks had reached 35 million bags, a level roughly equivalent to the world's annual consumption. The country's producers agreed to reduce their exports by 10 per cent, but they never enforced the agreement.

In 1962, the UN convened a conference in New York that led to the formation of the International Coffee Agreement (ICA). The US, still worried about communist infiltration in Latin America, gave their support and the agreement was ratified in December 1963. The Agreement set a world export quota of 45.6 million bags; Brazil had 18 million and Colombia 6 million bags. The Agreement also established the International Coffee Organisation (ICO), based in London, to act as the Agreement's enforcer.

The Agreement allowed quotas to be adjusted every three months, as long as a two-thirds majority of importing and exporting members approved the adjustments. Some importing member countries, principally Japan, China and the Soviet were exempt from the quotas, as were non-member countries.

Prices rose strongly during the negotiations because of a continuing drought and another frost in Brazil. Concerned that the US would fail to ratify the Agreement, producers agreed to increase quotas by just over 3 per cent. The Agreement was finally implemented in 1965.

Under the Agreement, every coffee shipment had to be accompanied by a certificate of origin, or a re-export certificate. However, the system had a significant flaw: it allowed coffee that was outside of the Agreement to be re-exported from exempt countries, particularly from the USSR. It became known as 'tourist coffee'. Besides, some coffee was exported (smuggled) from producing countries outside of their quotas. Many producers sold this coffee at discount prices, but they preferred to take a lower price for some of their coffee than respect the quotas and not sell it at all.

The Agreement had other problems. Production didn't fall as anticipated and stocks built up at origin, particularly in Brazil. By 1966, Brazil held 65 million bags, out of the world surplus of 87 million bags. History was repeating itself, but this time the government decided to burn coffee trees rather than the coffee itself.

In 1969, another frost hit Parana. Prices rose, and the Brazilian government reversed its policy of burning coffee trees, announcing a plan to plant 200 million new trees. However, in 1970, growers found leaf rust disease in Bahia, Sao Paulo and Parana; despite drastic efforts, growers failed to control the outbreak. During the 1970s, the disease quickly spread northwards into Central America.

In 1971, the US devalued the US Dollar, effectively lowering the coffee price in terms of producers' domestic currencies. The producing members asked for the ICA price to be revised upwards in compensation, but the consuming countries, led by the US, refused.

Two years earlier, in 1969, representatives from Brazil, Colombia, El Salvador, Ethiopia, Guatemala, Ivory Coast, Mexico, Angola, and Uganda had met in Geneva to push for an increase in their quotas; they failed. In 1972, this 'Geneva group' of producers agreed to under-ship their export quotas. Prices rose, and even though the increase may have had more to do with rust disease, importing countries blamed the new export restrictions. Long, acrimonious discussions followed, and the Agreement lapsed at the end of the year.

Three years later, in July 1975, a black frost hit southern Brazil, killing more than half of the country's coffee trees. Production was also hit elsewhere in the world with rust disease in Central America and civil war in parts of Africa, particularly in Ethiopia.

By March 1976, world coffee prices had doubled to $1 a pound and the US re-joined the ICA in the hope of stabilising prices. The move failed. There was little that the ICO could do except encourage exporters to export more, something that they were unwilling or unable to do. By May 1977, coffee prices were trading over $4 per pound.

Prices began to ease off into the summer of that year and gradually fell to around $2 per pound. Brazil stubbornly refused to sell anything at less than $3.20 a pound and even began buying physical coffee from other producing countries to try to limit world supplies and push prices back up. Their efforts failed, and by November they had given up. Although Brazil's growers maintained the fiction of a $3.20 minimum price, they offered discounts to sell their coffee and compete on the world market

The 1980s were a period of relative stability for the world coffee market with prices contained mainly within a range of $1 to 1.5 per pound, just outside the ICA's $ 1.20–1.40 target range. 1986 was an exception when a drought in Brazil pushed prices to a high of $2.5 per pound. The price spike led to a suspension in export quotas, and they were only reintroduced in October 1987 when the coffee price was on the point of once again falling below $1 per pound.

In 1989, exporters suspended the quotas after they failed to come to terms on new ones. Backed by the US, Central American states and Mexico pressed for a larger market share of export quotas, but the Brazilian and African countries refused. The Agreement collapsed for the last time.

There have been various attempts over the years to negotiate a new Agreement. In 1989, the President of Colombia wrote to US President George Bush to ask for his help to support coffee prices. The following year, President Bush told a Latin American drugs summit in Colombia that the US was committed to a new ICA. In 1992, Brazil gave the go-ahead to start negotiations for a new ICA. The talks collapsed with each side blaming the other for the failure.

Since then, there have been some further half-hearted and ultimately unsuccessful attempts to reintroduce an international price support system, but for the moment the ICO continues as a global information exchange without any provisions for price regulation.

Even if it had survived, it is, in any case, doubtful whether the ICA would have been flexible enough to deal with the growth in production in Vietnam. During the 1990s, Vietnam went from producing fewer than 2 million bags a year to over 25 million bags a year, making it the second-largest producer of coffee after Brazil. Other producing countries would have been unlikely to have agreed to reduce their ICA export quotas to allow Vietnam to grow.

However, others have turned this argument around, suggesting the growth in Vietnamese production was only possible because of – and a direct consequence of – the ending of the quota system.

Recently, there have been renewed calls for government help in dealing with current low prices. In 2019, the renowned economist Jeffrey Sachs and a team at the Columbia Centre on Sustainable Investment called for an annual $10 billion fund to stabilise the global coffee sector. But the authors of the report were realistic as to whether price stabilisation would work. They wrote:

'Historically, price support systems have caused market distortions, reduced domestic consumption, and either encouraged oversupply—with a consequent lowering of the world price of the subsidised product—or required complicated supply management efforts. Past coffee price support efforts at different levels have also failed to reach their objectives over the long-term.'

A conversation with Shirin Moayyad

Good morning, Shirin. Could you tell me a little bit about yourself?

I studied anthropology as an undergraduate and then began a master's programme in development studies. For that, I needed to do a practicum, and I somehow found a position in the highlands of Papua New Guinea, working with an anthropologist. I quickly realised that the academic life wasn't for me, so I took a job with a local trading company that owned coffee plantations, along with other businesses. The company was also the managing partner for what at the time was Volcafe's division in PNG.

My employers put me in charge of a small coffee estate, about a hundred acres. I lived on the plantation, so I learned coffee from the ground up - from the growing angle.

At that time, there were only two tiny coffee roasteries in Papua New Guinea. The company bought one of them and put me in charge of modernising it and developing exports. Our coffee ended up in supermarkets all over the South Pacific. It was quite a success as a model for value-adding in-country and a fantastic project in which to be involved.

After eleven years in Papua New Guinea, I moved to Singapore, where I was hired to set up the roasting plant for a chain of coffee shops. I commissioned the roasting plant and was both the roaster and green coffee buyer for them.

I then moved to Peet's to be their green coffee buyer. I was based in Oakland, California; I travelled the world looking for coffees for them. I was responsible for procuring the company's high-end coffee supply.

My job combined my anthropological studies and my love of the written word. I had not only to bring back the coffees but also the stories behind them. It was a dream position. I stayed with Peet's for seven and a half years.

When you were in Papua New Guinea, did you learn the local language?

I didn't have a choice. I was living on the plantation, so I had to learn the language!

I grew up in a multi-lingual home. As a child, you hear and absorb languages, and you end up speaking what you hear around you. We spoke mainly German at home, but my father was Iranian, so we also talked in Persian. We migrated to the US when I was almost four, so my sister and I were schooled in English. I had a whole lot of French cousins, and it was easier for me to speak French with them than Persian. We had this entire mishmash of languages in our family.

You started as an anthropologist but ended up in commerce. Is trade better than aid?

Absolutely! Papua New Guinea is immensely rich in natural resources. You could eat fruit, spit out the seed and see a tree grow there the following day. Papua New Guineans are not underprivileged in the ordinary sense for an LDC (Lesser Developed Country) – they aren't starving. When I lived there, what they lacked at the time was training, know-how, education, and skills that would help them navigate a modern world of trade. So, the business offered them the chance for learning.

I am completely behind the idea that teaching someone to fish is better than giving them fish. I felt quite strongly about what we were doing there: we were creating a business that was enabling people to do things, not handing out charity.

From Peet's, you were recruited by Nespresso in Switzerland?

I moved to Switzerland in January 2013. I landed in a snowstorm, and it carried on snowing for the next ten days. I had never seen anything so beautiful. If Disneyland did Switzerland, I thought, it would look like this.

What was your job at Nespresso?

When Nespresso lost their capsule patents, they found themselves up against a growing number of competitive capsules. They realised that they had to position themselves differently. They had to leverage their in-depth knowledge of coffee, their expertise.

My job was all about showing that Nespresso had something beyond a glamourous appearance. They have tremendous experience and an effective sustainability programme; the resulting quality is reflected in their capsules. My job when I was there was to tell the real-life stories behind the coffee, and to connect employees, agencies and ultimately customers with those stories.

Nespresso has this unbelievably good sustainable sourcing mechanism called the AAA Sustainable Quality Program. It's tightly controlled and monitored, and they ensure that almost all their coffees run through it. Only that way can they assure that their coffee is verifiable and produced according to their standards, not to mention the quality they need. When there are breaches, as there were recently with a couple of farms in Guatemala over child labour, they were instantly able to trace it back, to nail it down, and to deal with it.

Why did Nestlé buy Blue Bottle?

I met James Freeman, the founder of Blue Bottle Coffee in March 2005. At that time, he was roasting in a shoebox space, a potting shed, right off the patio of the Dona Tomas Taqueria in Oakland. In 2017, he sold 68 per cent of his company to Nestlé for $425 million. That's pretty impressive.

By December 2012, JAB had begun a series of acquisitions that would ultimately position it as being the world's second-largest coffee company, just a hairsbreadth behind Nestlé. I honestly don't know why Nestlé bought Blue Bottle; they might have been looking at JAB buying speciality coffee companies and felt that they had to do the same.

Nestlé is an expert in coffee, but they are expert in big coffee. I'm not sure they had any speciality coffee companies per se, except maybe Zoégas in Sweden - and of course Nespresso. Perhaps they were afraid that they might be missing out on something and wanted to dip their toe in the water of speciality.

Nestlé has tremendous coffee expertise, particularly the Nespresso division. Even so, a small roaster like James Freeman - who came up from nothing to having these exquisite boutiques – must have had something that Nestlé wanted.

I don't think they would have bought it, only then to turn it into a Nescafe clone. What would be the benefit of that? So, I'm assuming they're allowing Blue Bottle to continue to do what they are good at. However, I don't know what Nestlé has learned from buying Blue Bottle.

What about JAB – now the second largest roaster in the industry?

JAB, a privately held investment company, bought Peet's Coffee in 2012 for about $1 billion. The group already owned a significant stake in Coty as well as other leading luxury brands. At that time, Peet's had maybe 300 coffee shops in rented properties, so it looked as if JAB was buying a roasting plant and 300 espresso machines!

Why did they pay so much?

I suspect they saw unrealised value in the money tied up in the supply chain. I imagine it was all about using the supply chain to raise cash to grow the business. As well, Peet's had – and still has – a system of roasting to order and a grocery supply system that is second to none.

Peet's eventually bought out two of the third-wave coffee leaders, Stumptown and Intelligentsia. But from what I understand, they have respected their buying habits, treating those divisions in the same way that JAB treated Peet's and allowing them to continue what they excel in. They certainly didn't tell them to stop buying expensive coffee and to start purchasing commercial-grade coffees.

Did JAB change anything when they bought Peet's?

JAB is an investment company. They had no coffee expertise and had no interest in gaining any. They buy companies and leave them to do what they are good at. I suspect they saw an unleveraged opportunity in Peet's to expand the model. Peet's has a roast to order model, which is quite unusual in the world of quantity coffee.

Is the speciality coffee market still growing?

I sometimes wonder what coffee tasted like when it first came to Europe - and why the Viennese added milk and sugar to it. I suspect the answer is that it must have tasted ghastly at the time. There must have been no sorting; it was probably mouldy and full of rubbish – what we refer to as triage today.

Although I often wonder what it tasted like, one thing I'm sure of is I wouldn't want to go back to that. We have all become used to better coffee, and it's impossible to imagine migrating back to mediocrity.

So yes, the speciality coffee market is growing – and will continue to grow.

Do you classify Starbucks as commercial or speciality?

Starbucks is absolutely speciality. If you look at what Starbucks has done with their Reserve concept, it's incredible!

Of course, that's just the Reserve concept, and with their volume on the other qualities, they are obliged to buy many hundreds of different lots. However, their size gives them the power to scale quality, and that's part of the evolution of the coffee world as well.

Nowadays, as a roaster, it is rare to see rocks or pebbles in coffee; in the olden days, you used to see a lot. You would pull out bullets and nails and knives and all kinds of crap. Now you rarely see anything but coffee in bags of coffee.

It is a question of scaling quality. That's been a benefit for the whole industry, except perhaps for the grower. With prices as low as they have been over the last couple of years, it's arguable whether the growers are being remunerated sufficiently for all their effort.

Is quality continuing to increase?

Producing countries are continually trying to stand out in a crowded market, and one way they are doing that is by using different processing methods.

One example of this is Nicaragua and their honey processed coffee. Nicaragua used to be perceived as just bog-standard washed arabica that went into a commodities basket and was interchangeable with Mexico for soluble coffees. But all of that has changed as the country has innovated on processing methods to bring out different flavour profiles.

Most, if not all, producing countries are trying to differentiate themselves from their competitors, and this is driving an increase in the quality of coffee worldwide. So, the quality of coffee has not stalled—quite the reverse.

Can you use washed arabica as a proxy for speciality coffee?

Once upon a time, you used to be able to do that, but no longer. The quality of coffee, including robusta, has increased. Many countries - Nicaragua being just one example - have innovated so much in processing to help them gain value that you now have all of these unusual processes such as anaerobic fermentation, carbonic maceration etc. You have white, yellow, red and black honey processed coffees. You have wet-hulled coffees from Laos, which for decades was not seen as a quality origin.

In the late 1990s to early 2000s, it was Ethiopia that started the resurgence of full natural fully sundried coffee - but dried on raised beds and processed as carefully as a washed coffee. The resulting cup profiles took the speciality coffee world by storm.

Why is washed better than natural?

It isn't. It has a different set of attributes, but it is not better. It's apples and oranges, as with the arabica versus robusta debate. You can't make that judgment. You can't say one is better than the other.

Up until a couple of years ago, robusta was not considered a speciality coffee – it wasn't allowed to be considered a speciality coffee. The SCA still says it's not, but the Coffee Quality Institute, who own the Q grading programme, has brought in a programme for robusta. It is trying to raise the quality worldwide of robusta as well.

Tell me about your latest adventure.

At Nespresso, alongside my job as Coffee Expertise Leverage Manager, I was on the small panel of cuppers who were qualified to taste and evaluate all the green coffees they bought. I loved that, but we were in a large industrial setting where we didn't have our hands on coffee the way I did in previous jobs. I missed that. Then, in August 2018, personal losses and home stresses caused me to resign from Nespresso. A year later, in August of 2019, I finally decided to take the plunge and start my own little roasting company here in Switzerland: Sweet Bean Coffee.

Opening Sweet Bean Coffee has allowed me to get my hands back onto the primary material that I love. I love coffee. I adore coffee, and I realised I needed to be around the primary material.

What is your biggest challenge setting up a roasting business?

My biggest challenge is carving out space for myself as a small roaster. On one side there are the big companies with their massive advertising budgets. On the other are the growing number of tiny, third-wave style roasteries. Roasting is mushrooming in Switzerland, perhaps because it's perceived to have a low barrier to entry.

A lot of people look at it, and I think: 'I could do that.' They don't realise how complicated it is. Just because they roast coffee in third-wave light style doesn't mean they're necessarily producing an excellent tasting coffee.

So, it is a question of how to reach my target market. When I do, my customers inevitably think that my coffee is exceptional. And they keep coming back to buy more.

Larger roasters have their challenges in convincing their audience that they're not an evil corporation. We all have our challenges: mine is being heard in an ocean of noise.

Is roasting capital intensive in terms of machinery?

Yes, if you want the right equipment. The Rolls-Royce of all the equipment is German manufactured, and it is costly. The brand of the roasting machine that I use now is Probat. I think it's the oldest roaster manufacturer in the world. In Papua New Guinea, my roastery had a Probat machine that dated back to 1928; it had been recovered from a shipwreck. My second roaster dated from 1962. Probat is German-made equipment; it is expensive, but it will last forever!

Where do you buy your green coffee?

I buy from different origins. In the Americas, we have Brazil, Colombia and Guatemala. My absolute favourite is Guatemala. In Africa, I purchase from Kenya and Ethiopia. I also buy from Indonesia, Sumatra and Sulawesi, and, of course, Papua New Guinea. I couldn't imagine having a coffee business without Papua New Guinea!

I've been lucky to start sourcing some women-produced coffees from Mexico, Colombia and Sumatra. I've been an advocate of the women in the coffee movement for many years now, and I'm thrilled to be able to support it actively now.

Is it a gift to be able to cup coffee, or is it something you can learn?

For me, it's about discipline and training. I'm half-German, and I grew up with a lot of discipline in the household. I attack any work project with discipline and concentration. If you've cupped coffees as many thousands of times as I have, your palate becomes trained, disciplined and discerning.

I'm not a supertaster - someone with a large number of papillae on their palate - but I am a Q grader, qualified for both arabica and robusta. The robusta certification is still very rare. It's new and challenging. Both qualifications are insanely difficult, with 22 exams based on tasting, smelling and coffee knowledge.

I'm also on the Board of Trustees for the Coffee Quality Institute that created the certification. I didn't pass the exams because of that. I became a trustee after I passed!

How many cups does a taster cup on average a day?

When I was a buyer at Peet's, we would cup for 4-5 hours a day. When you cup a coffee, you begin when it's still hot, and you continue tasting it to trace its evolution through to room temperature. So, you might cup one coffee 20 times. You can translate that into hundreds of tastings a day.

We did different types of cupping at Peet's. We were tasting offers from the origin, pre-shipments, arrivals into the destination port, and then again into our warehouses. We would then taste prototypes for blends.

What qualities do you need as a roaster?

To be a good roaster, you need the ability to concentrate intensively for short periods. You have to be able to focus to the exclusion of everything else because you're roasting with your senses, your eyes, your nose and your ears. You're looking for colour. You're looking for expansion on the beans; you listen to the sounds that the beans make, you're smelling its roast progression. It's not the moment to be on your handphone!

What qualities do you look for in a green coffee?

It depends on the way that the customer will prepare the coffee. In Papua New Guinea, I'm looking for a particular flavour profile that has something almost akin to a mango, breadfruit or Jackfruit - tropical fruit notes at their very ripest level. That's what you can to get in the washed arabica from Papua New Guinea.

In a coffee from Sumatra, I'm going to be looking for a huge body and cured tobacco leaf notes that are particular to the terroir and the method of processing in Sumatra.

But when something exceptional comes along, I buy it anyway. I'll figure out what to do with it afterwards.

Which are better: blends or single origin?

Blends can bring complexity, but a pure origin can give you the spirit of the country. Smell is a powerful memory stimulant. When I roast coffee from Papua New Guinea, it takes me back to walking the streams of the Southern Highlands Province, going trout fishing in the remote bush a day's walk away from the nearest roads. I am smelling my memories in the bush, going through the coffee rows, the fresh milled crop being bagged for export and so many other memories. That's the beauty of a single origin; it transports you to that place.

How do you recommend your customers brew your coffee?

I don't recommend a brew method. I prefer to hear from my customers their preferred method, along with their taste preferences, and then work with them to give them recommendations based on what they like. I'm not prescriptive at all.

You expect your clients to grind their coffee fresh.

We will grind, but we don't pre-package ground coffee unless it's to order because it goes off so quickly. When we are at the market, we take a grinder with us. In the roastery, we only grind right before dispatching. We want our coffee to be as fresh as possible.

Which is your favourite coffee, and how do you brew it?

PNG is my favourite coffee. What else, of course?! I use a French press. I love the pure and unfiltered grit of the sludge at the bottom of my cup.

Thank you, Shirin, for your time and input!

Chapter 7: Merchant Traders

Seldom does the coffee drinker realise how the ends of the earth are drawn upon to bring the perfected beverage to his lips. The trail that ends in his breakfast cup, if followed back, would be found to go a devious and winding way, soon splitting up into half-a-dozen or more straggling branches that would lead to many scattered regions. If he could mount to a point where he could enjoy a birds-eye view of the these and a hundred kindred trails, he would find an intricate criss-cross of streamlets and rivers of coffee forming a tangled pattern over the tropics and reaching out north and south to all civilised countries. This would be a picture of the coffee trade of the world.

William Ukers – All About Coffee, 1922

Nine companies dominate the world's coffee trade. The Neumann group is the biggest, trading each year between 16 and 17 million bags. Olam and ECOM vie for second place, with both companies each trading an estimated 14 million bags per year. Volcafe and Louis Dreyfus fight it out for the fourth place, each trading an estimated 11 million bags per year.

Sucafina is not far behind in sixth place with an estimated 9 million bags per year. Dutch-based Mercon Coffee Group and the Japanese 'shoji' (trading house) Mitsui tie for seventh place, each trading an estimated 4-5 million bags. The Chinese company COFCO comes in ninth with an estimated 2-3 million bags per year.

If you add that all up you get to just under 90 million bags of green coffee traded annually, three-quarters of the 120 million bags that are shipped each year by the world's coffee exporters. Beware though that, like most commodities, coffee can pass through several different hands between mill and roaster. As such, the total traded volume of coffee is likely to be a multiple of that 120 million bag export figure.

Although they are direct competitors – and the competition is intense - each of these seven companies has its distinct business model and modus operandum. For example, at Neumann, each of the group's 50 companies in 28 countries operates as a separate profit centre. Olam, by contrast, runs its entire coffee business as one profit centre, while concentrating on the origin and owning plantations. ECOM refers to themselves as the 'least trader of the traders', while Louis Dreyfus prides themselves on their fundamental market analysis and their role in price discovery.

Neumann Group's (NG's) history began in 1934 when Hanns R. Neumann began trading coffee as a broker and agent in Hamburg. The company has remained firmly in the family's ownership since then. Its headquarters are in the Coffee Plaza in Hamburg's HafenCity, the site of the company's – and the world's first - green coffee silo, inaugurated in 1975.

Neumann bought out their German competitor Bernhard Rothfos AG in 1988. Also based in Hamburg, Bernhard Rothfos had a more extended history than Neumann. Gollücke & Rothfos was founded in Bremen by Mssrs Gollücke and Rothfos in 1922. The two partners split five years later, and Berhard Rothfos founded his firm, under his name, in Hamburg in 1927. Somewhat confusingly, the original company kept the name Gollücke & Rothfos. It still exists as a highly successful coffee trader in Germany, owned by Volcafe, while Bernhard Rothfos is now the green coffee trading arm of Neumann.

InterAmerican Coffee, founded in 1983 and based in New Jersey, is also part of the Neumann Group, focusing on importing both speciality and commodity coffee into the US.

In total, NG has close to 2,500 employees with export operations in 17 countries. The group also owns and operates three coffee estates: Finca La Puebla in Mexico; Kaweri in Uganda; and Fazenda Da Lagoa in Minas Gerais, Brazil – a total of 8,500 hectares.

Olam, as well as being a trading company, also owns coffee estates - in Brazil, Tanzania, Zambia and Laos totalling about 6,000 hectares of cultivated area. As a company, their business model is origin-based, not just in coffee, but in all the commodities they trade. One of their traders told me that their aim is 'to out originate their competitors'.

Olam is present all along the coffee supply chain from farming, origination and merchandising. It is also midstream, with soluble coffee manufacturing in Vietnam and Spain. Reluctant to compete with their retail brand customers, Olam only produces soluble coffee for private labels; it does not have its own brands.

The company traces its origins back to 1989 with Olam Nigeria Plc. The Group's agri-business was headquartered in London until 1995 when it moved to Singapore and listed as a public company. Temasek, Singapore's state investment fund, is a significant shareholder, as is the International Finance Corporation (IFC).

Interestingly – and this is worth a little detour - Olam is currently splitting into two parts. The first, Olam Food Ingredients, will be made up of cocoa, coffee, edible nuts, spices and dairy. The second, Olam Global Agri, will contain the traditional commodity businesses of grains, animal feeds, protein, edible oils, rice, cotton, and commodity financial services.

In an interview with Bloomberg in 2020, the company's CEO and co-founder explained that each new entity would seek to take advantage of two distinct trends. The first trend is the growing desire among wealthy consumers for healthy, sustainable and traceable products. The second trend is the dietary shift in developing countries, particularly in Asia and Africa, away from carbohydrates and towards meat and fats.

In other words, the company is to be split between bulk food, feed and fibre for developing countries, and traceable, sustainable food ingredients for developed countries. They are separating off the unglamorous, low-growth and cyclical commodity trading businesses from the sexy high growth food ingredients businesses.

The distinction between the two is not always a clear one. People in rich countries also need food, feed and fibre. People in developing countries also care (enormously) about food safety, and hence traceability. Meanwhile, coffee and cocoa can be just as cyclical as soybeans or wheat.

Jose Esteve founded ECOM in Spain in 1849 as a cotton trading business. ECOM entered the coffee trade in 1951, and its core businesses are now coffee, cotton and cocoa. The company is still family-controlled with four Esteve brothers owning 94 per cent of the shares. In the mid-1960s the family moved their global headquarters to Pully in Switzerland.

ECOM became a significant force in the coffee business in 2000 when they acquired Cargill's coffee trading operations. And this is worth another detour: Why did Cargill, one of the world's biggest coffee traders, exit the coffee business? A trader who was with Cargill at the time takes up the story:

'In 1997, Cargill had begun a strategic review of all their business units to question what each one should look like going forward. At that time, they had more than one hundred different activities. In particular, they looked at whether they could significantly grow each business to become one of the top three players in each sector. If they felt they couldn't, they questioned whether they should stay in the industry.

'Barriers of entry were one of the things that Cargill looked at specifically in coffee. They quickly realised that they were low. Anyone with a bit of experience and a bit of money could start trading a few containers of coffee, and, with lower overheads, they could undercut Cargill in terms of price. They also saw that smaller players could cut corners in terms of traceability and sustainability that Cargill, with their brand name, just couldn't afford to do.

'More importantly, Cargill realised that the investment hurdles were low: the capital requirement for a coffee wet mill was nothing compared, say, to what was required to build a sugar mill, flour plant or cocoa butter presser. As for port infrastructure, bulk loading facilities – such as they had recently constructed for raw sugar in Santos – could give the company an edge in terms of costs. Still, there was no edge to be gained in containerised coffee shipments.

'As for market coverage, Cargill was already the biggest within the US in terms of coffee. They felt they had no room to grow. They believed that they didn't have any particular advantage outside the US.

'Cargill approached a number of the bigger roasters to ask if they could manage their supply chains for them, but they were rebuffed. They had more success at the origin with a couple of agreements to market some production, but the volumes were small.

'The coffee team eventually identified that their only edge was in being able to trade the market better than their competitors, based on their trading experience, their global proprietary information flow, and in-depth knowledge of coffee fundamentals – the supply and demand.

'In 1997, the coffee price began to rally on talk of a drought in Brazil, but Cargill's internal analysts believed that the fears were overblown and the increase in price overdone. As the price continued to rise, the team sold short into the rally. They quickly reached their internal in-house position limit and then got permission to double it. The price rose from 85 cents/lb to 135 cents/lb, at which point the company's risk managers pulled the plug on the position, forcing them to cover.

'The team covered their shorts, in the process taking the price to a high of 148 cents/lb. By the following June, the market had fallen to 60 cents/lb, but it was the end of Cargill's coffee business. Management decided that their supposed edge in trading was not everything that the traders had made it out to be.'

Cargill initially offered their coffee trading business to Neumann and Sucafina, but they both turned it down. They eventually sold it to ECOM, propelling ECOM into the first division of the global coffee trade. In 2013, ECOM grew further when they purchased the commodity trading division of Armajaro Holdings, acquiring its physical coffee, cocoa and sugar business.

Volcafe can trace its roots back to 1851 when two brothers, Johann Georg and Salomon Volkart, founded a coffee, cotton and cocoa trading company with offices in Winterthur, Switzerland and Bombay, India. The Winterthur Erb Group acquired the business in 1989 and renamed it Volcafe; by 2003 it had become the second-largest coffee trader in the world. When the parent company got into financial difficulties in 2004, the British trading house ED & F Man bought them out. They integrated Volcafe into their existing coffee trading business but kept the Volcafe name.

ED & F Man was founded by James Man in 1783 as a barrel maker and sugar brokerage company, based in Harp Lane in Billingsgate London. (At that time, traders shipped raw sugar in wooden barrels.) The following year the company won the contract to supply the British Royal Navy with the rum for its daily rum tot, a tradition under which the Navy allocated all sailors a daily rum ration. This tradition continued until 1970, with the company holding the contract throughout. In 1802, the company added coffee and cocoa to the commodities that they traded.

The firm was renamed ED & F Man in 1869, based on the initials of James Man's grandsons Edward Desborough Man and Fredrick Man. E.D. & F Man listed on the London Stock Exchange in 1994. In 2000, the company divided into two separate businesses, with Man Group plc focusing on financial services and ED & F Man (the commodities division) taken private in a management buy-out. ED & F Man is mostly owned by its more than 6,000 employees spread across 60 countries.

According to their company website, Volcafe trades 11 million bags of coffee each year, placing them at perhaps number four in the pecking order of the international coffee trading houses.

While Cargill exited the coffee business, Louis Dreyfus Company, one of Cargill's main competitors in the grain trade, hung in there, growing their business and expanding both ways along the supply chain.

Léopold Louis Dreyfus was born in 1833 to a farming family in Sierentz, in the French Alsace region, just a few kilometres from Basel, Switzerland. He had twelve older brothers, and by 1851, at the age of 16, he realised that his prospects on the farm would be limited. Trying his hand at grain marketing, he began buying wheat from his neighbours, selling it in Switzerland.

Léopold was too young to incorporate a company under his name, so he set one up under his father's, Louis Dreyfus, in Berne, Switzerland. Sometime later, Léopold changed his surname to Louis-Dreyfus, with a hyphen. However, the company is still called Louis Dreyfus—without a hyphen.

Nearly 170 years later, the company that Léopold founded still exits. It originates, processes and transports approximately 80 million tonnes of agricultural goods annually, accounting for about 10 per cent of the world trade in farm products, and enough to feed and clothe 500 million people on earth. The company has approximately 18,000 employees and operates in over 100 countries. ADQ, an

Abu Dhabi investment group, bought 45 per cent of Louis Dreyfus Company in 2020.

LDC got into coffee in Brazil in 1989 and now has a global footprint of 19 processing, storage and logistic facilities and coffee origination offices across 12 countries. Always viewed as the most trading-orientated of the big coffee merchants, LDC now places more emphasis on supply chain management, edging along the chain in both directions in search of higher-value-added businesses.

In 2019, Louis Dreyfus began its first coffee roasting project, signing an agreement with Luckin Coffee – the Chinese retail coffee shop chain – to build and operate a joint venture coffee roasting plant in Xiamen, in China's Fujian province. Despite Luckin Coffee's recent financial problems, they expect production to start in mid-2021.

Like its competitors, Louis Dreyfus places great emphasis on sustainable sourcing. They are one of the drivers of the move beyond certification, only supplying certified coffee when their customers want to pay a premium for it. The company tells me that they have stopped using certification as a benchmark against which they measure themselves; certification has become just one of the three pillars of their approach to sustainable coffee.

Sucafina also emphasises sustainability and farmer wellbeing. The Tamari family established the business in 1905 in the coastal city of Jaffa, Palestine. The company exported oranges and imported foodstuffs, selling their goods throughout the Middle East and expanding with each generation. In 1977, the family founded Sucafina in Geneva, dealing in sugar (SU), café (CA), and finance (FINA).

Two generations later, Sucafina is, like Neumann, entirely focused on coffee. The company employs around 1,000 people across 40 locations in 28 countries, works with 178,000 growers and operates 28 washing stations. The company's family founders are also behind the Kahawatu Foundation which, like the Louis Dreyfus

Foundation, works at origin to improve farmer livelihoods. Sucafina is also the driving force behind Farmer Connect, a blockchain initiative to link coffee farmers directly with consumers.

Mercon is headquartered in the Netherlands with offices in Brazil, Guatemala, Honduras, Nicaragua, Panama, Spain, the US, and Vietnam. The company has been trading coffee for over sixty-five years and now markets between 3 to 4 million bags per year. The group runs its independent sustainability programme, called LIFT, to provide onsite training and technical assistance to small farmers.

Mercon began operations in Nicaragua in 1952 with their subsidiary CISA Exportadora, and they still have a significant presence in the country. Through MerCapital, they offer micro-financing to the country's coffee growers, and they are pioneers in the production of robusta in Nicaragua—creating a whole new industry for the country's growers.

In 2019, Mercon launched Novus Coffee Imports, a new division specialised in sourcing micro-lots, estate-grown, and premium coffees for small to medium roasters in North America. According to their website, their services also include educational workshops, business consulting, blending, roasting, packaging and Origin Experience Trips.

Mitsui is a Japanese global trading and heavy engineering company and one of the world's largest corporations. It was founded in the 17th century by Mitsui Takatoshi, the fourth son of a shopkeeper who specialised in miso, a Japanese seasoning made from fermented soybeans. Takatoshi waited 24 years until his older brother died before he could take over the family shop. He then opened a second shop selling kimonos, revolutionising the business by making the kimonos first, and then selling them in the shop. Previously, manufacturers only made kimonos to order. The retail side of the company was later split off and is now called Mitsukoshi.

Mitsui got into the coffee business in 1971 when it bought S. Schonfeld and Company, founded in 1953, later changing its name to Mitsui Foods. It is now a significant coffee trader, initially sourcing green beans for Japan's roasters, but now a truly international operation trading 3 to 4 million bags of beans each year.

In 2020, Mitsui sold its Mitsui Alimentos' roast and ground coffee business in Brazil for 210 million Reais (US$48.52 million) to 3Coracoes, a joint venture between Strauss Coffee and São Miguel Holding. Before the sale, Mitsui Alimentos was the fifth-largest player in the Brazilian coffee industry with a market share of 3.8 pct. The deal included two coffee factories, a distribution centre and several domestic brands. Mitsui will continue to export Brazilian green beans to Japan and other Asian countries.

COFCO International is a relatively recent entry into the top tier of international coffee trading companies. (COFCO stands for 'China Oil and Foodstuffs Corporation' and not 'Coffee Company' as one friend suggested!) Founded in 2014 as a majority-owned subsidiary of China's COFCO, a state-owned enterprise, the company already has revenues that approach those of LDC and a similar (estimated) market capitalisation. In 2018, COFCO International traded more than 100 million tonnes of foodstuffs.

COFCO got into coffee when they acquired Noble Agri, the agricultural trading arm of Singapore-based Noble Group. Noble Group Ltd had entered the world of agricultural commodity trading – including coffee - with the demise of Andre & Cie in 2001, when Noble bought André's grains business.

Noble Group Ltd was founded by Richard Elman, who named his company after James Clavell's 1981 novel Noble House, a tale of a trading house in 1960s Hong Kong. A wave of acquisitions turned Noble into a conglomerate, operating assets the world over: coal mines in Australia, sugar mills in Brazil and American fuel terminals.

In February 2015, an analyst group, Iceberg Research, run by an ex-Noble employee, published a critique of Noble's accounting practices, warning that some earnings wouldn't materialise and suggesting that the trader couldn't repay its debts. The company dismissed the criticism but later wrote down $1.2 billion, mostly from long-term coal contracts it had booked at an excessive price.

As its fortunes turned, Noble tried to stay afloat by selling assets, including the agriculture unit it had built on Andre & Cie's foundations. However, buyers understood the company's desperation, and the sales netted less than Noble had hoped. With $1.5 billion in debt to repay in the first half of 2018, the company had no choice but to restructure, a process completed in December that year.

Just as Noble had taken advantage of the demise of André & Cie in 2001, COFCO took advantage of the passing of Noble. Having acquired 52 per cent of Noble Agri in April 2014 for $1.5 billion, COFCO bought the remaining 49 per cent in December 2015 for $750 million. The company is now in the top tier of agricultural commodity trading companies and firmly in the top nine coffee trading companies.

A Conversation with Ben Clarkson

Good morning Ben and thank you for taking the time to chat. Could you please tell me how you got into coffee?

I studied history at the University of Bristol and then spent three years in finance in the City of London. I didn't enjoy it, and I began to get interested in commodities. I took a job with Armajaro in 2005. At that stage, they were principally a cocoa company but had recently started a coffee trading business.

I spent a lot of my time with Armajaro in Asia, first in Vietnam and then in Malaysia. I joined Louis Dreyfus in 2012 in Geneva, and I am now their coffee platform head.

Could you tell me a little about Louis Dreyfus (LDC) and coffee?

The company first went into the coffee business a little over 30 years ago. We started in Brazil in 1989 with a single origin. We now have 19 processing, storage and logistic facilities, and coffee origination offices across ten countries. We're one of the world's top green coffee merchants.

Vietnam is the largest producer of robusta coffee and is an essential part of our business. We have a significant operation there, and we are one of the leading exporters of Vietnamese coffee. We are also very active in Brazil. We have an extensive asset network in both Brazil and Vietnam. Still, we also have offices and large businesses in all the major producing counties, including Colombia, Honduras, Mexico, Uganda, India and Indonesia.

All our origin offices are staffed with agronomists, research analysts, traders, asset managers, quality, sustainability teams and logistics managers. We have factories, warehouses and origination teams, sourcing coffee from farmers on behalf of our customers. Most of our coffee platform employees are based in producing countries.

Louis Dreyfus has often been viewed as the most trader of the merchants. Do you consider your company more as a trader or as a merchant - a supply chain manager?

In the past, our coffee business might have been more of a trader than a supply chain manager, but I think this view is now out of date.

Over the last five to ten years, we've made considerable investments, and built a significant asset footprint, in all major coffee-producing countries. In that sense we have become much more of a supply chain manager, offering customers a reliable supply of a wide range of coffees by sourcing the right coffee from the right place, at the right time.

We still spend a lot of our time discussing price and the role of price because we believe it plays an essential part in encouraging the movement of commodities between surplus and deficit regions. In that sense, it is still vital that the market prices coffee correctly, and that the correct price signals are transmitted all along the supply chain.

So, we still believe that trading has a role to play, but the scale and the size of our supply chain and the diversified portfolio we offer our customers means that we are now much more than traders.

Are you worried that the market might become less efficient as companies move towards being supply chain managers and away from being traders?

I would be worried if 100 per cent of global production was in fixed-price supply chains. The market would be less efficient, and so too would our business. However, coffee supply chains still respond to price signals.

Yes, there are speciality coffees that trade on fixed margins in fixed supply chains, and this is important to support vulnerable communities and the supply of these coffees, but this does not apply to all supply chains. The majority of coffee flows are still commoditised today, and price signals transmitted along these supply chains are essential.

Are you seeing more of your supply chain trading on a fixed price now and less on a differential price?

No, not necessarily. The way that the pricing mechanisms work today is similar to how they have always worked.

We see a tremendous interest to work with us, and with farmers, to build sustainable supply chains from the origin, to ensure that coffee is responsibly sourced and fully traceable. LDC is a suitable conduit for that because of the scale of our business, and the scale of the investments we make at the origin. We provide reliability and insurance, but it's not necessarily about trading at a fixed price.

You mentioned scale. What type of infrastructure does LDC have in coffee?

In a significant origin, we would have warehousing assets throughout the country. We would have one or two warehouses near the ports, and then upcountry warehouses and buying points, which would be smaller assets. Typically, within that framework, we would have mills to process and clean raw coffee.

Different customers require different grades and types of coffee. Our facilities allow us to source these for our customers within the origin and then ship the coffee according to their requirements.

What is LDC's USP - Unique Selling Point - in coffee?

We spend a lot of time and resources to understand the flows of green coffee, and where the imbalances are, with a particular focus on research and agronomy, analysing the price drivers.

And as I mentioned earlier, we have a scale in, and a deep understanding of, all the significant origins, with access to 35,000 farmers through our sustainability networks, and we can source the right coffee for our customers in a very transparent way.

We believe our customers see the value in the investments we make - both in analysis and agronomy and in the origins and our supply chain. Together, these mean we can provide a service that is a bit different to everybody else.

Where are you looking to add additional value in the supply chain?

LDC started in coffee as a trader/originator. We think there is still scope for us to further develop our origin presence in certain places, and to continue our work with producers to secure coffee supply chain resilience for the future. We see origination as very important. So that's one end of the supply chain.

At the other end of the supply chain, we work closely with our customers to understand what they need, and what their customers need, and are looking to expand these flows.

We're looking to extend our involvement in the supply chain so that we are as close to the farmer as possible and as close to the consumer as our customers would like.

Can traders make money by merchandising from producer to roaster, or do they need to take positions on the market to be able to make money?

These things ebb and flow. If we have the right relationships and provide a service to our customers, then we can make money by merchandising commodities on their behalf. Sometimes these margins are decent, sometimes less so.

However, we find that as time goes on, customers increasingly understand the scale and maturity of our operations, along with the different services that we can provide along the supply chain, and that this is something they are prepared to pay for.

So, the answer to your question is: 'Yes'. We believe there is value in our merchandising activities, but also that there is additional value in taking trading positions. As traders, we have a role to play to make markets efficient and to move commodities from where they grow to where they are needed.

Trading and merchandising can work in parallel. There is a lot of overlap between the two.

Back in 2000, Cargill got out of coffee trading because they felt the barriers to entry were too small. Is that still the case?

It was probably still the case four or five years ago, when it was relatively easy for a small coffee trader to buy FOB (Free on Board) from a local exporter, and sell FOB or CIF (Cost, Insurance & Freight) to a roaster.

But this is changing. Customers nowadays need a lot more than just coffee on a boat. They need to know where the coffee comes from. They need guarantees of traceability and food safety, and they need to know that their coffee has been sourced according to high ethical and environmental standards.

As a top-tier agribusiness, LDC has considerable responsibility in this area, and we take it very seriously.

We also believe that LDC now adds much more value thanks to our origin footprint and the investments we've made over the last five to ten years. These capabilities create barriers to entry that perhaps were not so apparent ten years ago.

Traceability is becoming a barrier to entry.

The coffee supply chain is complicated. What we're trying to do is to simplify it through traceability, so that the producer can see the consumer, and the consumer can see the producer. We believe that LDC is well-positioned to provide this transparency.

Does blockchain have a role to play?

We believe blockchain will be an important lever for supply chain traceability and transactional efficiency - and we're working on it within LDC and with industry peers and stakeholders. For the moment, it's more relevant for the commodities that are moved in bulk rather than in containers.

In addition to blockchain, technology, in general, has a role to play in the coffee business, be it for precision agronomy, logistic efficiency or traceability.

I saw on your website that you have what you call a 'three pillars approach' to sustainability? Could you briefly explain what that is?

We currently work with 35,000 farmers globally. The three streams to our sustainability program are certification, collaborative initiatives and responsible sourcing.

Certification is about boosting the supply of certified and verified coffee. We work with farmers to do so, under all the principal certification and verification schemes.

Our collaborative initiatives are about extending our focus beyond certification to support the farming communities that need it the most, through independent projects on the ground. We work with these farmers to help them increase their income and productivity sustainably while empowering their local community and protecting the environment. We've done this through many different projects run with various partners, such as the Louis Dreyfus Foundation, other non-profit organisations and also roaster customers.

Finally, responsible sourcing is a more blanket approach to our entire supply chain. Our teams have introduced our Coffee Supplier Code of Conduct across all coffee origination countries. This document builds on our global Sustainability Policy and Group Code of Conduct. It aligns with International Labour Organization conventions, applicable local laws and regulations, as well as various codes of conduct and sourcing policies developed by our customers.

The objective is not to exclude any farmers or suppliers, but rather to encourage them to commit to a long-term and continuous improvement process, supported directly by LDC and its partners.

What can be done to improve farmers' incomes in producing countries?

For LDC, collaborative initiatives and responsible sourcing efforts are critical.

Our scale and presence at origin mean that, together with our customers, we can make a difference in farmer communities, improving their livelihoods and the long-term sustainability of their businesses. It is especially important in the more vulnerable communities globally, who are at risk of exclusion due to a lack of resources and knowledge of acceptable agricultural practices.

Is counterparty risk a significant issue for you?

No, it's not a significant issue, but it is something that we consider every day, with more focus at origin rather than the destination, but this is by no means a rule.

When we think about counterparty risk at the origin, we're typically thinking about market risk. When we buy coffee from source, we sell futures against it. This creates futures market risk if the coffee is not delivered. At the destination end, we have quite sophisticated customers, which reduces the default risk.

To what extent does financing play a role in your business?

Different origins do different things—some origins trade with minimal financing, others with a bit more.

Has the consolidation among the roasters over the last five years increased their power to impose their credit terms on the supply chain?

Yes, it has. Many of our customers now ask for some kind of credit terms; to be a serious actor in the coffee business, you have to consider supplying them. To some extent, this is another barrier to entry, and, because of our size and our creditworthiness, we can offer credit terms.

Do you have long-term contracts with any of your origins?

Brazil operates with long-term contracts, as do some of the other arabica origins. It is much less likely in the robusta origins.

On a typical long-term contract with our customers, we will agree on the differential, also known as the 'basis', but not the flat price. Some customers want to lock in the supply but fix the differential later. However, that is the exception rather than the rule.

The physical differentials seem to be as volatile as the flat price; how do you hedge your basis risk?

We are not trying to hedge our basis risk, but instead, we hedge the flat price risk in our physical transactions. Generally, we are very comfortable with basis risk, and this is the foundation of our trading book - in other words, the relationship between the physical coffee and the futures contracts. For example, we look to understand the relationship between Brazilian arabica and the New York arabica futures contract. That is our core business as traders.

As coffee merchants, we need transparent rules and liquidity in the futures contracts into which we hedge our physical transactions. These futures contracts need to look like the coffee that we're transacting, thereby creating a genuine relationship between the two.

Is the Brazilian domestic price/world price a big arbitrage play for traders?

Brazilians are big consumers, producers and exporters of coffee. They have flexibility as to what they put into their domestic blends. When Brazilian robusta prices are low, they will increase the amount of robusta in their domestic blends; when robusta is expensive, they will reduce the amount of robusta, while increasing the amount of arabica.

Does that have a significant effect on global prices? Indeed, it will adjust the ratio of arabica and robusta shipments, but it is only one part of the arbitrage puzzle.

Is the London New York arbitrage actively traded?

Yes. The New York arabica contract - the C-Contract - is the most liquid and best-known market, certainly for a non-coffee specialist. That's what people reference for coffee prices. As a merchant, we use both the London robusta and the NY arabica futures contracts to hedge our price exposure for the associated coffees, and we trade the relationship between the two.

Recently, we see external money - hedge funds and the like - becoming more interested in the relationship between robusta and arabica.

LDC has always had the reputation of being the most fundamentally driven trader. Have the hedge funds had an impact on your business?

When you join LDC, you quickly understand that there is a continuous conversation about the supply and demand for coffee and coffee prices. It is a core skillset in trading, and we have these conversations all the time.

Although hedge funds may have altered the timing of the influence of fundamentals to price, we still absolutely believe that the price of the futures market, the price of the basis and the price of the spreads will in the medium term align with the fundamentals.

How important are the calendar spreads in coffee?

The futures markets are consumer market warehouse contracts, and the calendar spreads are critical. The futures contracts should reflect the price of coffee in these warehouses and ports, as well as the supply and demand for coffee to and from these ports. When there is too much coffee, the spreads will typically allow owners to carry coffee profitably in these ports until tighter times. In times of deficit, the spreads will strengthen; how much they strengthen depends on the size of the deficit. The calendar spread should then attract more coffee to these ports, thereby solving the shortage.

As a coffee trader, do you regularly cup coffee for quality?

Yes, every team and department globally regularly cup coffee. Understanding the qualities and delivering the correct qualities to our customers are absolutely core skills in our business.

It is critical in our business. We typically buy a raw coffee in the origins, and we turn it into a deliverable product. Every single customer will want a different coffee, and sometimes these differences are very subtle. We manage large origin assets that we dedicate exclusively to differentiating grades and quality to meet customer requirements.

Second to last question: what is your favourite coffee?

A strong Italian espresso.

Last question: does coffee keep you awake at night?

I have two children and a dog - they cause me more sleepless nights!

Thank you, Ben, for your time and input!

Chapter 8: Roasters

'You either sell up, or you grow. There is no alternative,'

- Lavazza CEO, Antonio Barravalle
(Quoted in the FT, 2016)

Coffee people like to compare coffee to wine, but more recently, the sector has had more resemblance to beer than wine.

Both the coffee-roasting and beer-brewing sectors have seen significant consolidation over recent years. InBev has been driving the consolidation in beer while JAB has been driving the consolidation in coffee. When Olivier Goudet became CEO of JAB in 2012, he remained chairman of In Bev, only resigning in 2019 to spend more time focusing on JAB. He took to JAB the knowledge he'd acquired in building the world's biggest brewer.

Before its merger with InBev in 2008, Anheuser-Busch was the world's biggest brewer with a market share of 8.5 per cent. Today, AB InBev is still the world's biggest brewer, but with an estimated 21 per cent market share. Today's top five brewers represent more than 50 per cent of the global market; this compares to 32 per cent in 2003.

Cost-cutting through economies of scale has driven the consolidation within both the beer and coffee sectors. Some of these economies have been found in processing and packaging facilities, but most have been in research and development, marketing and brand management.

Many argue that a larger market share also brings the market power to negotiate favourable terms from suppliers and to obtain a larger share of the value chain - a larger slice of the cake.

Bloomberg wrote in 2019: 'The revolving door between the beer and coffee empires has also influenced JAB's business model. Like the brewer, it's moving to tap the advantages of scale. By moving to pay suppliers as many as 300 days after purchasing their beans, it's squeezing trading houses while leaving the company sitting on more cash. That frees up money to help with takeovers.'

I wonder, though, to what extent size and market share affect green coffee purchasing. Chris von Zastrow mentions in his conversation later in this book that Starbucks' size helps them to effect positive change among growers in terms of sustainability and quality. However, in a commodity market such as coffee, price is set by the market, not by any individual player. Unless buyers get together to form a cartel, suppliers usually have a choice as to whom to sell. They have options. There is typically another buyer knocking on their door.

As such, the oft-repeated notion that big roasters lean on helpless coffee growers to get lower prices is usually untrue. The opposite is more often the case. The price is set by the market, as are the differentials for the different origins and qualities. However, nothing precludes a buyer from paying a premium over the market.

Chris tells me that back in 2002, when market prices were around $0.50/lb, Starbucks was paying over $1.00/lb in many countries to keep origins from disappearing. Indeed, Costa Rica has told Starbucks that by doing that, they saved their coffee industry.

Developing countries such as China, India, and Brazil have been driving the demand for both coffee and beer; for coffee that growth has mostly been in instant and RTD products. Meanwhile, the consolidation within the beer industry has been accompanied by the emergence of a plethora of new craft beer producers, just as speciality coffee roasters have accompanied the consolidation within the coffee sector.

JAB is possibly the world's largest roaster in terms of financial turnover at an estimated $12 billion, split equally between JDE Peet's and Keurig Dr Pepper (see below). Nestlé is possibly still the largest roaster in terms of volume. Although none of the roasting companies publishes their volume figures, trade sources estimate that Nestlé roasts 16 million bags of coffee per year compared with JAB with 14 million bags. The two companies are, without doubt, the dominant players in the sector.

Starbucks comes in at number three on the list with an estimated 6 million bags a year, just edging out Smucker's in number four position at between 5 to 6 million bags per year. Strauss and Lavazza come in at joint number five with an estimated 4 million bags, while Kraft comes in at number seven with 3 million bags. If you add all that up, the top seven roasters account for 46 per cent of the market. The top two roasters account for 25 per cent.

Let's start with JAB, a privately held German conglomerate, headquartered in Luxembourg. JAB stands for Joh. A. Benckiser. Its portfolio has expanded rapidly since its formation. It now includes investments in companies in the areas of consumer goods, forestry, coffee, luxury fashion and fast food, among others. Although you may never have heard of JAB, you will undoubtedly have heard of some of the famous brands it owns, such as Krispy Kreme, Panera, Caribou Coffee, Au Bon Pain, and Pret A Manger, as well as Keurig Dr Pepper and bottled-water brand Core.

The history of JAB dates back to the early 19th century when the Reimann family established Benckiser, a chemical and industrial manufacturing company, in Germany. During the first part of the 20th century, Benckiser was a small to medium-sized business, primarily a supplier to the food industry; its main products included processed cheese, salts for blood treatment, supplements for baby food, and chemicals to soften water.

During the 1980s, the company expanded as it acquired and integrated its European and North American household products business and cosmetics companies, before spinning off cosmetics into Coty Inc. in 1996. Three years later, Benckiser merged with Reckitt & Colman to form the consumer goods business Reckitt Benckiser.

As mentioned earlier, JAB has been extraordinarily active in coffee; it has been driving the consolidation in the sector. Some sources estimate that JAB has spent more than $30 billion, expanding their coffee empire. Their frenetic activity reached a zenith in 2020 when JAB cashed in some of their chips and raised $2.5 billion by taking JDE Peet's public on the Euronext Amsterdam stock exchange in a deal that valued the company at $17.3 billion.

As well as owning JDE Peet's, JAB also invested in coffee through Keurig Dr Pepper Inc. The investment firm bought Keurig Green Mountain for $13.9 billion in 2016.

Green Mountain Coffee Roasters (GMCR) was founded in 1981 in Vermont, and over the years gradually expanded its footprint both nationally and internationally. In 1993, GMCR invested in a Massachusetts start-up called Keurig that was developing a single-cup coffee brewing system. Four years later, Keurig and GMCR launched the Keurig Single-Cup Brewing System, and in 2006 GMCR bought the remaining shares in Keurig to acquire full ownership. In 2014, Green Mountain Coffee Roasters changed its name to Keurig Green Mountain.

In 2018, Keurig Green Mountain acquired Dr Pepper Snapple Group for $18.7 billion, and the merged company changed its name to Keurig Dr Pepper, the third-largest beverage company in North America. It trades on the New York Stock Exchange.

But let's go back to JDE Peet's. How did it get to where it is today?

The company has its origins in De Witte Os, a general grocery shop that Egbert Douwes established in 1753 in Joure, Netherlands. In 1780, he transferred the company to his eldest son Douwe Egberts. It developed into a company dealing in coffee, tea, and tobacco, and in 1925, it had changed its name to Douwe Egberts.

Consolidated Foods Corporation, later the Sara Lee Corporation, took over Douwe Egberts in 1978. In 2012, Sara Lee split off the company's coffee division into a company called D.E Master Blenders 1753. (The DE stands for Douwe Egberts; 1753 is the year the company was founded.) Meanwhile, the Sara Lee company changed its name to Hillshire Brands.

By coincidence, that same year, 2012, JAB bought Peet's Coffee and Tea for about $1 billion. A year later, they purchased D.E Master Blenders 1753 for $9.8 billion. The company appointed new management and delisted from the Euronext stock market, merging with Peet's to form JDE Peet's.

But they didn't stop there. Within 12 months, JAB had merged JDE Peet's with the coffee division of American food conglomerate Mondelez International.

JAB was still hungry. In 2015, the group paid more than $300 million to buy Espresso House, the leading coffee chain in Sweden and Norway. That same year JAB acquired majority shares in both Stumptown Coffee and Intelligentsia Coffee & Tea, although they left the original owners as managers and operators of the businesses.

Nestlé looks positively staid by comparison. Like JAB, the company's origins date back to the 19th century. In 1866, Charles and George Page, two brothers from Illinois, USA, established the Anglo-Swiss Condensed Milk Company in Cham, Switzerland. In 1867, in Vevey, Switzerland, Henri Nestlé developed milk-based baby food. The following year, the company helped Daniel Page, the inventor of milk chocolate, to establish a new process for its manufacture.

In 1877, Anglo-Swiss started making milk-based baby foods. The following year, the Nestlé Company started making condensed milk, making the firms direct rivals. In 1879, Nestlé merged with milk chocolate inventor Daniel Peter.

Henri Nestlé retired in 1875, but the company retained his name as Société Farine Lactée Henri Nestlé. In 1905, Nestlé merged with the Anglo-Swiss Condensed Milk Company to become the Nestlé and Anglo-Swiss Condensed Milk Company.

The company only adopted its current name in 1977. It is still based in Vevey, Switzerland, and is now the world's biggest food company with a market capitalisation of around $350 billion. Nestlé currently manages over 2,000 brands ranging from bottled water to pet food.

The company first got into coffee at the request of Brazilian producers who were looking to dispose of surplus stocks after the failed price support effort in 1929. It took Nestlé almost ten years to come up with a solution, and they launched Nescafé in Switzerland on 1st April 1938. Sales increased rapidly during the Second World War, when Nescafé became standard issue to US soldiers, but then dropped sharply again after the war ended. Sales picked up slowly during the 1950s and received a boost with the introduction of Nescafé Gold Blend in 1965. Gold Blend contained some arabica coffee, to improve its flavour; it was freeze-dried and had a golden-brown colour, as opposed to the nearly black colour of Nescafé.

Nescafé instant coffee, produced in their factory in Dole, Switzerland, accompanied NASA's Apollo 11's astronauts to the moon in 1969.

Nestlé concentrated exclusively on soluble coffee until 1986 when it founded Nespresso as an independent entity. In 2006, Nescafé launched a new coffee machine system Dolce Gusto, allowing consumers to make various styles of coffees at home. Unlike other Nescafé products, Dolce Gusto coffee beverages use roasted and ground coffee beans, instead of instant coffee.

In 2017 Nestlé bought a majority stake in the up-market Oakland, California-based Blue Bottle Coffee, paying about $425 million for a 68 per cent stake. At the time of the purchase, Blue Bottle operated 40 shops in the US and Japan, as well as selling direct to customers.

The acquisition took the coffee world by surprise, first because of the valuation placed on Blue Bottle, but also because, as one observer mentioned to me, 'there is nothing that Blue Bottle can teach Nestlé about coffee.' Perhaps it was a question of strategic positioning. At the time, the company's CFO explained the move: 'We didn't necessarily want to make a big entry in coffee shops, but it made sense for us to do a test in the super-premium area with Blue Bottle. It is interesting for us to understand what is going on in that space that is more about service while we focus more on products.'

In 2018, Nestlé again raised eyebrows when the company paid $7.15 billion for the right to distribute Starbucks coffee through retail outlets outside Starbucks stores. Kraft Foods previously had this 'right', but Starbucks had repurchased it though an arbitrated process for around $2.1 billion.

Nestlé's objective was to use their powerful retail distribution system, particularly in China, to expand Starbucks' sales and to put Starbucks coffee into Nestlé's single-serve systems: Nespresso and Nescafé Dolce Gusto. Starbucks sources the green coffee for these systems, but Nespresso now roasts the beans.

Starbucks' CEO described the move as 'the definitive global coffee alliance in the industry'. Nestlé's CEO was more open about the reasons for the deal, telling CNBC: 'We were late in the US coffee market and this deal allows us to catch up.' The company's CFO, meanwhile, explained the alliance in terms of the airline industry:

Nescafé is for Economy Class passengers; Starbucks is for Business Class passengers; Nespresso is for First Class passengers.

Some commentators wondered at the time whether Nestlé was just putting their toe in the water before acquiring Starbucks outright, something that they have the financial muscle to do. (At the time of writing, Starbucks has a market capitalisation of $77 billion compared to Nestlé at $350 billion.)

If you live outside of the US, you may have heard of Starbucks, but you have probably not heard of Smucker's who come in at number four in the roaster top-ten.

Smucker's is a fifth-generation family-owned company founded in 1897 by Jerome Monroe Smucker. He began by selling homemade cider and apple butter from the back of his horse-drawn wagon. The company grew steadily and became a significant force in jam, peanut butter, jelly, fruit syrups, beverages, shortening, ice cream toppings, oils, and other products in North America. Smucker's headquarters are in Orrville, Ohio.

Smucker's entered coffee in 2008 when it bought Folgers, at that time the number one brand in the US for ground and packaged coffee. In 2010, the company expanded its footprint in the sector when it acquired Rowland Coffee Roasters along with their Café Bustelo and Café Pilon brands. In 2012, Smucker's bought a majority of Sara Lee's North American foodservice coffee business to become the leader in the $10 billion US at-home retail coffee category.

William Bovee founded the Folger Coffee Company in 1850 in San Francisco as the Pioneer Steam Coffee and Spice Mills. It was the first company in the US to produce and sell roasted and ground coffee ready for brewing. Previously, consumers purchased green coffee beans and roasted and ground them at home. Folgers may be able to claim to be the oldest coffee-roasting company in the world.

To help build his mill, William Bovee hired James Folger as a carpenter. James had arrived from Nantucket Island at the age of 15 during the California Gold Rush. He worked there for a year before heading out to look for gold. James carried samples of coffee and spices with him, taking orders from grocery stores along the way. In 1865, he returned to San Francisco and became a partner of The Pioneer Steam Coffee and Spice Mills. In 1872, he bought out the other partners and renamed the company J.A. Folger & Co.

Under the mid-20th century leadership of Peter Folger, the brand became one of the principal coffee concerns in North America. Procter & Gamble acquired Folger's in 1963 and removed the apostrophe from its name. During their ownership, Folgers became the number one coffee brand in America. P&G sold Folgers to the J.M. Smucker Company in 2008.

Moving further down the list of the world's largest coffee roasters, we come to number six, the Strauss Group, a conglomerate with 14,000 employees worldwide. It was founded in Israel in the late 1930s as a small dairy company by Richard and Hilda Strauss; today it is a significant player in the global food and beverage market. Although the Strauss Group is a public company, it is still a family-run business, with Ms Ofra Strauss as Chairperson of the Board.

Strauss Coffee began operations in 2000 and is the world's fifth-largest coffee company in the world in terms of the volume of green beans that they roast and distribute. It has over 16 brands, more than 6,000 workers and operates in 10 different countries around the world.

It is the largest roaster and distributor in Brazil, through the Três Corações company, a 50/50 joint venture between Strauss Coffee and the São Miguel Group, roasting as many as three million bags of green coffee per year. It also has a strong presence in the Former Soviet Union, as well as in Eastern Europe. In Russia, Strauss owns the Ambassador brand, once owned by Sucafina.

Strauss Coffee is managed from the company's headquarters in Amsterdam and has an extensive research and development unit based near Tel Aviv, Israel. They do all their green coffee procurement from Zug, Switzerland.

Lavazza probably ties with Strauss Coffee in terms of roasted volumes. The company was founded in Turin in 1895 by Luigi Lavazza and has stayed privately-owned. The third and fourth generations of the Lavazza family now run the company. The company has a market share by sales of over 36 per cent in Italy, 3,800 employees and revenues in 2019 of €2.24 billion.

Lavazza credits itself with inventing the concept of blending, combining different types of coffee from various geographical areas. In 1979, it established the Luigi Lavazza Centre for Coffee Research, devoted to the study of espresso. It has since evolved into the Lavazza Training Centre, a network of over 50 coffee schools worldwide, where 30,000 people receive training each year. As far as technology is concerned, there is even a specially designed zero-gravity Lavazza espresso machine on the International Space Station!

In 2018 Lavazza told Reuters that it had turned down offers from both JAB and Nestlé and that it intended to stay independent. The company has been on an acquisition spree in recent years, buying Canadian organic coffee firm Kicking Horse, Italy's coffee pod firm Nims, French coffee brand Carte Noire and Denmark's Merrild. In 2019, in partnership with PepsiCo, Lavazza launched canned ready-to-drink cappuccino in Europe.

Heinz Kraft is the world's seventh-largest coffee roaster with their Maxwell House brand. Introduced in 1892 by wholesale grocer Joel Owsley Cheek, it was named after the now-closed Maxwell House Hotel in Nashville, Tennessee, Cheek's first major customer.

General Foods bought Maxwell House in 1928 and introduced a soluble version of the brand in 1942. By 1953, Instant Maxwell House had leapfrogged Nescafé to become the biggest selling instant coffee in the US. Until the late 1980s, it was the country's highest-selling coffee brand – both instant and roasted.

In 1985, General Foods was acquired by Philip Morris Companies (now Altria Group, Inc.) for $5.6 billion. Three years later, Philip Morris acquired Kraft, Inc., and, in 1990, combined the two food companies as Kraft General Foods (KGF). They dropped the 'General Foods' moniker in 1995 and rebranded the company as Kraft Foods Inc.

In 2012, Kraft Foods Inc. spun off its North American grocery business to a new company called Kraft Foods Group, Inc. The remainder of Kraft Foods Inc. was renamed Mondelez International, Inc. Three years later, in 2015, Kraft Foods Group Inc. merged with the H.J. Heinz Company, owned by 3G Capital and Berkshire Hathaway Inc., to form the Kraft Heinz Co., the world's fifth-largest food and beverage company

Kraft Heinz put its Maxwell House coffee brand up for sale in 2019 for a rumoured price of more than $2.5 billion. Several suitors have since looked over the company's books, but it appears that the price tag may be too steep. One source told me that Maxwell House was rather like Folgers: 'It is in the unsexy, slow-moving corner of the coffee ring. Attention now is on the premium sectors of speciality coffee and out-of-home consumption, rather than old-fashioned in-home consumption.'

In 2020, Maxwell House's owner, Kraft Heinz Co. took a $15.4 billion write-down on assets in an acknowledgement that changing consumer tastes had destroyed the value of some of the company's most iconic products, including Maxwell House.

I bet that if you were to ask your friends and family to name the world's top ten coffee companies, they would never come up with the list above. However, I have to wonder whether this frenetic M&A activity and the rapidity of the consolidation within the coffee sector means that these commercial giants are still coffee companies. You may argue that they are, first and foremost, finance houses and brand managers.

I will let you make up your own minds on that.

A conversation with Martin Löfberg

Good morning, Martin. Could you please tell me a little about Löfbergs?

Löfbergs was founded in 1906 by the brothers Anders, John and Josef Löfberg. They began roasting coffee in Karlstad in 1911. Today, we are one of the Nordic region's biggest family-owned coffee businesses, producing the equivalent of more than 10 million cups of coffee every day. Löfbergs is still wholly owned by the Löfberg family, now in its third and fourth generations. I am one of that fourth generation.

With all the consolidation in the sector, how have you managed to stay independent?

That's a good question! We have to be flexible and dynamic to stay close to our customers and clients. It's a balancing act to be long-term-oriented and at the same time to adapt quickly to a changing environment.

I imagine that other groups have approached you.

We are attracting attention, but we are focusing on passing the business on to the next generation – and make it attractive enough for them to want to take it over. We are fully committed to staying 100 per cent family owned.

The company roasts about 32,000 tons of green coffee a year. That's slightly over half a million bags. Is that right?

A little bit more.

Where does that put you in the pecking order of coffee roasters? You are relatively small relative to Starbucks at 6 million bags.

It depends on how you look at it. We are in the top five in sustainably certified, Fairtrade and organic coffees. We only roast 100 per cent certified coffees. We are also a significant player when it comes to Rainforest Alliance.

You joined the company in 2008. What's it like working for a family company?

As children, our parents brought us up in a coffee environment. When I was younger, I loved going with my father to the factory, learning about the machinery and all the aspects of coffee.

How young were you when you first drank coffee?

I don't remember, but my younger brother started drinking coffee when he was eight. Maybe I started a little bit later.

Did you have any choice about joining the family company?

We have a family policy that we need to work five years outside the company in a different industry – to gain experience – before we can join. I was fortunate that my sister joined the company before I did and paved the way for me.

We worked within the family business network to help with the generational transition from my father and his brother to our generation. The process took more than ten years to complete; talking to other family businesses helped a lot.

How many family members work in the company?

Actively, on a day-to-day basis, it's only me. We are six persons in the fourth generation, who are involved in different ways. My older sister Kathrine is, for example, chair of the board.

So, the CEO of the roasting company is not a family member. Is that right?

That's correct. He has been working for us for more than 20 years, and CEO since 2008.

Do you think your children will join the company?

I think it's up to us to make the company group attractive enough – and exciting enough - for them to join. We also need to grow the company to enable a bigger group of owners to enter. They are three times as many as us, so the company needs to be at least three times bigger!

Let's move on now to your procurement roll. What does that entail?

I spend a lot of time in the coffee origin countries. Out of the twelve years I have spent with the company, I reckon I have travelled for one year of that. I have primarily been focusing on the co-operative side, Fairtrade, organic and Rainforest Alliance certified cooperatives, mainly in Central and South America.

I do a lot of cupping: three times a day for a total of 300 cups. That's an integral part of my role. Cupping allows me to be actively involved and not just manage the procurement process from a distance. I need to be inside the flow. It allows me to keep an ear to the rail tracks: to listen to what's going on; to understand the challenges in producing countries; to stay on top of how our farmers and partners are doing. Although it may sound counterintuitive, being hands-on allows me to look at the business more strategically.

Throughout my day, I also have to keep on top of the coffee price and follow the futures markets.

What percentage of your coffee do you buy against the futures and what percentage on a flat price?

We buy close to 99 per cent of our coffee on a differential basis against the futures. We only buy our speciality coffees at a flat price.

About 15-20 per cent of the coffee that we buy is Fairtrade. For several years now world prices have been low, and these purchases have been at the Fairtrade minimum price. These coffees are priced on a differential basis, but a minimum price applies. It is 140 cents/lb for washed arabicas, with a 30-cent premium for organic, plus a 20-cent social premium. That gives a minimum price of 190 cents/lb, to which you may have to add a quality premium.

In the past three years, the world price has been higher than that for only one day - in December 2019! Apart from that one day, the Fairtrade minimum price has applied.

What criteria are most important to you in your buying decisions?

It's an optimization between the three standard procurement elements: the quality; the price/financing needs and delivery performance; together with sustainability. You need to optimize those to be successful as a coffee buyer.

Which countries mainly supply your coffee?

As a Scandinavian roaster, we have a long heritage with Brazil. Colombia is also an essential partner for us. We also work closely with cooperatives in Peru, Honduras and Nicaragua. Then in East Africa, we buy from Ethiopia and Kenya, and sometimes from Uganda. Most of our coffee comes from Latin America.

And it is mainly arabica?

Yes, it is. Since we expanded internationally, we now have to cater to local tastes, and we do buy a small portion of fine robusta. It plays a role in a few of our blends. It is something that has changed in the last 10 to 15 years. Our competence within robusta has increased year by year, allowing us to tailor some of our blends.

When you buy coffee, do you buy with a particular blend in mind, or do you sometimes buy a coffee and work out where to put it later? Is it the coffee that's driving the blend or the blend that is driving the coffee?

Some consumers like a consistent taste profile over the seasons and the years. If a new-found coffee fits into our blends, we are happy to introduce it. However, we operate on a more strategic basis for the blends. The blend drives the coffee.

It is not as easy as it sounds; every new crop is a new page in a book. It's never the same as the previous crop, and it takes a long time to get an understanding of that. It takes at least five years to become a rookie in this business. It's always changing. We continually try to be proactive and to see how the crops are progressing - what qualities are being produced. We have a very narrow tolerance in our blends.

Some consumers like to buy specific origins or regions, or single estates or even single lots, part of an estate. Sometimes, we come across something unique. When we do, we buy it and then test it through our two coffee shops, which are a little bit our centres for innovation, to see if the consumers like it.

There's a treasure chest of findings throughout my travels that I have been able to introduce. We can use our significant flows of coffees to put a few bags inside a container to make it easier for us to import.

Do you buy from origin or do you buy through traders?

We always try to buy as close as possible to the source. However, we sometimes need a facilitating help when it comes to the trade. Trade houses can play an important role when it comes to financing. They can also help with the hedging, which some of our partners are not able to do.

We usually do our buying directly with the local exporting entities, or even with the farmers and estates. We then facilitate that flow with the trading houses.

In most cases, the producing entity, whether a farmer or a cooperative, is a small-scale family business. They can't export on their own. There needs to be some aggregation of coffees at the origin.

Although speciality coffee is relatively small for you, you know the origin of all of your coffee.

Yes, we do. Sometimes it takes a bit longer to track it down, of course, but it has been facilitated with the introduction of independent certifying standards like Rainforest Alliance and Fairtrade.

We have always been keen to keep track of our coffee. Coffee has an International Coffee Organisation lot number on each bag, which states the lot number of the exporting country. It's an easy code that can be followed if you use it properly.

We had a target to buy 100 per cent certified coffee by December 2020, and we have already reached it.

Some people have complained that there are too many certification agencies. Have you found this?

We don't see this as a problem, particularly with the merger that is now underway between UTZ and Rainforest Alliance. They should complete the union by 2022, but from July 2020 we can cross-use coffees from farms and estates under both schemes.

We are in favour of the merger as it can be a challenge for farmers to handle too many standards. It's costly for them to be part of a certification scheme, not just in money but also in time. It is also confusing from the consumer side. Having too many certification standards dilutes the picture.

However, having more than one certifying agency means having access to a broader market. UTZ and Rainforest Alliance were quite similar in their standards.

Fairtrade is different because of its focus on the premium and the minimum price. Fairtrade is strong from a social perspective. Then you have the organic coffees which are very strong from an environmental perspective.

Rainforest Alliance and UTZ operate on the bigger farms where Fairtrade doesn't work. Fairtrade is small scale.

We see certification as necessary. It is one of many tools, but for us, the Löfbergs brand is more important. Our brand is the guarantee and the trust of consumers and partners that we build into it. Certification symbols and so forth are sometimes important for consumers, but Löfbergs is the true seal.

Do certification agencies concentrate too much on social sustainability and not enough on economic sustainability?

That might be a problem in some areas in the world. Certification is not perfect, but it addresses issues and - if the tool is in the right hands – it does make things better.

Sustainability is about optimizing the resources and maximizing the impact. If you don't see the effect happening, there's no incentive to keep doing it. It is about improving farmers' incomes through fewer inputs and more outputs. It's about helping farmers to become better business units. It's about allowing farmers to become more performance-driven commercial entities.

As I mentioned earlier, the Löfbergs' seal is critical. We always make sure that our supply chain is economically, socially and environmentally sustainable.

Could you tell me a little bit about International Coffee Partners and any other sustainability programs you support?

Some challenges around sustainability are so massive that no one company can address them and make enough of an impact. So, some twenty years ago, we joined forces with other family roasting companies that shared the same values to form International Coffee Partners (ICP). We are much stronger together.

Our vision is to train farmers, to make them stronger so that they can then eventually move on to certify themselves. We have, for example, an exciting project in Trevino, in Guatemala, on the border of El Salvador and Honduras. We have also been to Tanzania, Brazil and Honduras and many other countries. My sister Kathrine is the chair of the board of ICP.

Climate change is a crucial issue for coffee, and the ICP has launched the 'Coffee and Climate Toolbox', also bringing in outside partners.

Is climate change the main challenge faced by the industry?

Climate change and the next generation of growers are the two strategic challenges for the industry.

We need to provide incentives for the next generation of farmers to keep growing coffee. Even if Brazil and Vietnam produce beautiful coffee, we can't rely on only those two.

Coffee is grown in remote places in distant mountains with a variety of different processing techniques, creating a richness of flavour and a lot of different taste profiles. I fear that the diversity of coffee is a little endangered.

Climate change is an existential threat to the whole industry. If you are a farmer, you either have to adapt or move.

Can you tell me a little bit about your Next Generation coffee retail initiative?

I think our Next Generation retail blend is a bit of a lighthouse in the industry in terms of attracting attention to the problem. The message has been well received by consumers, especially younger consumers. We have also recently applied an assessment of Blockchain in a joint venture project together with the University of Copenhagen and WWF, amongst others.

Generational issues are not confined to coffee countries. They are also a concern in Scandinavia where rural populations are moving to urban centres. It is the same in our family business – transitioning between generations and attracting young people into the sector.

Young coffee growers need a decent income and access to essential services such as schools and medical centres. We want to give the younger generation the freedom to choose whether they want to stay in coffee farming in remote mountains. For that, we need to provide them with income and services.

Coffee has a unique role to play in meeting the UN's sustainable development goals. The money doesn't get stuck in the cities but is distributed up into the mountains. Coffee is a commodity where private entities can fill the gaps that governments don't cover.

From a business point of view, you can choose acceptable practices. The choices you make can help steer these countries into becoming better societies.

I believe you have two coffee shops. Do you think you'll end up with a chain and be competing against Starbucks?

You never know, but we are very much the tortoise compared to the hare! We see our coffee shops as places where people can come together to enjoy coffee, and I am sure that we will develop. I would expect that we will have more than two shops in the coming years, but to call us a competitor to our dear industry friends such as Starbucks, maybe that is too distant a scenario!

Do you see the RTD sector as an opportunity for growth?

Indeed. Ready-to-Drink coffees are attracting the next generation of consumers. We try to stay on our chosen course of always providing natural things and staying away from, say, artificial sweeteners. That is our heritage.

I see you use plant-based plastics for your capsules.

Yes, they are industrially compostable. However, the most ecological delivery system for coffee is the vacuum-packed ground coffee in brick packs. They are the best packaging solution if they are applied to the latest packaging technologies, both environmentally and logistically.

How is coffee mainly brewed in in Scandinavian countries?

Most of our coffee is sold ground in vacuum packs. The filter is still the prevailing brewing technique, but we've seen a trend towards whole beans and home grinding.

What's your favourite type of coffee? And how do you prepare it?

It depends on the day and the time of day! My most common technique is to self-grind and then use a filter. But I also use a French press and an Aeropress.

As for which coffee I prefer, it's like choosing between your kids. It's impossible! I do have my favourite espresso, though. It's a natural Brazilian one. If I don't get it at least once a week, I will die!

Final question: does coffee keep you awake at night?

More the business than the drink!

Many thanks, Martin, for your time and input!

Chapter 9:
Speciality Coffee

I came to the richest country in the world, so why are they drinking the lousiest coffee?

- Alfred H. Peet

Alfred H. Peet is known as the 'grandfather' of the speciality coffee movement. He was born in 1920 in Alkmaar, in the Netherlands, where his father owned a small coffee wholesale business. In his book, *The Coffee Visionary: The Life and Legacy of Alfred Peet*, Jasper Houtman tells the story of how the young Peet worked with his father to roast and grind coffee and, in particular, to maintain the machinery. At the age of 18, he moved to London, where he found an apprenticeship in a coffee and tea trading company. He returned to the Netherlands at the outbreak of the Second World War and ended up in a German labour camp.

After the war, he continued in the coffee trade, spending time in New Zealand and Indonesia before moving to San Francisco in 1955, where he eventually found a job with a coffee and tea importer. Peet was appalled at the quality of the coffee in the US; he felt he could do better. He started his business in 1966, opening a retail coffee bean outlet on the corner of Vine Street and Walnut Street in Berkeley, California. In an interview with Inc Magazine in 2001, he took up the tale:

'By the time I started my business, in 1966, I was 46 years old. I had learned all the pieces of running a company. I learned about selling. I sold coffee for my father. I didn't understand why people didn't buy my father's coffee. It was so much better than the big roasters' (coffee). I learned I had to sell myself and then sell the product. I spent at least ten years in different import-export firms. Trading is where you make money in the coffee business, but it's also where the game is really rough. What you learn from that is immense.'

Peet's business quickly took off, but as the business grew, the pressure became too much for him. He sold the firm in 1979, remaining with the company as a buyer and consultant until 1983. He told Inc Magazine: 'I worked too hard because I couldn't delegate. I wanted to oversee everything. I was burnt out, so I had to sell. Do you know what it's like when you've given so much, there's nothing left? I sold my business. At the time, it broke my heart. Coffee was my life.'

Peet's was the first coffee bean and brewed coffee retailer to offer speciality grade coffee. He roasted the beans longer, producing a coffee that was darker, more bitter, with less of the sour taste of the coffees offered in the US at the time. Peet's continues to have devoted followers, sometimes known as Peetniks.

Starbucks owes much of its success to Alfred Peet. He trained the founders of Starbucks and supplied them with coffee when they opened their first store in 1971. In an interview with the LA Times, Jerry Baldwin – one of the three founders of Starbucks – said: 'He generously shared with us how to cup, to roast and to blend, and instilled his uncompromising standards. I'll always be in his debt.'

Many people define the speciality coffee movement in terms of waves. Depending on who you talk to, we are currently in the third, fourth, or even fifth wave.

Most people date coffee's first wave back to the mid-1800s when coffee consumption first began to take off in the US. Consumers at that time cared more about the caffeine than the quality: the flavour was less important than convenience and accessibility. During this first wave, producers and roasters concentrated on increasing agricultural yields, lowering costs at origin and getting the product to market as cheaply as possible. Soluble coffee was a product of this first wave.

Somewhat unsurprisingly, this lack of focus on quality gradually drove consumers away. Per capita, coffee consumption in the US fell from around 16 pounds in 1960 to 6 pounds by 1995. Meanwhile, the market was becoming increasingly concentrated as roasters reached for economies of scale. The number of independent roasters in the US fell from around 2,500 in 1945 to 162 in 1972. By 2005, the big three roasters, Procter & Gamble, Kraft, and Sara Lee, controlled over 80 per cent of the retail market.

Alfred Peet is widely credited with starting the second wave in the mid-1960s with Starbucks taking up the baton in the 1970s. Consumers began to appreciate coffee more; they wanted to taste better qualities.

Coffee specialists sometimes refer to this second wave as 'the democratisation of speciality coffee'. Over time, coffee shops started creating more coffee-based drinks, such as Frappuccinos, to appeal to a broader and younger audience. They transformed the coffee culture into a more relaxed one. Retailers designed their coffee shops to make their customers feel more comfortable, while the improved quality of the coffee made them more willing to pay higher prices.

You can best describe the third wave of coffee as the time when coffee started to become more like wine. Coffee drinkers began to become more interested in how to grow it, how to process and roast it, and how to brew it. The quality of the coffee became critical, as did a growing focus on economic, social and environmental sustainability along the supply chain.

In 1982, a group of roasters got together to form the Speciality Coffee Association of America (SCAA) as a non-profit trade organisation representing different segments of the speciality coffee industry, including producers, roasters, importers/exporters and retailers. In 2017, the SCAA merged with the Speciality Coffee Association of Europe to form the Speciality Coffee Association (SCA).

The SCA has defined a grading scheme based on cup-tasting: anything that scores above 80 points out of 100 is considered speciality. Coffee that scores between 90-100 is deemed to be Outstanding; coffee that scores 85-89.99 is Excellent, while coffee scoring 80-84.99 is Very Good.

The SCAA knew that they couldn't address the quality in the cup without first addressing the way coffee is grown and processed at the origin. They knew that the quality of coffee depended first and foremost on the growers who not only had to survive but to thrive. In the words of Ric Rhinehart, the former head of the SCA, 'even if a coffee results in a great tasting beverage, if it does so at the cost of the dignity, value or well-being of the people and land involved, it cannot truly be a speciality coffee.'

To further their objectives, and to address quality and income issues at the origin, the SCAA set up in 1996 the Coffee Quality Institute (CQI). First founded as a committee of the SCAA, it is now an independent not-for-profit organisation. Its goal is to improve quality through training and education: 'Providing coffee producers with the tools they need to compete in the world marketplace.' Its mission is: 'To improve the quality of coffee and the lives of those who produce it.'

The CQI runs the Q Program that has a common standard for evaluating the quality of speciality grade arabica and fine robusta. The organisation runs educational certification programmes along the supply chain, from the mill to the buyers, roasters and baristas.

The CQI has helped to drive the speciality coffee movement, as too has the Alliance for Coffee Excellence (ACE). This Portland Oregon not-for-profit organisation owns and manages the Cup of Excellence® (CoE) programme, begun in 1999 to help farmers receive more money for their high-quality coffee. As well as running the CoE programme, ACE also conducts training, testing, research projects and other activities designed to increase the appreciation of speciality coffees and reward farmers who produce them.

CoE competitions are held each year in producing countries and have become a benchmark for quality coffee. The prices that the winning coffees receive at the auction can be extraordinarily high. As an example, in 2020, the 17th El Salvador Cup of Excellence auction resulted in a record-high price per pound. The 22 winning green coffee lots scoring 87+ points earned an average price of $22.53 per pound, widely eclipsing the previous high of $13.65 per pound set in 2017. None of the winning lots received less than $12 per pound. The top-scoring lot sold for $80.10 per pound, the second for $60.10 per pound.

However, this is still far below the record high price of coffee of $1,029 for a pound attained at auction in 2019 by Wilford Lamastus Jr., a fourth-generation Panamanian coffee producer.

So, if those are the three waves of speciality coffee, what are the fourth and fifth waves? Definitions are a little fuzzy, but they broadly involve more of a focus on the science and the marketing of coffee: how it is grown, processed, roasted and brewed. Fourth wavers want to understand, participate in and control all these stages, from the way growers manage their farms to the way they prepare the coffee in the coffee shop. The fourth wave is about the science of coffee with an obsession to detail, leading to a perfect taste experience.

The fifth wave is about improving the consumer experience by maintaining a focus on serving quality coffee in upmarket environments, with additional attention paid behind the scenes in terms of investment opportunities and chain development. Daily Coffee News cites as examples Starbucks' investment in its Reserve concept, as well as in mergers-and-acquisitions activity such as the Nestlé acquisition of Blue Bottle Coffee.

In a report, the UK-based market research firm Allegra wrote:

'This artisan scene that developed in the mid-2000s has become widespread, and the market is now entering a new era of exceptional professionalism — dubbed the 5th wave, the business of coffee. The 5th wave is a compelling combination of all four previous waves demonstrated by a more advanced set of business practices, delivering high-quality boutique concepts at scale. In the future, market-leading chains will need to demonstrate a capacity for innovation and adaptability to survive in an increasingly competitive marketplace.'

Speciality coffee, when defined as coffee that scores over 80 on the SCA scale, accounts for between 5 and 10 per cent of total coffee sales in developed markets. Demand for speciality coffee is continuing to increase as people get used to – and to insist on – better quality coffee. Indeed, Allegra predicts that the speciality segment will continue to grow at around 3 per cent per year over the next decade.

This annual growth rate of 3 per cent on the 5-10 per cent of the market that is speciality coffee is not much when you compare to the 2.2 per cent yearly growth rate in the total global demand for coffee. Speciality coffee gets the attention in the media, but it is commodity coffee that is doing all the heavy lifting. The consumers in Asia and the coffee-producing countries of the Southern Hemisphere are the ones driving world demand.

Speciality coffee does, however, punch above its weight. Speciality coffee is changing the image of coffee not just in developed countries, but the world over. Coffee has become cool, modern, and young. For the time being, new consumers in Asia and coffee-producing countries are drinking soluble and RTD coffees; as tastes mature, consumption should switch to better-quality speciality coffees. It would be good news for everyone in the supply chain, but especially for farmers because of the quality premia that they should receive. (But more on that in a later chapter.)

Many people outside of the coffee trade mistakenly think of speciality coffees as novelty coffees such as the Kopi Luwak from Indonesia.

Kopi Luwak dates from a time when the Dutch colonial rulers forbade Indonesian farmers from harvesting coffee cherries for their use. Instead, they looked on the ground for fallen cherries, often finding beans in the dung of civets, small mammals native to the region. The civets eat the coffee cherries and then pass out the beans through their digestive systems.

In the past, Kopi Luwak was almost exclusively produced by wild civets. The animals would graze in the wilderness, picking the choicest cherries at their leisure, and coffee producers would hunt for the dung. That's all changed now. There's such a massive demand for the coffee that most Kopi Luwak producers use civets that have been captured, put in cages and force-fed coffee berries.

In his book The Monk of Mokha, Dave Eggers quotes George Howell, a well-known roaster, as describing Kopi Luwak as: 'Coffee from assholes, for assholes.'

Black Ivory coffee is produced through a process similar to Kopi Luwak, but by elephants in northern Thailand. Unlike Kopi Luwak, the coffee is produced in cooperation with an elephant refuge, and a percentage of coffee sales go to fund the elephants' healthcare. It is an expensive coffee about which you can feel good.

But it's probably best to go with a quality coffee that hasn't already been partly digested before it gets to your cup!

A conversation with Ric Rhinehart

Good morning, Ric. Could you tell me a little bit about yourself and how you got involved in coffee?

I got into coffee by accident. I am an engineer by education, but early on I realised that I wanted to do anything except being an engineer. After leaving university, I found myself in the food and beverage world, specifically in the hotel business. I was a food and beverage director for Four Seasons Hotels, and I was always looking for coffee for my hotel.

I found a local guy who supplied fantastic coffee. He told me that if I ever got tired of hotels, he had a place for me in the coffee business. One day I got tired of working every holiday and every weekend, and he took me into the coffee business. That was 30 some odd years ago, and I never left.

Until recently you were CEO of the SCA. Could you please tell me a little bit about the SCA?

The SCA emerged as a result of a merger between the SCAA - the Specialty Coffee Association of America - and the SCAE, the Speciality Coffee Association of Europe.

A group of small business folks who were pursuing the speciality coffee trade founded the SCAA in 1982. They felt that the US National Coffee Association was not addressing their needs or their perceptions, so they started an all-volunteer organisation in 1982. They hired their first full-time staff person in 1991, and that was right about the time that the US speciality coffee movement began to boom.

Our goal has always been to promote the understanding and consumption of speciality coffee in the US, and then ultimately at a global level. Our focus was on educating folks in the coffee business. Our thinking from the outset was that if we could educate the interface with the consumer, then that interface would educate the consumer.

The educational offering is now broader. It is directly aimed at roasters, buyers and producers all up and down the chain.

How does your membership break down between baristas, roasters and producers?

The old SCAA was mainly centred around roasters, but today the organisation is more centred around baristas. There are more producer members than there used to be, but the economics of a membership organisation is challenging for producers. We have more producer associations, along with some of the larger-scale farms. We also have a lot of cooperatives.

Has the speciality sector been the driver of the growth in US coffee demand?

Absolutely. In the mature markets, particularly in the US, coffee consumption had peaked in the early to mid-1960s. It was in decline until the mid-90s when the speciality coffee movement began, and people started returning to coffee.

With the growth of coffee bars and shops, there was also a new venue of consumption. People began drinking coffee outside of their home and their workplace. Out-of-home consumption had previously been centred around the workplace. Still, in the early to mid-90s, we started to see cafés appear everywhere, and people began to consume coffee outside the home and the workplace. That changed the market.

And is US demand growth continuing?

Yes, US coffee consumers now drink an average of three cups per day, and that's back up to practically to where it was at its peak. Consumption continues to be on the rise, and it continues to be mainly driven by the speciality sector.

Coffee consumption in kilos is still just a little less than 70 per cent at home, but in dollar value, it's probably 55 per cent outside the home now, mainly because a kilo is cheaper than a cup.

Are you're worried about demand with cafés closed because of the coronavirus?

Coffee has two noteworthy characteristics from an economic standpoint. One is that its price elasticity is low. If you are a coffee drinker, coffee is a relatively high priority for you at a relatively low-price basis, so you're willing to defer other expenses to continue to drink coffee. Conversely, if coffee were suddenly free, you wouldn't increase your consumption to say nine or ten cups a day. You'd still maintain your three or four cups.

Coffee has also been remarkably resilient in economic downturns. That was true in the global recession in 2008 when coffee consumption stayed relatively healthy. It is the venue of consumption that shifts. When you're in an economic downturn, people tend to return to drinking more coffee at home and drinking less coffee out-of-home.

Consumption bounced back very quickly after 2009 when out-of-work people were looking to get out of the house and have some social interactions. The coffeehouse became an affordable and friendly place to do that.

We saw a relatively short period where the venue of consumption shifted from cafés and other out-of-home opportunities to in-home consumption. It returned to out-of-home consumption reasonably quickly.

The current scenario is quite different in that the cafés have no choice but to close because of social distancing. I suspect that a lot of marginal operations will disappear, never to return.

What percentage of the US market is speciality coffees?

It's hard to determine, in part because most of the data that supports this is reliant on self-identification. Consumers identify products as speciality or gourmet beverages or products.

As I mentioned earlier, in dollar value, it's about 55 per cent of the US market through self-identification. In kilos, it's been hovering around 20 to 25 per cent of the total consumption. That just tells you that the in-home and institutional consumption tend to be at a lower price, while consumption in restaurants and cafes tend to be at a higher price.

We think of all businesses whose principal product is coffee – so, for example, all the Starbucks cafés - as speciality coffee.

Could you tell me a little bit about your new role now you've left the SCA?

I am now semi-retired. I was the executive director and CEO of SCAA and SCA for a total of eleven years. The studies suggest that CEO effectiveness peaks between five and seven years. I started to feel that after so long in the role, I was not as effective as I would have liked to have been. As a baby boomer, I was also looking at the generational transition between my cohort and the next, and it just started to feel like it was time to cede some of the responsibilities.

The timing lined up with the burgeoning price crisis in coffee, and the board asked me to spend my terminal year focusing on that price crisis. We launched a price crisis response team within the organisation to try to understand what drives the cyclical low prices in coffee, and what we might do about it.

Coffee farmers, smallholders in particular around the world, were frequently producing and selling coffee at below their cost of production. It was just so counterintuitive to us, but in many cases, there are not a lot of other options for producers. Their terrain doesn't allow for an alternative good cash crop. For many smallholders, coffee is a cash crop that augments subsistence farming at the same time.

So, we were trying to come to grips with that and see how we might find ways to change the nature of the business so that coffee was a better deal for producers.

My impression is that coffee prices are low because Brazil and Vietnam are efficient producers, and they are the ones who set the prices.

There's no doubt that the market is working as you would expect. The more efficient producers are gaining market share and forcing out the less efficient producers. It raises a couple of questions and creates some externalities.

We have just talked about the speciality market, but neither Brazil nor Vietnam produces speciality coffee. They are commodity producers. They are looking at how low they can take production costs – as well as sales costs – while maintaining an acceptable level of quality.

So, it's a constant battle for them to push the quality down to the point of broad market acceptance, where there's no downturn in consumption: where you get equilibrium around consumption but continue to drive down costs at the same time. It's happening in coffee; we've seen the quality of coffee at the commodity level drop to the lowest acceptable level.

But hasn't the demand growth in the developed world been principally in speciality coffee?

What's happening here is that roasters have gotten much better at marketing their coffee as speciality, even when it's a commodity-based product. You can see the writing on the wall; ultimately, a couple of things will happen. The highly efficient producers will survive. Inefficient producers will fail.

Oddly those inefficient producers are the ones who generate most of the unique speciality coffees. They'll likely disappear, and their coffee will disappear with them.

Coffee consumption has risen over the past 30 years in part because coffee started to taste better, particularly in the US. Consumers who had left coffee in the 70s and 80s because it didn't taste good anymore returned to coffee because it's starting to taste good again.

As I mentioned earlier, the trend towards better-tasting coffee has been offset by a tendency towards better-marketed coffee. The big CPG (Consumer Packaged Group) companies and the big roasting companies have invested a lot of money in convincing their customers that their coffee tastes good, because it's got the right packaging, a recognisable label, and it's convenient. They've abandoned the search for better-tasting coffee. The long-term trend is that ultimately consumers will reduce the amount of coffee that they drink.

No consumer gets up one day and says: 'I don't like coffee anymore.' If you put frogs in a pot of cold water, they will not notice a gradual rise in temperature until it is too late. Coffee consumers are like that. They say: 'I don't need another cup today; the last one wasn't that great.' Eventually, their consumption will decrease over time. This is the reverse of what happened in the past when people said: 'Wow that was a great tasting coffee; I'll have another one!'

Isn't there room for both commodity and speciality coffee?

Global coffee production has grown from about 85 million bags in 1985 to about 175 million bags today. Virtually all of that growth in production and consumption can be attributed to robusta and natural arabica. Washed arabica production and consumption have stayed level at roughly 35 million bags.

We can use washed arabica as a proxy for speciality coffee. You're starting to see a bifurcation in the markets where a small number of individuals appreciate expensive coffee. In the more mainstream segments, washed naturals and robustas have offset arabica. I don't see that changing. A few successful farmers who can market their product and maintain a high quality of coffee and get market access will persist. The rest of the washed arabica will likely start to crumble.

Let's take a look at some numbers. Costa Rica at its peak produced about 3 million bags of washed arabica coffee; production this year is 1.3 - 1.4 million bags, almost half of what it used to be.

Panama, probably the most remarkable success story in speciality coffee, produced about 300,000 bags of coffee at its peak; they exported most of it. Today Panama produces somewhere around 150,000 bags: the domestic market absorbs 90,000 bags, leaving exports at about 40-50,000 bags. Most of the exported coffee sells at very high prices, somewhere around $6-7 a pound. That's a great price, but it's only 40-50,000 pounds. Thirty or forty producers in Panama are doing well at $7 a pound, but there's no mainstream production left there.

We can look across the board at traditional washed arabica producers; practically all of them are in decline. The only place we've seen growth in washed arabica production is in Colombia. Honduras has had a significant uptick in production, but mainly at the expense of other Mesoamerican producers. Salvador's a disaster. They were four million bags at their peak of production, but they're at about a half a million bags today. Guatemala has gone from four and a half million bags to three and a half million bags.

Mexico has struggled, and they see their production increase primarily in robusta to feed the growing soluble market.

Speciality coffee will persist but at an ever-declining narrowing base of both production and consumption and increasing prices. That doesn't bode well for the long term.

What's the solution?

Unfortunately, I know more about the drivers of the problem than I know about the solutions.

I believe that the most significant driver has been the shift in the approach to economic activity from pre-Friedman capitalism to post-Friedman capitalism. The concept that those unrestrained markets were the solution to development and economic prosperity gathered steam until it almost became a religion. Instead of Ten Commandments, there were two: first, that the market shall be unrestrained; second, that shareholder value should be paramount. That became the religion of economics worldwide.

I am a fan of capitalism but on a restrained basis. The invisible hand of the market is dangerous if it doesn't have the opposing force of the public sector to constrain its worst impulses.

I believe we're now at a moment of inflexion. I think the incoming generation is looking at the results of these 50 years of unrestrained market approaches to capitalism. We've got a planet on the verge of death. We've got a population facing a pandemic for which we were woefully unprepared, and we cannot respond.

The market, this fabulous market that fixes all things, is utterly debilitated and unable to respond; it is begging for public sector rescue. The younger generation is saying: 'Who are you to tell me that the public sector is inept, and the private sector can fix everything?' I think the system will change.

It seems that the pendulum is swinging back towards stakeholder rather than shareholder capitalism.

That's excellent news for the coffee industry and all of the farmers around the world. You've got to look after your stakeholders. You have to price in all the externalities.

We can work with that swing of the pendulum to revitalise our institutions, to be outspoken about the need for a stakeholder rather than a shareholder approach to capitalism, to be overt in saying that utterly unrestrained markets as they are today are not only impractical but dangerous. The most important is to reassess how we form our values as a separate issue from how we assign value.

It is a complex problem, and there is no simple solution. It's going to be a myriad of solutions: values rather than value; institutional strengthening; a recognition that the private sector and the public sector have to have a balance.

What can be done to eradicate child labour from the supply chain?

I think you'd be hard-pressed to find anybody who would say child labour is always wrong. In a small family farm today in California, perhaps the most regulated place in the US, it is culturally appropriate and ethically correct for 15-year olds to work summers on the family farm. There's nothing inherently wrong with that.

The issue is when children are employed out of economic necessity and at the expense of their health, education or welfare. It's almost impossible to discern that dividing line in any meaningful way in emerging economies, or in rural agricultural economies where access to health, education and welfare is relatively low already.

Our response has been to decree that all child labour is terrible. It is a hypocritical response, but it is too complicated and too expensive to do otherwise.

However, the problem is not child labour. The problem is a system that keeps prices at a level that I call 'sustainable poverty'. We keep people just poor enough to exist, but not so poor that they die, and never sufficiently wealthy to break free from their subsistence existence.

What are the sustainability issues in coffee?

In terms of coffee's environmental impact, smallholder coffee is between neutral and positive. Coffee tends to grow best under shade in terms of quality. Coffee is a hardwood tree that grows pretty fast and does an excellent job of sinking carbon, especially if it displaces pasture. It tends to be an outstanding contributor to genetic diversity. It does well with other companion growths.

Coffee can have a negative impact when it's grown in scale, as in Brazil. Farmers may uproot virgin timber to plant coffee trees, and they may use more chemical inputs to produce it. There could also be downstream damage from the effluent from coffee processing.

Environmentally, coffee is more beneficial than detrimental. That could change if we move from a broad distribution of smallholders to a narrow band of highly technical intensive farms.

Is it true that people view someone with a cup of coffee in their hand as friendlier and less threatening?

A study tested how people were perceived with and without a cup of coffee in their hand. It found that if you have a cup of coffee in your hands, you're viewed as a warmer and friendlier person.

It is a fundamental question for anyone in coffee: 'Why do we humans like coffee?' It's a non-nutritive food product. It doesn't taste good at first, and we have to learn to like coffee. It's got some psychotropic additive value because of caffeine, but it's not very good. There are better caffeine sources, and there are certainly more exciting psychotropics.

I don't know why coffee is so well-received and so well-loved by humans, but I am anxious to find the answer. Someday we'll know, but I suspect there's something in our biology that loves coffee for a particular reason.

What is your favourite coffee?

It is generally true that the way you've come to coffee is the way you stay with coffee. I grew up a drip-coffee drinker, and I am a drip-coffee drinker today. I like espresso, but it's not my principal consumption. If you're an Italian who comes to the world as an espresso drinker, you are likely to leave the world is an espresso drinker.

As to which is my favourite coffee, it's like asking me which out of my four children is my favourite. I don't have a favourite, but I'm a big fan of Ethiopian coffees.

Thank you, Ric, for your time and input!

Chapter 10: Café Culture

What on earth could be more luxurious than a sofa, a book, and a cup of coffee?

– Anthony Trollope

In 1981, a kid from Brooklyn walked into a coffee store in Seattle, Washington. He had flown in from New York and was on the West Coast trying to sell household goods, including coffee-making machines, for a Swedish importer. He had stopped off in Seattle on a whim, checking out the terrain and hoping to make a sale.

Howard Schultz had attended Northern Michigan University on a football scholarship. He graduated in 1976, spent a year working at a ski lodge, and then got a job with Xerox as a photocopier salesman, before joining a Swedish household goods company.

While in Seattle, he stopped in at a store that had been set up by three friends. The three friends had met when they were students at the University of San Francisco: Jerry Baldwin was an English teacher; Zev Siegl was a history teacher; Gordon Bowker was a writer and partner in an advertising agency. When they got back to Seattle after college, they were unhappy with the quality of the coffee that they found there and decided to set up a store similar to the one that Alfred Peet owned and ran in San Francisco. The three friends tried to come up with a name for the store and somewhat bizarrely settled on Starbuck, the character of the chief mate in the book Moby-Dick. They opened their first store in 1971, at first roasting and selling green coffee beans purchased from Peet's.

Howard Schultz was so impressed by the store the three friends had set up that he asked them for a job. He believed that his sales experience would help them expand their business to restaurants and hotels. He continued to badger them for a job for more than a year before they finally agreed to take him on, sending him to Milan, Italy, for a trade fair. Schultz was blown away by the Italian café culture in Milan and wondered how it might translate to the US. On the flight home, he came up with a concept that he called 'the third place' – somewhere between home and work where people could hang out in a safe, welcoming environment.

Back in Seattle, he tried and failed to convince the three founders to sell beverages as well as beans; they don't want to get involved in running cafés. He eventually convinced them to test the concept, and they let him have 500 square feet in a new 1,500 feet store that Starbucks opened in 1984 in downtown Seattle. The idea was a success, but the three partners were unimpressed and decided that their future lay in the sale of beans, not beverages. They doubled down and, in 1984, bought Peet's.

Schultz left Starbucks a year later to set up his own coffee chain; he called it Il Giornale, after the Milanese newspaper of the same name. Starbucks was a founder investor for $150,000 of the $400,000 he needed to start his business, while a friend of his wife invested another $100,000. He had difficulty raising the rest of the money, pitching the idea to more than 240 potential investors. He eventually raised the money and opened three cafés.

In 1987, Starbucks' founders offered to sell their company's six stores to Schultz for $3.8 million, giving him three months to raise the money. He just managed to do it, but only after Bill Gates' father intervened to persuade an alternative bidder to back out.

Schultz resigned as CEO of Starbucks in 2000 but stayed on as chairman. By then, the company had grown to 3,500 stores around the world, and Schultz was complaining that he spent all his time dealing with lawyers and HR. It was, he said, 'no fun anymore'.

The company continued to grow exponentially and, by 2008, had more than 15,000 stores. However, these new stores were beginning to cannibalise business from existing stores, and the company was burning cash. 'People had got sloppy and lazy,' Shultz later explained. 'Success has to be earned. It is not an entitlement.'

Starbucks' share price hit a record low during the financial crisis of 2008, and Shultz stepped back in as CEO. He closed 900 stores, many of which had only been open for a few months. He shut down all the remaining stores for an afternoon to retrain staff. He summoned 10,000 of his store managers from around the world to attend a meeting in a football stadium. He told them that if nothing changed, the company would be bankrupt within seven months. He asked for their help to turn the situation around. They gave it to him.

BY 2018, when Schultz stepped down for a second time as company CEO, Starbucks had a turnover above $25 billion and a market capitalisation of over $50 billion. At the time of writing, the company has stores on six continents and in 79 countries and territories, with 31,256 outlets. Its market capitalisation is above $85 billion.

Schultz argues that the quality of the coffee had a part in Starbucks' success, but it was more to do with the relationship his company had with its customers; the stores had become the third place he first envisaged on his that trip to Milan in 1983.

He may be right. I remember the first time I visited a Starbucks coffee shop – in Canterbury in the UK on a trip to visit my parents. It had only recently opened, and I remember the comfortable armchairs where I could hang out there with the children while my wife and mother window-shopped together.

I also remember how I used Starbucks as an office when participants from the international sugar trade assembled in London for their bi-annual dinner. I would visit London-based clients in their offices, but I would meet overseas clients in the Starbucks café opposite the Hilton Hotel on Berkeley Street. I would spend a lot of time there, and not once did anyone ask me to leave or push me to buy another drink. As one friend said: 'The price of the coffee might be high, but it includes the rent.'

Coffee shops have often been centres of commerce. In 1652, a French visitor to London was so impressed by the city's coffee shops he wrote: 'You have all manner of news there; you have a good fire, which you may sit by as long as you please. You have a dish of coffee; you meet your friends for the transaction of business and all for a penny if you don't care to spend more.'

As William H Ukers wrote in All About Coffee: 'The coffee houses became the gathering places for wits, fashionable people, and brilliant and scholarly men, to whom they afforded opportunity for endless gossip and discussion.'

Lloyd's Royal Exchange, famous for its shipping intelligence and marine insurance, dates back to 1688, when Edward Lloyd opened a coffee house in Tower Street, later in Lombard Street, in the City of London. It was apparently 'a modest place of refreshment for seafarers and merchants', but Edward Lloyd handwrote ships' lists that informed his customers which vessels were insured and by whom. It was the beginning of the two institutions that have grown to dominate world shipping: Lloyd's Register of Shipping; Lloyd's Royal Exchange. Edward Lloyd died in 1712. The coffee house moved to Pope's Head Alley, where it was called New Lloyds, and in 1784 it moved again to the Royal Exchange.

Still on the theme of shipping and world trade, London's Baltic Exchange traces its origins back to 1744 and the Baltic Coffee House on Threadneedle Street in the City of London, which served as a central meeting place for merchants and shipowners. Its first rules were established in 1823, and in 1857 it became known as The Baltic Company. In 1900, it merged with the London Shipping Exchange and became known as the Baltic Exchange.

Coffee houses were also centres of commerce in the US. In New Orleans, all the business of the city was for a long time transacted in the coffee houses along Canal Street. In New York, the Exchange Coffee House, built on Broad Street in 1731, became the city's unofficial auction room and the centre of the commodity trade. It was rivalled by the Merchants' Coffee House, built in 1737, on the northwest corner of Wall Street, in which the Chamber of Commerce began to hold regular meetings. Meanwhile, in Boston, the Exchange Coffee House, which opened in 1808, was modelled on Lloyd's of London. It quickly became the centre of marine insurance and intelligence in the city.

Coffee houses were not just centres of commerce; they were also hotbeds of revolution. Café Precope opened in Paris in 1689; it quickly established itself as a literary salon, a gathering place for the city's actors, authors and musicians. It was also a regular haunt for Benjamin Franklin, so much so that when he died, in 1790, the owner draped the café's walls in black in mourning for 'the great friend of republicanism'. Café Precope also played a role in the turbulent years of the French Revolution, as a meeting point for Robespierre, Danton and other plotters. Napoleon Bonaparte was also a regular as a young artillery officer; he once had to leave his hat behind as security against an unpaid bill.

The French Revolution began not in the Café Precope, but on 12th July 1789 in the Café Foy where the journalist Camille Desmoulins climbed onto a table and incited the café's customers to march from the café and, two days later, to storm the Bastille.

Across the Atlantic, the basement of the Green Dragon coffee house on Union Street, Boston, became the headquarters of the American Revolution. Samuel Adams met there with like-minded republicans – the 'Sons of Liberty' - to win freedom for the colonies. They planned the Boston Tea Party there, and they sent Paul Revere from there on his famous midnight ride to Lexington to warn Patriots that the British were on their way.

In the words of William H Ukers: 'One of the most interesting facts in the history of the coffee drink is that wherever it has been introduced, it has spelt revolution. It has been the world's most radical drink in that its function has always been to make people think. And when people think, they become dangerous to tyrants and foes of liberty of thought and action.'

Coffee shops have often been luxurious. The first coffee shops in Constantinople were richly furnished, while in Damascus they were decorated with silks and damasks. This tradition continued with the gilded mirrors found in Parisian and Venetian cafés through to the palms in the Waldorf Hotel. They were already often the third place that Howard Schultz sought to recreate in his cafés.

For most Starbucks customers, the comfy chairs are just a backdrop, the setting where they order their coffee to take away. You could argue that the customers seated in those chairs are just a backdrop that makes the take-away customers feel good about the place. One friend of mine once argued that Starbucks should pay people to sit in their cafés, like extras in a movie. Rather sadly, most people sitting in a Starbucks café are not chatting with friends as in Central Park, in the TV series Friends. Instead, most are glued to their computers or smartphones. But perhaps we shouldn't blame Howard Schultz for that.

In any case, Starbucks is the largest coffee chain in the world, generating ten times more revenue than its closest competitor. Starbucks is also the world's third-biggest coffee roaster, by volume, after Nestlé and JAB. One of the most extraordinary things about the Starbucks phenomenon is that traditional coffee players let it happen. They didn't see the demand, nor did they share the vision. The rest of the field is now trying to catch up, but they have a long way to go.

Dunkin is the world's second-biggest coffee shop chain, with nearly 13,000 franchised coffee shops in 42 companies around the world. The business was founded, in 1948, by William Rosenberg in Quincy, Massachusetts as the Open Kettle; he changed its name two years later to Dunkin Donuts. (The brand dropped the 'Donuts' in 2019.) As the name suggests, the company specialises in baked goods. Still, it was also the first chain in the US to serve only arabica coffee, introducing US consumers to a more refined coffee taste.

Baskin-Robbins' holding company, Allied Domecq, acquired the chain in 1990 and changed its name to Dunkin' Brands. In 2005, they sold Dunkin' Donuts and Baskin-Robbins to a private equity consortium for $2.4 billion.

The Canadian-based Tim Hortons is the third-largest coffee house chain in the world. Tim Horton, an ice-hockey player, opened the first store in Hamilton, Ontario, in 1964, under the name 'Tim Horton Donuts'. Ron Joyce, a former Hamilton police constable, took over as manager of the store in 1965 and, two years later, became a partner. By the time Tim Horton died in a car crash in 1974, the company had become a chain of 40 stores across Canada. Joyce bought out the Horton family's shares for $1 million and expanded the chain, opening the 500th store opened in 1991.

The Horton and Joyce partnership carried on with the marriage of Joyce's son, Ron Joyce Jr., to Tim Horton's eldest daughter, Jeri-Lynn.

In 1995, Tim Hortons merged with Wendy's, the American fast-food company, and overtook McDonald's as Canada's biggest hamburger chain. In 2006, Wendy's spun off Tim Hortons as a separate company, by which time it accounted for around 60 per cent of the Canadian coffee market. Starbucks, in the number two position in Canada, had only 7 per cent.

In 2014, Burger King acquired Tim Hortons in a deal worth about US$11.4 billion, and it is now part of Restaurant Brands International. The chain currently has almost 5,000 coffee shops spread across 14 countries.

Costa Coffee, founded in 1971, the same year as Starbucks, is the fourth largest coffee shop chain in the world with around 3,900 outlets.

The two brothers, Bruno and Sergio Costa, were both born in Parma, Italy and moved to the UK in the 1960s. They began their company in Lambeth, London as a wholesale operation supplying roasted beans to caterers and specialist Italian coffee shops. They moved into retail in 1978, opening their first store in Vauxhall Bridge Road, London. In 1985, Sergio bought out his brother's shares, and in 1995 he sold the company and its 41 stores in the UK to Whitbread, a beer company.

Costa Coffee continued to expand under Whitbread's ownership, opening its 1,000th store in the UK in 2009. That same year, Costa Coffee bought the Polish chain Coffeeheaven, adding 79 stores in central and eastern Europe. Ten years later, Whitbread sold the chain to the Coca-Cola Company for close to $5 billion.

You have to move to Asia to find the next biggest chains. The fifth in size (by the number of outlets) is South Korea's Paris Baguette. The chain was founded in 1988, and now has over 3,300 retail stores in South Korea, 57 stores in the US, and an additional 185 retail stores in China, Vietnam, Singapore and France.

Still in South Korea, Ediya Coffee is the sixth-largest chain in the world. Founded in 2001, the privately-owned company now has over 3,000 franchised outlets in Asia.

Thailand's Café Amazon is the world's seventh-largest chain with more than 3,000 outlets located around the world. It began as a subsidiary of PTT, Thailand's national oil and gas conglomerate, and was initially the retail business of PTT's network of petrol and gas stations. It now operates as a standalone enterprise at department stores, supermarkets and roadside locations. The chain sources its coffee from Thailand's plantations.

China's Luckin Coffee is the eighth largest coffee chain by the number of outlets, with over 4,500 outlets (as of 2020); it has more outlets in China than Starbucks. The company opened its first shops in January 2018 in Beijing and Shanghai and by October 2018, had opened 1,300 stores in the country. In January 2019, Luckin Coffee listed on Nasdaq at $17 a share.

A year later, Muddy Waters Research published a report claiming that Luckin Coffee had falsified financial and operational figures. The company denied the allegations but in April 2020 admitted that it had inflated its sales figures by over $300 million. The US stock market halted trading in its shares after they had plummeted more than 80 per cent. The shares began trading again in May 2020 but fell by a further 20 per cent.

You will find the world's next largest chain of coffee shops in India. As well as running retail outlets, Café Coffee Day owns 4,500 hectares of coffee plantations in the country and is the largest producer of arabica beans in Asia. (Tata is the largest Asian coffee producer if you combine arabica and robusta.) Café Coffee Day opened its first outlet in 1996, and it now has more than 2,500 café outlets in India, as well as in Austria, Czech Republic, Egypt and Nepal.

In an interview in 2016 in Outlook, an Indian weekly, the company's founder, V. G. Siddhartha said: 'I wanted to be Robin Hood to rob the rich and give to the poor, but then I realised India was a really poor country. There was nothing to rob. It was better to make your own money; to get into business.'

Siddhartha went missing in July 2019, and police found his body in a nearby river. The authorities classed his death as suicide, a possible result of taking on debt too often financed by shady black-market lenders. At the time of writing, the company has appointed Ernst & Young to look for potential buyers for the beleaguered chain.

The Coffee Bean & Tea Leaf Company is the tenth-largest coffee chain by the number of outlets, with over 1,000 self-owned and franchised stores in the US and 31 other countries. Herbert Hyman founded the company in 1963 as a coffee service for offices. He opened the first Coffee Bean store in 1968 in Los Angeles. By the 1970s, Coffee Bean had ten stores in Southern California.

Starbucks tried to purchase Coffee Bean in 1991, but Hyman turned them down. In 1996, the Hymans sold the Asian franchise rights to Singaporean brothers Victor Sassoon and Sunny Sassoon, and two years later the two brothers bought the parent company. They sold it in 2019 to the Jollibee Foods Corporation, a Filipino multinational company based in Pasig, Philippines.

What is the difference between a coffee shop and a fast-food restaurant? McDonald's, for example, launched the McCafé concept back in 1993 in Melbourne, Australia, and by some accounts, McCafé is now more profitable than McDonald's itself. As well as coffee, they also sell snacks, shakes and drinks. As to how many outlets McCafé operate, I have seen estimates varying from 5,000 to 10,000. Similarly, some people would argue that Dunkin is not a coffee shop but a fast-food restaurant. It is somewhat arbitrary as to where to draw the line.

What does the future hold for coffee shops? Some say that the coronavirus pandemic of 2020 will accelerate the decline of the large coffee shop chains, arguing that consumers will boycott stores and use their smartphones to order their coffee for delivery to their homes or offices.

At the time of writing, Starbucks is replacing some of its stores with kiosks and drive-throughs. The company had already begun to do this before the pandemic hit, but the epidemic is accelerating the transformation. In a June 2020 press release, Starbucks CEO Kevin Johnson said: 'Starbucks stores have always been known as the third place, a welcoming place outside of our home and work where we connect over a cup of coffee. As we navigate through the COVID-19 crisis, we are accelerating our store transformation plans to address the realities of the current situation, while still providing a safe, familiar and convenient experience for our customers.'

The pandemic might also lead to the loss of many of the small independent coffee shops around the world. But there again, the epidemic might only accelerate a trend that was happening anyway, with more people working from their homes and meeting, not in coffee shops, but on Zoom.

Communities around the world must wrestle with the question: 'What do cafés offer us in addition to good coffee? And what will we lose if they close their doors for good?'

A Conversation with Chris von Zastrow

(Chris recently retired from Starbucks where he was coffee sustainability director. All views are his own and not necessarily those of Starbucks.)

Good morning Chris. Thank you for taking the time to chat. I think you grew up on a coffee farm. Can you tell me a little about that?

My father managed coffee farms in Kenya and Tanzania before buying his farm on the slopes of Kilimanjaro in Tanganyika (Tanzania) in 1959. I was born in Kenya in 1953, and apart from my time in boarding schools in Tanzania, Ethiopia and England, the farm was my home until I was 19 years old.

We had 150 acres (60 hectares), but soils were poor and the land rocky. Mechanisation wasn't possible; we did all the work manually. Operating costs were horrendous. We grew arabica coffee under rather heavy Gravilea Robusta shade canopy, as was the custom at the time. We sold the coffee through the local auction system. There were very few direct sales back then.

Shortly after Tanzania gained independence in 1961, the government more or less doubled the minimum agricultural wages. We couldn't maintain the same workforce; it made it difficult to run the farm profitably. As operating costs increased and rain patterns changed - without irrigation, the farm was reliant on the rains – the revenue from coffee sales rarely covered the operating and living expenses.

My mother started raising chickens to supplement our income. Also, both my parents led birding and wildlife safaris for a little extra revenue. My parents concentrated more on the safaris in the last couple of years before I left, and, as a teenager, I ended up running the coffee farm in their absence.

Why did you leave Tanzania?

I was kicked out of the country in April 1973, when I was 19 years old. I'd driven into Arusha to buy farm supplies and renew my multi-year resident visa. Instead of renewing the visa, they simply cancelled the old one and informed me I had to be out of the country by midnight. It was already 4.30 pm, and I still had a 90-minute drive to get home and then another two-hour drive to the Kenyan border.

My parents weren't allowed to take their Land Rover across the border, so they had to leave me there. Finally, just before midnight, I managed to hitch a ride to Nairobi with a priest in the back of an old Peugeot wagon.

Once I arrived in Nairobi, I had to beg and borrow from family and friends to get a flight to London. In London, I then did the same and managed to scrape enough money together to buy a ticket to the US.

Did your parents stay in Tanzania?

The government nationalised my parents' farm in October 1973. My parents, like many others, had only one bank account – the farm account – and everything went through it. The account was considered part of the farm assets and was blocked.

With no access to the bank account and no money for food or fuel, my parents ended up having to sell furniture and personal belongings to survive; they eventually left the country in February 1974.

When you went to the US, did you get back into coffee?

It took me about ten years to get back into coffee. In America, I was totally out of my depth. I had no idea what I could or wanted to do in such a new and foreign environment. I attended a couple of junior colleges and bounced around in different jobs: bank teller, driver, washing dishes, hamburger cook, changing tires, and roughnecking on oil drilling rigs. When, in 1982, the US oil industry collapsed, and jobs were tough to find, I had to admit that I needed to further my education. In 1983, I enrolled at the University of Utah, where I spent the next three years earning a degree in business law and communication.

On leaving university, I got a job with J. Aron & Co., a subsidiary of Goldman Sachs. They trained me for three months in New York and three months in London, and I quickly learned how little I truly knew about coffee and the industry. They then sent me to Nairobi, where I opened my own little coffee buyer-representative company, financed by Goldman Sachs.

From the end of 1986 through 1994, I represented J. Aron & Co. as a regional buyer. I purchased coffee from eastern African countries. In 1991, I bought over 16 per cent of the Kenyan crop, which at that time was one of the largest purchases made by one company in Kenya.

It may surprise younger people to hear that Goldman Sachs was once in the coffee business.

In 1981, Goldman Sachs bought J. Aron & Co., a trading company founded around the turn of the century and based in New Orleans. It was historically a coffee trading company, but over the years it had expanded and become successful trading, amongst other commodities, precious metals, mainly gold. Goldman Sachs integrated

J. Aron's trading operations into the group and moved the business to their New York offices.

In the 1990s, J. Aron went through a difficult period in coffee, finding themselves on the wrong side of the market two or three times, especially on Brazils. J. Aron traded mostly in large commercial quantities through the Exchange, and although the margins were small, the volumes more than made up for it. Speciality coffees represented a tiny segment of their trade. The coffee industry was changing rapidly, with many mergers and also bankruptcies amongst the trade houses. If I remember correctly, futures losses amounted to many millions in the short span of a few years. They decided to cease coffee trading operations after nearly 100 years of trading.

In 1993, I took up an offer to join the Neumann Group, to open a second coffee trading office for them in Moshi, Tanzania. It was at the same time as the Burundi/Rwanda genocide. They asked me also to help keep the Burundi office open. I spent quite a bit of time travelling back and forth to Burundi. Coupled with family health issues, it was a challenging period, and, in 1995, we decided to move back to the US.

Back in the US, I opened a small speciality roasting company called Kilimanjaro Coffee in Coeur d'Alene, Idaho. It was a struggle. Looking back, I was ahead of my time for the speciality coffee trend in that part of the country. I kept the business going for two years but then ran out of money. I took a job in the insurance business in Boise, Idaho.

I eventually managed to get back into the coffee business with a roaster in Minnesota; it was relatively short-lived for financial reasons. I kept myself afloat by trading green coffee in the Midwest for a West Coast coffee importer. In 2003, the CQI (Coffee Quality Institute), at that time part of the Speciality Coffee Association of

America, was starting a series of training programmes in Africa. They asked me to join a group them. It was during one training session that I met the chief of party for the sponsoring NGO: later that year he offered me the position of technical advisor for coffee.

In late 2003, I moved from Minnesota to Uganda for the East African Fine Coffee Association (EAFCA), in conjunction with USAID, to promote African coffees and to provide extension service advice to farmers. As part of the promotion process, we set up an East African coffee conference to bring foreign buyers to the region. The first conference took place in Nairobi in February 2004. The meetings are still held in a different African country each year.

How did you end up with Starbucks?

I had previously been in touch with Starbucks to help them navigate some issues in Ethiopia.

In March 2007, Starbucks asked me if I would be interested in managing the African side of their global coffee strategy programme. They specifically wanted to establish and manage Farmer Support Centres (FSCs) in Rwanda, Tanzania and Ethiopia. I joined Starbucks in November 2007 and promptly visited their first FSC in Costa Rica, to learn a little bit more about the company, as well as the work and the mission of the FSCs.

Starbucks funded the FSCs 100 per cent; they tasked them with helping farmers and cooperatives improve the quality of their coffees through improved husbandry and lower cost of inputs.

In 2011, Starbucks invited me to move to Switzerland to expand the FSC initiative. It led to the creation of additional FSCs in China, Sumatra, Guatemala, Colombia and Mexico. Each FSC had anywhere from two to ten people, agronomists or technicians, depending on the needs of the country. By the time I retired, there were 35 people on the team.

You also looked after the Starbucks CAFE Practices sustainability scheme.

CAFE Practices (CP) is implemented and managed by Starbucks, rather than being a third-party programme. That said, certified independent third parties conduct the auditing aspect of the supply chains and constituent farms. In that sense, it has similar to the Nespresso AAA programme.

Starbucks made considerable commitments to the CP programme, and in 2015/16 succeeded in purchasing more than 99 per cent of its coffee requirements from supply chains that met the CP requirements. It was a first for any major roaster, and as far as sustainability programmes go, it is one of the best, if not the best and most comprehensive programme in the industry.

What are the main environmental challenges facing coffee production?

Climate change. Areas that were suitable for coffee 20-30 years ago are now becoming marginal. Coffee production is tending to move higher up mountains, especially smallholder production in Central America, but also in Colombia, Peru and Ecuador. It leads to deforestation - in many cases deforestation of primary forests, which in turn leads to changes in weather patterns, landslides, long-term soil infertility, etc.

Water is another challenge. Washed coffee uses a lot of water. I don't believe that we should necessarily be retaining the washed coffee method; it can have quite a negative impact on the environment and water quality. Although washed coffees tend to be much better in the cup, I do believe there are alternative methods such as pulped naturals.

Many producers produce pulped naturals, where the berries are de-pulped and dried with the mucilage – the fruity part. The mucilage partially ferments on the beans and can add more dimensionality and a fruitier flavour to the cup. I like it, but many don't. They consider the taste as over-fermented - it can be a fine line. This process would require more work to prevent over-fermentation, but I believe the process could more than offset the costs of water and water treatment – if the water is treated at all. That said, a lot of effort has been made to improve the situation.

What about the ongoing shift from shade-grown to full-sun?

Shade trees have various functions. They absorb CO_2. They provide shade, reducing the surface of the earth exposed to the sun – just think about the temperature difference the next time you move out of the sun and under a tree. They also recycle nutrients into the soils and prevent soil erosion and water run-off. Shade trees also provide a habitat and corridors for birds and insects.

So, yes, I am a proponent of shade-grown coffee or at least some level of shade. In Costa Rica, we saw that retaining shade and a minimum amount of undeveloped land encouraged a balanced level of biodiversity, all of which also helped reduce the insects that were detrimental to coffee.

Colombia has a different problem because of its cloud cover and its lack of luminosity. They say they need full sun to maximise their production. Brazil has over the years developed full-sun varieties that would most likely also have reduced yields if grown in the shade. Additionally, the planting of shade trees in the vast Brazilian plantations would make it more difficult to harvest and might increase farming costs. There is no one answer or solution; it is more a question of arriving at an overall beneficial balance.

The CAFE Practices programme has shade as one of its components; points were awarded depending on the percentage level of shade canopy on the farm. Both Brazil and Colombia producers had issues with shade and possible loss of points, but that's an economic choice that has to be made.

What are the main issues on the social side?

I would say child labour, and that goes back to general economic issues and poverty levels in producing communities. Low coffee prices haven't helped. The kids are working on the farms due to the high poverty levels in coffee communities; adult workers are unable to achieve sufficient income levels to feed and educate their families. They have no choice but to send their children into the fields to make up the deficit.

In one African country, which I prefer not to name, there are over 5 million kids in the land between the ages of 5 and 15 who work and do not attend school. In most cases, they are members of families that are having a difficult time surviving. Sometimes, they are even heads of households because the parents have died, and as children themselves, they're trying to support younger siblings.

If you stop the kids from working, you are taking food away from low-income families. Many coffee-producing countries are confronted with this problem, and not just in Africa. If consumers want to enjoy a product, then a living-wage price needs to be paid that can help alleviate the issues. Consumers can't just mandate that there is no child labour without providing and supporting alternatives. The underlying problems need to be tackled.

That brings us to economic sustainability.

Before the International Coffee Agreement (ICA) lapsed in 1989, the minimum trading reference price under the quota system was $1.15 per pound. From a relative purchasing power perspective, that would be the equivalent today of around $2.45 per pound. The C-market price is currently $1.10 - $1.20 per pound.

Despite all the aid, and all the social and economic programmes that have been implemented over the years in producing countries by industry and governments, coffee farmers are half as well off today as they were 30 years ago.

Admittedly, they have found ways to cut their costs, such as higher use of relatively cheaper pesticides, herbicides, etc. to increase production – not healthy for humans, wildlife biodiversity or the environment.

The wealth in the coffee supply chain now sits with the trade houses, the roasters, and the coffee shops. It's not at the farmer level.

What is the solution?

The simple solution is for roasters to pay more for their coffee. They have to pay more than the cost of producing the coffee – and that should include a farmer's cost of living, schooling, clothing etc. Most farmers don't count their own or their family's time when calculating their cost of production.

Higher prices would, in many cases, motivate an educated younger generation to stay in coffee farming, treating it more as a business rather than a subsistence form of living. I saw an example of this on a Starbucks sponsored project in Colombia, where, with help and advice, a farmer could earn four to five times the minimum wage on a well-managed one-hectare farm. And he owned the land, his house and had his vegetable garden.

Many roasters and traders tend to resort to funding third-party implemented projects, such as food programs, water wells, hygiene, agronomy training, or donations of seedlings.

All of these efforts are beneficial to some degree or another, but if you're a farmer, yes, you'll take what you can, but you don't want aid. You have a certain amount of pride and self-respect, and you would much prefer to earn your living by growing and selling coffee or other products at a fair price, as opposed to getting a lousy price and then having to rely on some kind of handout later in the year. The other things are great, but they are not a replacement for cash in your pocket.

Many projects cost millions of dollars, but quite often it is the project implementers who keep the lion's share of the funds through consultancy fees, salaries, international and domestic travel expenses, vehicles, housing and general operating expenses. I say, let's use some of that money to pay higher prices directly to the farmers.

What about governments: do they have a role to play?

Governments in producing countries need to be actively involved in any project or programme. Without local government support, programmes lose traction and die off. They are not sustainable in the long term.

Higher incomes to farmers suggest higher foreign exchange earnings at the national level. The more foreign exchange earnings coffee generates, the higher the government's interest would likely be in actively supporting its production. In one African country, coffee was the primary export and foreign exchange earner in the 1960s and 70s. Today, although millions are involved in the local industry, it ranks close to the bottom, generating only around 4 per cent of foreign earnings.

Looking back over your career, do you have any regrets?

I have no regrets. Starbucks was one of the best companies for which I ever worked. I hope I used - and implemented - my experience for the good of farming communities and my former FSC colleagues. I enjoyed both learning from and coaching my team members, as well as working directly with farmers and supporting them wherever possible. It was always great to see a farmer or group of farmers become successful.

One such experience happened in Rwanda when a farmer and washing station owner walked into our office, asking for help; he was close to bankruptcy and about to close everything down. Even though he was not a Starbucks supplier, we worked with him and his group of 300 farmers for the next 2-3 years; he went on to win Rwanda's Presidential Prize for Quality.

We established our Farmer Support Centres for the long-term. They have become a valuable and reliable resource for the local coffee industry.

Starbucks is among the top five roasters, buying more than 6 million bags of coffee per year. For better or worse, few trade houses or farmers can afford to not have Starbucks as one of their buyers. It gives the company tremendous leverage to do good and to implement positive changes.

Last question: what coffee do you drink now?

Starbucks coffee, of course! I make it in a French press or a stove-top espresso. I enjoy their House Blend and their single-origin coffees from Guatemala, Ethiopia and Colombia.

Thank you, Chris, for your time and input!

Chapter 11:
Economic Sustainability

When we rise in the morning... at the table we drink coffee which is provided to us by a South American, or tea by a Chinese, or cocoa by a West African; before we leave for our jobs, we are already beholden to more than half the world.

- Martin Luther King, Jr.

The UN Food & Agriculture Organisation (FAO) defines a sustainable agricultural value chain as follows: 'Profitable throughout, has broad-based benefits for society, and does not permanently deplete natural resources.' A supply chain is not sustainable unless it is economically sustainable. At current world prices of around $1 per pound, the coffee supply chain is probably only economically sustainable in just three countries: Brazil, Vietnam and Colombia.

Economists argue that, over the long term, commodity prices revert to what they call an 'equilibrium price', the price at which the marginal supply of a commodity equals the marginal demand for that commodity. This equilibrium price is usually said to be the cost of producing an extra (or marginal) unit of that commodity in the most efficient producer; economists call this the 'marginal cost of production'. No matter how high or low commodity prices might go in the short term, they should revert over time to a price equal to the marginal cost of production in the most efficient producer(s).

The world's marginal producers of coffee are Brazil, Vietnam and (arguably) Colombia. As the most efficient, lowest-cost producers, these three countries set the world price for commodity coffee. If other producers want to sell coffee onto the world market, they have to accept the price set by the larger producers or differentiate their product in such a way that it is no longer a commodity.

Even the most prominent coffee growers in Brazil, Vietnam or Colombia are too small to make a difference to the price. Individual coffee farmers in those countries have to accept the world price. One farmer may reduce his production but, operating individually, he will have little impact on price. So, although three countries collectively set the world price for coffee, each producer within those three countries is a price taker, not a price setter.

Unlike services or many manufacturing industries, the supply chain for commodities is a zero-sum game. The market sets the price. If one participant in a commodity supply chain makes more money, someone else in the supply chain has to make less. The same applies to market share. As demand is growing only slowly, if one producer sells more, another must sell less.

Over the centuries, market power has moved downstream along the agricultural commodity supply chain. When world agrarian production increased due to higher yields and new areas opening up in the New World, farmers lost pricing power within the supply chain.

Farmers initially lost market power to the merchants who moved the food to market. As information became cheaper and quicker, the merchants, in turn, lost market power to food processors and retailers. The growth of the Internet and, in particular social media, has, in turn, weakened the power of the brands and the supermarkets, empowering consumers at the expense of farmers, merchants, processors and retailers. The market power now lies firmly with the consumer.

In a zero-sum supply chain, the only way to increase your profits without picking others' pockets is by reducing your costs. Unfortunately, what may work for an individual company (or farmer) may not work collectively. A farmer can take advantage of innovation and technology to increase yields. It will allow him to grow the same size crop from a smaller area, but his instinct will be to plant all his available land and produce more. A coffee cooperative might build a larger mill to capture economies of scale, but it will look to maximise throughput to reduce unit costs.

Over the past half-century, farmers have had to adapt to their loss in market power by becoming more efficient and lowering their costs. Farming is arguably the part of the agricultural commodity supply chain that has benefited the most from innovation and technology. Hybrid seeds, more efficient farm machinery, improved pesticides and insecticides, as well as drone and GPS technology, have all helped to reduce costs.

However, the best way to reduce unit costs is to increase throughput. As a result, there is a tendency for cost-cutting in a commodity supply chain to lead to increased supply. And increased supply usually results in lower prices. Acting alone, an individual player in the supply chain may be able to increase his margins by cutting costs through higher production but, if everyone does it, the resulting extra production could result in a fall in price that negates the saved expenses.

So, when looking at a supply chain, you have to ask: 'Who has the market power?' If you are talking about Apple Inc, it is the producer. If you talk about apples, it is the consumer. Where there is no product differentiation—and there is none in commodity coffee — the market power lies with the consumer and not the producer.

The only way for the upstream players in the coffee supply chain to restore margins is by recapturing the market power that they have lost over recent decades. Crop failures or other disruptions might restore margins in the short term. Still, in a zero-sum commodity supply chain, the only way to regain market power is through decommodification. That is happening with speciality coffee, but it is still only a tiny part of total world coffee consumption.

The Columbia Centre on Sustainable Development's report on the economic viability of coffee production found that under a business-as-usual scenario, more and more smallholders will get out of coffee production. Unless something changes, Brazil, Vietnam and Colombia will continue to increase production, while output in the rest of the world will contract, reducing the supply of coffee from different origins. Brazil and Vietnam have already produced an estimated 80 per cent of the extra coffee needed to meet increasing consumer demand over the past 30 years.

During this period of structural change, many small growers are hanging on as best they can. They will continue to do so as long as the coffee price covers their variable costs of production. Rather than plant new trees, they will endure reduced yields on their ageing trees. When the time comes that growers have to replace their trees, they may not bother. They may abandon their farms, sell them to better-financed neighbours or corporations, or grow a different crop. An example of the latter is Kenya, where pineapples and flowers for the European market have taken acreage from coffee.

If coffee is a smallholder's only cash crop, some growers may hang on for longer. In many parts of the world, cash generated from growing coffee has paid for schooling for the next generation. Unfortunately, coffee prices are so low now that farmers (particularly in Africa) can no longer afford to pay for education and have taken their children out of their classes. In many parts of the world, low coffee prices are embedding poverty, not just for this generation, but also for future generations.

Is there a solution?

As we saw earlier, Jeffrey Sachs at the Columbia Centre for Sustainable Investment suggested that a Global Coffee Fund (GCF) – with an annual budget of $10 billion - be set to support smallholder growers. He indicated that $2.5 billion per year could come from a levy of around 34 cents per kg of coffee. In contrast, the rest would come from private donors, producing-country governments, and competitive private sector investments in a public-private partnership. The idea would be for funds to be allocated to coffee-producing countries, taking into consideration their country-specific needs, while prioritising development goals in the poorest countries and among the poorest producers.

I asked a leading coffee producer what he thought of this proposal. He said that it would mean efficient producers (say in Brazil) financing less efficient producers, keeping them in business and helping them to maintain or expand their market share.

He added that, although all producers would have to pay the levy, it wasn't clear that they could pass on the extra costs to consumers. He argued that the only way to make sure that consumers in rich countries, rather than producers in developing countries, paid the levy would be if a global tax were imposed on coffee. As that was unlikely, he told me the scheme was 'dead in the water'. He suggested that smaller, less ambitious projects were more likely to be successful.

Indeed, they already are.

The Fairtrade programme already pays a 30 cents per pound premium, roughly the same amount as suggested under the GCF. As we will see later, Rainforest Alliance is also now including an economic element to their certification scheme.

Other schemes are currently in the pipeline that will allow consumers to tip a farmer directly by scanning a QR code on a coffee pack or cup and then transferring money directly to the farmer's (or cooperative's) bank account. After all, it is the consumer now that has the power in the supply chain, so the consumer should have the ultimate responsibility for the wellbeing of the farmer that supplies him his coffee.

These are well-meaning initiatives that are better than nothing, but tipping is in itself sometimes unfair. A handsome young waiter will get loads of tips, but the cook in the kitchen will get none. That is why many restaurants in Europe charge a fixed service fee that is (in theory at least) distributed among all the staff. Adding a service fee to all coffee sold would bring us back to the levy on consumption that Jeffrey Sachs suggested.

Jason Clay, the head of the World Wildlife Fund's work on agricultural markets, has told me that without decommodification, inefficient and uneconomic smallholders will have no choice but to leave the sector.

Jason himself grew up on a subsistence farm in the US, a farm that was too small to be economically viable. Jason's father was killed in a tractor accident when he was 15, and he took over managing the farm with his mother. He quickly realised that it was an impossible task; he sold the farm, finished high school and studied at Harvard.

He told me: 'What no one wants to talk about is that many poor farmers work plots that are simply too small or too marginal to be viable. I know, because I was one once. This is a global issue. Smallholders need to get better or to get out; it's not a good life for them, and it's certainly not a future for their children.

'We have a lot of well-meaning people who've never set foot on a farm but have strong opinions about maintaining small farmers, and by extension, whether they realise it or not, poverty. We have certification programmes that, in effect, certify poverty. That can't be justified. The poorest performing producers either need to improve or get out.'

Jason was talking about palm oil and bulk grains, not coffee. Palm oil is much the same wherever it is grown, but this is not true for coffee. In coffee, each origin, altitude or even farm has its terroir and its characteristics. Corn is the same, whether it is grown in the US or Brazil.

If coffee consumers want to maintain choice along with their favourite coffees, they will have to pay the price that provides a living wage for growers. It is happening to a small extent with speciality coffees, but it is not enough.

There is, however, hope.

Companies now serve the interests of all stakeholders — not just investors, but also customers, employees, partners, suppliers, and society at large. Stakeholder capitalism means strengthening the weaker members of the supply chain, which, in the case of the coffee supply chain, means the growers. Stakeholders are already doing this by providing many growers with training and advice.

But what about coffee growers who cannot afford to send their children to school? The obvious solution is to increase the price that we pay them for their coffee. Although this may work in the short term, it is likely to encourage increased supply in the longer term. It applies to both speciality and commodity coffee. Speciality coffee is subject to the same laws of supply and demand as commodity coffee.

There is a saying: 'If you are a hammer, everything looks like a nail.' If you are in the coffee business, it is tempting to think that the coffee business can solve the world's problems. Jeffry Sachs concluded in his landmark report that you will usually fail if you try to solve social problems by increasing the price of a commodity; sometimes, you will make things worse.

Markets are blunt instruments of social policy; attempting to solve social issues through market intervention often backfire. If coffee farmers can no longer pay school fees, the solution is to make the school free, not to increase the price of coffee. And, as Jason Clay argued, the only way for smallholder farmers to break out of their cycle of poverty is for their children to go to school.

If governments and civil society want to improve rural incomes, they have more efficient tools in their policy toolbox than the price of coffee. One such tool is to provide direct payments to low-income families. The Lula government did just that with Bolsa Família, a programme that makes direct payments to families whose children attend school and are vaccinated against disease. Accompanied by investment in education, these payments can do more to alleviate poverty than temporarily high coffee prices.

A Conversation with Daniel Watson

Daniel Weston is Nestlé's General Counsel for Sub-Saharan Africa, Oceania and Asia. Up until end May 2020, he was Global Head of Creating Shared Value (CSV) at Nespresso with responsibility for the company's sustainability strategy and programmes.

Good morning Daniel. Could you tell me how you ended up at Nespresso?

I joined Nespresso in 2011 from Nestlé's Health Science business. My initial role was General Counsel, but that grew over time. In 2012, I took over responsibility for Corporate Communication and Public Affairs and, in 2015, I took on responsibility for CSV - sustainability along the entire Nespresso supply chain.

What does CSV - Creating Shared Value - mean?

Michael Porter, from the Harvard Business School, was the first to use the phrase. It is different from CSR – Corporate Social Responsibility - where a business does some good for society through philanthropy or charity. CSV is the belief that a company can only be successful in the long term by creating value both for shareholders and communities. Sustainability is deeply rooted in Nespresso's DNA and is a real example of CSV in action.

Nespresso has a distinct coffee sustainability programme from the Nestlé. Is it better?

Nespresso's programme is distinct from other sustainability programmes as it brings a strong focus on quality in addition to productivity and environmental/social sustainability. The Nespresso

AAA Sustainable Quality™ Program is a tailor-made approach to sourcing high-quality, sustainable coffee, co-created with the Rainforest Alliance in 2003.

Through the AAA Program, Nespresso works directly with over 110,000 coffee farmers around the world. Over 400 agronomists in the field support and train farmers on best farming practices to ensure quality and sustainability. Nespresso buys from the same farmers in the AAA Program year after year; this guarantees the aromatic profile and the quality of our coffees for our customers.

The terroir of coffee and the coffee varietal are critical in determining its taste and quality. Nespresso wants the Ispirazione Firenze Arpeggio coffee, for example, to have a consistent taste, so we need to buy from the same farmers on the same terroir year after year. It brings stability to the farmers.

The name of the AAA Program derived from the 'AA' standard, a hallmark of coffee quality found in Kenya and other high-quality coffee origins. Nespresso added the third 'A' to represent environmental, social and economic standards. Today, each 'A' of the AAA Program stands for the three foundations of the Nespresso approach: quality, sustainability and productivity.

The taste profile of the coffee and its quality are the primary entry criteria for the AAA Sustainable Quality™ Program. To be part of the AAA Program, a farmer must have an interest in continuous improvement in quality, the environment and social protection. Once farmers are in the AAA Program, an assigned agronomist works with them to increase their yield of high-quality, sustainable coffee; they are assessed against a set of criteria and given free training and technical assistance. They are under no obligation to sell their coffee to Nespresso, but they earn a premium for the higher quality coffee they sell to us.

Over time, farms in the Program can qualify for certification with certification bodies such as the Rainforest Alliance. If the farmer chooses to do that, then we pay them an additional premium for their certified coffee on top of the AAA premium.

Today, more than 50 per cent of the coffee Nespresso buys is Rainforest Alliance or Fairtrade certified. We pay the certification premium to farmers regardless of whether the certification label features on the pack.

Certification agencies such as Rainforest Alliance do not have any quality criteria. Do farmers sometimes concentrate too much now on certification and too little on quality?

Every farm will produce different levels of quality. A certified farm is no exception. We created our AAA Program because we wanted to add the element of quality to sustainability. Our AAA premiums are paid based on quality and sustainability.

I am confident that Nespresso is doing the right things for the right reasons and is driving positive change on a large scale. Nespresso does not buy all the coffee produced on AAA farms, as we will only accept the coffee that meets our quality criteria. It means that our investment and the sustainable farming practices implemented as part of the AAA Program benefits the broader coffee industry.

Nespresso seems to have a considerable emphasis on quality at the farm level and on building relationships with farmers.

When you buy a Nespresso capsule, you are not only purchasing the ground coffee in that capsule, but you're also purchasing the extensive and long-term work that Nespresso is doing together with the coffee farmers. Through the AAA Sustainable Quality™ Program, Nespresso works with coffee farmers to help them grow high-quality coffee and increase the productivity of their farm while revealing the unique characteristics of the coffee's terroir. Quality starts at the origin, through the growing practices. You cannot add it later. It is why this work is so crucial in producing countries.

You exclude farms that employ forced or child labour. Wouldn't it be better to engage with them rather than ban them?

We exclude from the AAA Program any farm that has any evidence of either child or forced labour. The premise behind your question is that exclusion does not solve the problem, and we agree. It's not a good thing to exclude permanently, but it's essential to give a serious message to the farm that this issue is critical, and unless it is fixed, we will not work with them.

Nespresso often pays the highest price for coffee in a region. For Nespresso to exclude a farm from our Program usually means a considerable loss of income for them. So, we feel a strong responsibility to work with the farmers to remediate. Still, if they're outside the Program, it's an incentive for them to fix the problem and fix it fast. Some farms may decide that they don't want to remediate; in which case we don't work with them again.

The Program's inclusion criteria are based on the willingness of the farmer to improve. If there is a problem, and the farmer agrees that they want to resolve it, we will agree with them a roadmap to go from where they are today to where they want to go, and we support them on that journey. As an example, this could involve making sure that farmers have school certificates for any children who help on the farm at the weekends or during the holidays.

It is a stick and a carrot. Of the limited number of cases that we have identified over the past four years, every single issue (except one) has been remediated, and the farm brought back into the AAA Program.

How many origins does Nespresso work with?

Today, we work continuously with 14 origins. We have start-up operations in additional countries such as Zimbabwe, where we work with 400 farmers and two coffee estates as part of our Reviving Origins programme that aims to restore coffee production in regions where it is under threat. Coffee almost disappeared from Zimbabwe due to economic and political instability. Nespresso started to work there to bring it back in 2018. The amount of coffee is limited, but once the coffee capsules reach the market, we sell them out in a matter of weeks! And every year, we will bring it back as a seasonal coffee.

You mentioned Zimbabwe. What about South Sudan?

Along with Ethiopia, South Sudan is the cradle of coffee. Coffee grows wild there. In 2011, George Clooney suggested we visit the country and take a look. We did, and we were amazed by the quality of the coffee from varietals that we hadn't tasted before.

Coffee production had declined dramatically during the civil war, and the country was importing coffee from Uganda. We helped set up three cooperatives in the region, imported some small-scale processing equipment, helped upgrade their processing, and introduced the washed method. We were there for three seasons, buying coffee and establishing relationships with the farmers.

We sold the first edition exclusively in France and the second edition in ten countries. Both times, it was sold out in less than a week. We were excited about the potential of the coffee, and you could see the transformational effect that it was having.

But then civil war broke out, and many of the farmers fled across the border to DRC and Uganda. It just wasn't safe for our agronomists or our buyers. We had to stop.

Recently, we've gone back into the town of Yei with our partner *TechnoServe* to start recreating some of the nurseries so that we're able to resupply the farmers when they come back. Some of the farmers have returned and are starting to produce again. As soon as it is safe, we will be operational again.

We know we'll be back. We'll continue to invest there because consumers want those coffees, and the local community wants to grow those coffees. It's a virtuous circle.

Nespresso, because of its resources, can go to origins where there were some extraordinary coffees, but which have started to disappear whether for economic, political or environmental reasons. We put this into practice through our Reviving Origins programme, applying the AAA Sustainable Quality™ program.

We're interested in finding unique coffees and then helping to recreate a local coffee economy. It brings enormous benefits to the local economy while at the same time providing Nespresso consumers with great coffees. It also delivers a sense of purpose to the company. The whole company is rightly proud of the AAA Program.

Some coffee companies build roads, schools or clinics. Does Nespresso do that, or do you concentrate on coffee agronomy?

We focus on the way the coffee is grown, harvested, and processed.

Perhaps it's easiest to share an example. In Jardin, Colombia, we had rejection rates of around 50 per cent because the farmers would process their coffee on the farm and then sell parchment coffee to the cooperative. They were great farmers, but during the processing step, they were damaging the coffee and reducing its intrinsic value. We worked with local community leaders to create a small community wet mill, and we now have a rejection rate of zero. They also sell their coffee at a higher price, and this has increased farmers' revenues.

On rare occasions, we do provide funding to ensure that roads reach the communities that need them. Still, we are much more interested in investing time in improving the skills of the local farmers and investing financially in processing infrastructure.

Let's talk about waste -- the elephant in the room. I know that you argue that capsules are more sustainable than other brewing methods such as filtered coffee or French press. Can you explain why?

When you look at the life cycle of a cup of coffee, roughly 45 per cent of a cup of coffee's GHG emissions occur in the home.

Portion coffee helps to reduce those emissions. It uses precisely the right amount of coffee for one cup, so there is no overdosing, something that often happens with other systems. It also heats precisely the right amount of water for each cup. With other brewing methods, it is quite common for people to heat too much water, and that energy is then wasted.

It varies depending on where you are. A cup of coffee in France with nuclear energy has a lower GHG emission than a cup brewed in Germany, where the energy mix is mainly carbon-based.

Portioned coffee does require individual packaging, so at the end of the process, you are left with the packaging material. We recognise that. We have created a recycling infrastructure that is readily accessible to our consumers. We currently have more than 100,000 points to collect used capsules globally, enabling 91 per cent of our consumers to recycle.

I am surprised that 45 per cent of the GHG emission is at the consumer end of the supply chain.

Yes, it's perhaps counterintuitive. You have the use of the machine and the water that it uses, but you also have the materials used to produce the machine. You have to divide that up by the number of coffees that the machine will make. You also have to include the materials that were used to make the cup, as well as the hot water for washing the cup afterwards.

At 2 per cent, distribution and transport account for a relatively small part of a coffee capsule's GHG footprint. 'End of life' – disposing and recycling the capsule after use – accounts for only 5 per cent. Coffee farming accounts for 19 per cent; the production of the packaging accounts for 18 per cent; and roasting and grinding accounts for 3 per cent.

How many of your capsules get recycled?

As of the end of 2019, slightly more than 30 per cent of our capsules were recycled. It's not easy to drive significant increases. It requires consistent investment in infrastructure and consumer communication, but I am glad to say that it is increasing year on year. It's also quite a complicated figure to calculate - not all capsules come back through our hands; some go through public recycling systems in countries where this is possible, such as Germany.

Today, our recycling programme is available in 53 countries, and our ambition is to have our aluminium capsules included in established collective recycling schemes. We are working with governments and local authorities to achieve this.

When you recycle capsules, the highest cost is the reverse logistics. You move 1 gm of aluminium, 6 gm of coffee and maybe 3 gm of water per capsule. At the end of the process, out of that 10 gm of material, you can sell 1 gm of value – the aluminium content. As a result, recycling is a cost for us: it is not financially profitable. But of course, recycling systems must recapture as much aluminium as possible to create a circular system.

How does Nespresso recycle the capsules?

In the case of Switzerland, the postman picks up your used capsules from your letterbox. They get delivered to our recycling centre in Moudon, where they are dried and stripped down. The coffee grounds and the aluminium are separated, and both go on to a second life.

The coffee grounds are mixed with slurry from nearby farms to power biogas reactors. Coffee grounds have a high calorific content, while the slurry is less concentrated. Once the gas has been produced, the residual compost is used as fertiliser.

The aluminium is either sold back into the upstream aluminium value chain or melted down to be used to make new capsules or iconic objects. We do this to try and connect consumers with recycling. For example, we collaborated with Victorinox, the Swiss Army knife maker; they made penknives with a casing from recycled Nespresso capsules. We also have a collaboration with Caran d'Ache for a recycled capsule-based body for their iconic 849 ballpoint pen.

In cities like Paris or Vienna, we've worked with municipalities to make sure that their recycling systems can pick up small metal items like our capsules. The result of this collaboration is that crushed soft-drink cans, yoghurt lids and bottle tops are now being appropriately recycled as well. As a result, recycling systems in these cities work better than before – and our investments create a broader positive impact beyond the limited scope of our own business.

Which capsules are better: aluminium or plastic?

There are pros and cons to every packaging option, but I prefer aluminium as it can be recovered and reused. Recycled aluminium saves something like 95 per cent of the embedded energy content of virgin aluminium. So, there's an enormous gain for the environment in reusing aluminium, and it has a high resale value.

There is not a substantial market for recycled plastics. It's starting to develop, and Nestlé, along with several other players, is putting a lot of effort into it. Still, today the economics aren't as attractive as for aluminium, especially for capsules.

A home-compostable capsule would be a good system, but currently, most products on the market must be composted industrially. And there are very few industrial compostable facilities operating today, which suggests that a recyclable product is a better choice.

Quality is also a key factor. Aluminium protects the coffee from oxygen, light and humidity better than other materials. It helps maintain the aromas that developed during the roasting.

You are currently Chairman of ASI – the Aluminium Sustainability Initiative.

Back in 2009, we had traceability in our supply chain for coffee, but not for aluminium. We set out with several other interested parties from civil society and business to see how we could address it. One decade later, we have the ASI standards. We now have traceability; we can follow aluminium from the mine through to end-use. We can now trace its environmental footprint. Equally importantly, we can ensure that it has been produced in a way which protects human rights and respects indigenous people.

I am incredibly proud of ASI. Aluminium is the only industrial metal that has a functioning responsibility standard. Several standards are being developed, but the ASI standards are live. They were approved at the end of 2017.

Nespresso did not drive this on its own. Still, I like to think we were one of the grains of sand that fell into the oyster of the aluminium industry, which ultimately led to the pearl that is ASI – something beautiful and valuable. We brought a simple argument to the table: if responsibility and traceability were possible for coffee, why couldn't the same be done in other supply chains?!

Are you using recycled aluminium now in your capsules?

Yes. Recycled aluminium uses less energy than primary aluminium, so we focus a lot on recycled content as a way of ensuring that we're reducing the footprint of our capsules.

We also work to build the circularity story where we try to 'nudge' the consumer to do their part and send the used capsules back for recycling. Aluminium used for packaging has a higher 'velocity' than the aluminium used in the construction or automotive industry. We need to get that aluminium back from consumers after use and return it to the upstream value chain.

We have recently started producing capsules with 80 per cent recycled aluminium content. To achieve this, we have moved to a different grade of aluminium, where recycled content is more widely available. We launched the first capsules made with this aluminium in May 2020. We will cover our full range in the coming months.

Is there anything else you'd like to add?

Before I started working for Nespresso, even though I was an avid consumer, I had a slight tinge of guilt. I was concerned about the environmental and social sustainability of our coffee capsules. I worked for the company for nine years, and I had the privilege to see the real impact of the company's investments in terms of environmental and social sustainability. I also saw first-hand the tangible benefits that the company brings to farmers and their communities by increasing quality, increasing yields of sustainable coffee and ultimately increasing revenues.

I am a middle-aged millennial if such a thing is possible! It is not enough for me to work for money alone; I need a sense of purpose and to work for an organisation that makes a positive impact. I certainly achieved that at Nespresso, and I hope to build on that in my new role with Nestlé.

Thank you, Daniel, for your time and comments.

Chapter 12:
Social sustainability

I had some dreams; they were clouds in my coffee.

- Carly Simon

In 2016, the Danish independent investigative journalism and research centre DanWatch published a report on the Brazil coffee sector, Bitter Coffee. Working alongside government officials, the investigators found that on plantations where coffee was picked by hand the majority of the pickers were seasonal workers, and about half worked without contracts. In the primary coffee-growing state of Minas Gerais, the investigators found that 40 per cent of agricultural workers were paid less than the minimum wage.

Migrant workers generally had more inadequate working conditions than seasonal workers from the local area, and they often worked long hours seven days a week. According to Brazilian law, agricultural workers may not work more than 44 hours per week, and never more than 10 hours per day. The investigators found some working 14 hours a day.

The investigators also found that some plantations only harvested on the weekends. Workers either came from outside of the coffee sector or were working legally on another farm and looking to earn a little extra money. Most weekend workers had neither a contract nor protective clothing.

Every year, the Brazilian authorities find migrant workers on coffee plantations living and working under what the Brazilian criminal code calls 'conditions analogous to slavery'. These can include having to sleep on coffee sacks on the floor or being trapped in a debt spiral that makes it impossible for them to leave the plantations.

Conditions analogous to slavery are not only found on Brazilian coffee plantations. Every year, inspectors from the Brazilian Ministry of Labour and Employment liberate workers from farms growing other crops, as well as from different kinds of workplaces, for example, the textile industry. Slavery-like conditions are especially widespread in Brazil's sugar, construction, livestock and charcoal industries.

The investigators also found instances of child labour. Children are typically brought to the plantations by their parents working in the coffee harvest. Some parents pay for someone to look after their children, but children sometimes work alongside their parents. Some of the children go to school while they work the harvest; others don't. It is illegal in Brazil for children under 16 years old to work on a coffee plantation, although teenagers between 16 and 18 years old may do so as long as it does not interfere with their schooling.

According to the Brazilian Institute of Geography and Statistics (IBGE), 116,000 children aged 5-17 years old worked in agriculture in 2013 in Minas Gerais, Brazil's largest coffee-producing state. Of these, 60,000 were under 14 years old.

In 2019, the Thomson Reuters Foundation uncovered extensive slave labour in the Minas Gerais' coffee sector. Their report attracted the attention of US Customs and Border Protection (CBP), which has the power to stop any goods they suspect were made by forced labour from entering the country.

The Brazilian government maintains a 'dirty list' of employers that have engaged in slavery. It is seen as one of Brazil's sharpest anti-slavery tools as blacklisted firms cannot get credit from state banks or receive other public money. As of August 2019, 18 of the 190 companies on the dirty list were coffee producers - 13 of them based in Minas Gerais. Only the cattle industry had more companies on the list.

Brazil's current anti-slavery laws are strict: coffee plantations found to have used slave labour risk fines of over R$1 million. However, the Reuters Foundation found that only 121 coffee farms had been investigated in Minas Gerais since April 2014. The state has at least 119,000 coffee plantations and only 245 inspectors. In 2017, Brazil's previous government cut funding for labour inspections by about half while the country's current President has publicly stated that child labour is not harmful. He has also complained that the legal definition of slave labour under Brazilian law is too broad.

Conditions on certified farms are better than on uncertified farms. Even so, Starbucks cut ties in 2019 with a Rainforest Alliance-certified farm that had been added to the country's dirty list after 25 workers were found in slavery-like conditions.

Also, in 2019, the UK Channel 4 Dispatches programme found evidence of child labour on Guatemala's coffee farms. Posing as researchers, the Dispatches' team visited farms that supplied Starbucks or Nespresso. They found children as young as 11 or 12 years old working long hours in harsh conditions for as little as £5 per day.

Most of the children were working to help feed their families. The programme rightly highlighted what it called 'the piteously small amount of money' that coffee farmers receive for their beans. The programme concluded that families often have no choice but to send their children out to work at a young age.

Although it is no excuse, this situation is not new. In the book Uncommon Grounds, Mark Pendergast writes: 'Children begin helping with the harvest when they are seven or eight. Though many Campesinos keep their children out of school at other times for other reasons, it's no coincidence that school vacation in Guatemala coincides with the coffee harvest.'

It is not clear whether the Dispatches team filmed the children during school vacation, or whether the children were skipping school to work. Still, both Starbucks and Nespresso have made clear that child labour is unacceptable at any time in their supply chain.

In a statement, Nespresso's chief executive said that the company had launched an investigation to find out which farms featured in the TV programme and whether they supply Nespresso. 'We will not resume purchases of coffee from farms in this area until the investigation is closed,' he added.

I grew up on a smallholder farm where I regularly helped out after school and during school vacations. I learned how to drive a tractor at eight and how to plough a field at ten. In the developed world it is still generally viewed as 'a good thing' when children help out their parents on a farm. In the developing world, it is considered to be an absolute 'no-no', even though the family may desperately need their children's help.

Farmers in the developed world have their children help out on their farms secure in the knowledge that they are also well educated. Farming parents in the developing world do not have that luxury.

Some people argue that child labour is a necessary evil if poor farming families are to survive in the coffee sector. I would say that child labour is an unacceptable evil. It is only by educating their children that low-income families will be able to pull themselves out of poverty and enable their children to have better lives than their parents.

A conversation with Jorge Cárdenas Gutiérrez

Jorge Cárdenas Gutiérrez has been the leading figure in the Colombian coffee industry for over half a century. Born in 1930 in Medellín, he studied Law and Political Science in his hometown; then he did a master's degree in Administration at the University of Syracuse. He has held various public positions in his country, but his lifelong passion has been the promotion of the Colombian coffee sector, both domestically and internationally.

For many years he was head of the Colombian Federation of Coffee Growers where he fought to improve coffee cultivation in Colombia, to improve the quality of life of the country's coffee growers and the quality of coffee for consumers.

Good morning, Jorge. How important is coffee to Colombia?

Coffee has been a leading product in the Colombian economy for 120 years. For many years it was 10 per cent of the gross domestic product, 30 per cent of agricultural output and 40 per cent of the external income.

Revenues from coffee exports have enabled Colombia to develop its industry, railways, ports and a good part of the national infrastructure.

Today coffee's economic importance to Colombia is lower. However, it is still the country's most important source of rural employment: 500,000 families in 2.5 million hectares produce a coffee harvest worth US $ 2.5 billion, which is 3 per cent of Colombia's GDP. Its social impact is fundamental.

What role has the National Federation played in maintaining the competitiveness of the sector?

The Government of Colombia has worked since 1927 in full agreement with the National Federation of Coffee Growers to develop public policies that build progress in the coffee-growing areas: road services, potable water, electricity, health and education.

The Federation administers the National Coffee Fund, which has existed since 1940. The Fund is for the development of these public policies and the promotion and modernisation of coffee cultivation. It also promotes coffee consumption internationally. The National Coffee Fund is a fundamental instrument of all coffee policy.

The Federation has 350,000 affiliated producers; since 1930, all producers have to pay a parafiscal contribution to the Federation by law.

To what extent has coffee had to compete with cocaine in Colombia?

The Federation has carried out extensive campaigns to combat illegal crops, and there are no significant coca crops in the coffee-growing areas. The farms are small in the coffee zone. Coca crops are in areas of little agriculture and very far from population centres.

What are the main challenges that the coffee sector faces in Colombia?

The main problem is the size of the farms: most plots are of 1 to 3 hectares. The production costs in these small farms are high compared to those obtained in larger areas.

What is the Federation doing to improve things?

The Federation of Coffee Growers has a Coffee Research Centre (Cenicafé) that carries out permanent research on innovation. It has helped introduce coffee varietals that are resistant to pests and are higher yielding. It has helped Colombia to maintain production of between 12 and 14 million bags of 60 kg for the past several years.

What lies behind the success of Colombian coffee?

Colombian coffee is competitive due to its quality; this is, in turn, the result of the care with which it is grown and processed.

Since the creation of Juan Valdez in 1960, the Federation of Coffee Growers has a unique niche in the world market. Juan Valdez gave a name to a generic product.

How does Colombia maintain a sustainable living for its coffee growers?

From 1940 to 2000, Colombia had an internal price for coffee that did not change more than three times a year. Export earnings and producer contributions to the National Coffee Fund made this sustainable and stable price possible. Besides, the various international coffee agreements provided price stability to global prices.

Since 2000, the domestic price reflects the international price of coffee. Only in times of low global prices have the Government and the Federation given growers a premium as part of the internal price of coffee.

The Colombian government has recently introduced a new Stabilisation Fund which seeks price stability as in previous years; for the time being, it does not yet have the necessary resources.

What about the international Fund proposed by Jeffrey Sachs?

Jeffrey Sachs' proposed Fund is attractive, but in my opinion, there is no support for it from consumers.

Are you optimistic about coffee in Colombia?

The National Federation of Coffee Growers continues in its task of innovating in the cultivation and harvesting, and the producers accompany these efforts.

The Federation celebrates 93 years of its founding and continues to be a leading rural service organisation. It has the support of the Government and the backing of producers.

Roasters the world over continue to view Colombia as a highly reliable supplier.

Today's consumers are increasingly moving towards high-quality coffees, which is very favourable for Colombia.

The future of Colombian coffee is bright.

Thank you, Jorge, for your time and comments!

A Conversation with Ricardo Arenas

Founded in 1895 by the Arenas family, Finca La Perla is an isolated farm located in the Western Highlands of Guatemala. Ricardo Arenas, who runs the business with his nephew, divides his time between La Perla and Guatemala City where he was until recently President of Anacafé, the Guatemalan Coffee Association, as well as President of the Rural Coffee Foundation.

In 2020, the President of Guatemala appointed Ricardo as the Ambassador of Guatemala for all issues related to coffee. The President also asked him to be the Presidential Commissioner for the prevention and eradication of the child labour in the country's coffee sector.

Good morning, Ricardo. How important is coffee to Guatemala?

It is essential. Coffee is the only agricultural activity that is present in all of Guatemala's 22 departments. It is the biggest employer in the country.

There are about 125,000 coffee producing families in Guatemala, all living in rural areas. With between five to nine people in each family, this adds up to nearly one million people who depend directly on coffee. Of those 125,000 families, 121,000 are small producers.

Coffee used to be the country's number one export in terms of dollar revenues, but sugar has recently taken that number one slot. And now, I have to say, the primary source of dollars for the country is remittances from our more than two million emigrants, working mainly – and legally - in the US.

Coffee is important in many producing countries in Latin America and Africa, but for Guatemala, it is essential. I would go as far as to say that the country's social and political stability depends on coffee.

Are the 125,000 coffee-growing families able to live with these low coffee prices, or are they suffering?

They are suffering.

We have had a perfect storm these last ten years. We won a battle against coffee rust disease in Guatemala in the 1980s, but new varieties of rust have appeared in the past ten years. It is a challenge.

We used to be the biggest producer in the region of Mexico, Central America and the Caribbean, but we have now fallen to second place behind Honduras. Honduras' President is a coffee grower, as are many members of his government, as well as many regional mayors. They have been supporting the development of the coffee sector in Honduras. Here in Guatemala, we do not have any form of financial support for the industry from the government.

The currencies of both Brazil and Colombia are low; this helps their agricultural exports. It means that even with the world price so low, producers there are covering their costs. They are happy with world prices at these levels. Guatemala's strong currency is a big problem for us.

We have the highest minimum wage of all the countries in Latin America except for Costa Rica and Panama. Even so, we have difficulty in getting labour. Coffee is a labour-intensive crop, but Guatemala has lost a lot of workers through emigration to the US, and also because the labour demand of Honduras to pick their coffee crop.

The low international price is the main problem. Many of our coffees are speciality coffees that trade at a premium to the world price, but I would say that 95 per cent of our growers are suffering. Coffee prices in dollar terms are the same today as they were in 1983, but a dollar then is worth only 63 cents today.

Our production costs are higher than the current world coffee price and higher than in other coffee-producing countries around the world. Our costs are between $2.00 and $2.50 because of our minimum wage, strong currency, financial fees and higher taxes. Growers in Central America produce coffee for between $1.75 and $2.00 per pound.

Coffee production in Guatemala is not economically sustainable. This is for sure. If the international market -- buyers, roasters -- want our farmers to keep producing coffee, then they will have to pay us a price that makes it economically sustainable.

If prices are below the cost of production, why are farmers still growing coffee?

In Guatemala, we grow our high quality and speciality coffees at high altitudes where the cold weather and the broken topography in the mountains mean that, apart from coffee, you can only cultivate corn and beans.

As I mentioned, small producers in our country represent 121,000 of the 125,000 coffee producers' families. They are sustainable only because they operate in the informal economy.

Because of the low prices, they are unable to work the plantation as they should. They are probably organic by default as they cannot afford pesticides, herbicides or fertilisers. They are not spending any money to battle the rust. And they don't pay the minimum wage.

These are family farms where everyone in the family helps; they don't pay themselves or their families the minimum wages.

Is child labour a problem in Guatemala?

You must remember that school vacations in Latin America were historically timed so that the children could help out with the coffee harvest. School finishes in October in time for the harvest. It creates a problem now because the kids are at home during the harvest; the parents don't want to leave them at home while they go to the farms to pick coffee. So, they take them with them. It is not slavery nor forced labour. It is a family and a cultural matter.

People are moving to the US because we don't have enough job opportunities here, and they want a better life for their families. It disintegrates families. If the father and the elder brothers leave, the mother stays with the little ones. She has to continue working, so she takes the young ones with her to the coffee plantation.

The Rural Coffee Foundation of Guatemala has created a programme called 'Coffee Kindergarten' where parents can leave their young children when they go to work.

Earlier this year, the UK's Channel 4 Dispatches programme found children as young as 11 or 12 working long hours in a couple of Guatemala's coffee farms. As a result of that programme our President has set up a commission to look at this issue; he has asked me to head it. We will be reporting back to the President soon. We still have child labour, and we have to be honest and recognise it, but poverty is the cause.

The first step that I took when I became President of the commission was to get a law passed in Congress that stated that the official position of the country was zero tolerance to child labour. It also sets out a directive for its prevention and eradication.

Under our old laws, people could work from the age of fourteen. The International Labour Organisation sets the working-age at 15 years old. This new law increases the working-age so that it is in line with the ILO at 15 years. It also includes measures that bar young people from working in specific industries.

Even though Guatemala is doing much better than the other coffee producer countries in the regions of Central and South America, our goal is to be at zero per cent child labour. Hopefully, one day soon!

Is poverty prevalent in coffee-growing areas?

We have poverty in the rural areas of Guatemala. Many farmers can't afford to pay outside workers to pick their coffee, so their children do it instead. Poverty drives child labour, and that goes back to the price that buyers are willing to pay for their coffee. If coffee prices were higher, we would have less rural poverty.

Child labour is an economic issue as much as a social issue. I am not against the roasters and the coffee shops from making money, but they must allow producers to make enough money to support their families without their children having to work on their farms.

Is there a domestic market for coffee in Guatemala?

Twenty years ago, the coffee that you could taste here in Guatemala was lousy. We exported the best. We now have much better quality, and our coffee shops and restaurants currently serve lovely coffee. We are working to increase domestic consumption

Why do you call coffee from your plantation 'Coffee of Peace'?

Guatemala had 36 years of internal war against the communist guerrillas. It started in the late 1960s and ended in 1995. It was 36 years of horrible times for the whole country.

Our estate is situated in one of the worst areas of this guerrilla movement. The guerrillas killed my father on 7th June 1975. They killed many of our workers, stole our payrolls and burned our buildings.

When the war ended, we thought we should honour all our workers, and all the people of Guatemala, by celebrating the peace, so we called our coffee Café de la Paix.

You are located in the western North-Western Highlands far from the nearest towns and ports. How do you get your coffee to the markets?

My parents bought La Perla a hundred years ago. My father's business was cattle, but there was a deep economic depression, and the banks had taken possession of many of the country's coffee plantations. My father was thinking of buying a coffee plantation located a short drive outside Guatemala City, in Antigua. Still, he heard from a friend that La Perla was also for sale.

That same day, he took my older brothers to visit that far away land, lost in the high mountains of the State of El Quiche, in the IXIL Region. He identified himself immediately with La Perla, which the Indian people call 'Xamac'; it means 'Sleepy Women' in their Maya-Quiche language. Xamac and La Perla are the same coffee plantation, and Xamac is a 'pearl'!

My mother's family comes from Spain, and she studied in Madrid for many years. She wasn't used to rural life, but she supported my father and lived on the estate, without leaving it for seven years. My younger brother was born there. She loved the people, their customs and culture, the majestic mountains, the beautiful rivers, and the incredible peace that you feel there. It is a lovely place. I can see why my father fell in love with it. But it is also excellent for coffee growing.

At that time, it took four days to reach the plantation from the city: one day's drive and three days by mule. Transport is better now. You can get to La Perla in 45 minutes by small plane and 8 hours on mostly asphalted roads. That's better than four days!

My father had 300 mules. Trucks or cars were useless because there were no roads. The mules would take the coffee from the plantation and bring back whatever was needed. During the war, we had to bring out the coffee by light plane. At that time, our annual coffee production was about 1,400 tonnes. We were also producing about 500 tonnes of cardamom. It all had to come out by plane.

We flew the plane to a small town about 60 km from La Perla, a seven-minute trip. We put one tonne, maybe a little more, on each flight; it took three minutes to unload the coffee, and then we went back again. We flew from 6 am to 2 pm, when it starts raining. It was costly!

Do you sell your coffee directly to international traders?

Anacafé gives licences for 'Exporters' as well as for 'Producer Exporters'. We are 'Producer Exporters'.

We won our first Cup of Excellence in 2001, and we have been in the top ten in Guatemala in terms of quality since then. The competition has positioned La Perla's Coffee as one of the best coffees in the world. It has given us a massive opportunity in new markets.

Our best clients now are from Japan and Taiwan. We have lovely clients in Australia as well. We also sell directly to a roaster, Taylors of Harrogate, in the UK. They supply the Marks & Spencer chain. We also sell to Canada and the US, but not to Starbucks or Nespresso. We sell to smaller companies. They pay better!

Our entire production is speciality coffee because of its characteristics: the high altitude and the microclimate that comes from the Gulf of Mexico. We do roast some of our coffee through Anacafé and sell it locally, but we export 98 per cent of our coffee.

Is coffee tourism significant in Guatemala?

I used to be the director of the Tourist Commission. Guatemala should be one of the world's best tourist destinations. We have so many beautiful volcanoes and lakes; the people are lovely; the weather is fantastic.

We had 36 years of civil war, but Guatemala is now calm. We border Mexico, and we have drugs moving up from Columbia to the US through Mexico. Tourists, however, should not have any problems. Yes, we have issues, but they are the usual problems.

Anacafé is looking to develop the coffee tourist sector, but unfortunately not to La Perla; it is too far away!

Thank you, Ricardo, for your time and comments!

Chapter 13:
Environmental Sustainability

We stand now where two roads diverge. The road we have long been travelling is deceptively easy, a smooth superhighway on which we progress with great speed, but at its end lies disaster. The other fork of the road – the one 'less travelled by' – offers our last, our only chance to reach a destination that assures the preservation of our earth.

- Rachel Carson, Silent Spring, 1962.

In 1833, the English economist William Forster Lloyd published a pamphlet in which he described shepherds sharing a common parcel of grazing land. The land became overgrazed because, for each additional sheep, a shepherd could receive benefits, while the group as a whole shared the resulting degradation of the earth. If all shepherds made the individually rational economic decision of putting more of their sheep on the common land, it would be depleted or even destroyed, to the detriment of all.

In 1968, the ecologist Garrett Hardin explored this dilemma in his article The Tragedy of the Commons, published in the journal Science. The essay derived its title from the pamphlet by Lloyd, which he cites, about the over-grazing of common land.

It is in the self-interest of individual farmers to invest in environmentally sustainable practices if that investment reduces their production costs or increases the value of their land. As long as they own the land, farmers may be more closely aligned with collective self-interest than consumers.

Farmers are custodians of their land for future generations. They know that they and their children can only continue to farm if they act responsibly and do not take short-term measures that damage their land and their ability to grow food. Individual consumers do not face the same costs; they can consume unsustainably, and everyone will share the costs.

This distinction is particularly relevant when it comes to coffee. Roughly half of coffee's GHG emissions occur not when or where it is grown and processed – or when it is being shipped – but when it is being prepared and drunk. Coffee's total carbon footprint depends more on how consumers prepare their coffee than on how farmers grow it.

The carbon footprint of your coffee largely depends on whether you take your coffee black or with milk, the quantity of milk you add, and whether it is cow's milk or non-dairy milk. In his book, How Bad Are Bananas? The Carbon Footprint of Everything, Mike Berners-Lee estimates that if you prepare your coffee at home – and you only boil the exact amount of water that you need – the carbon footprint of a cup of black coffee is around 21 gm of CO_2.

If you add milk, then the carbon footprint increases to 53 gm of CO_2. If you boil twice the amount of water you need (which we all tend to do), the carbon footprint increases to 71 gm of CO_2. The carbon footprint rises with the amount of milk you add: a large cappuccino has a carbon footprint of 235 gm and a large latte 340 gm. The best way to reduce your coffee's carbon footprint is to drink it black.

Drinking four black coffees a day, boiling only as much water as you need, works out at 30 kg of CO_2 a year – the same as a 40-mile drive in an average car. Three large lattes per day, by contrast, and you're looking at almost twenty times as much carbon, equivalent to flying halfway across Europe.

What about instant coffee – is it better or worse than fresh brew? The answer is that although instant coffee requires more energy to produce it, it has a slightly lower carbon footprint because there is less waste than with fresh brew. When you prepare fresh-brewed coffee, there is always a tendency to make too much, leading to waste. You have to add the carbon emissions of the coffee you throw away to the carbon emissions of the coffee that you drink.

It is a problem not just with coffee but with all the agricultural supply chains. The UN FAO estimate that about one-third of all food is wasted, with the waste happening on the producer side in developing countries and on the consumer side in developed countries. You have to add GHG emissions from wasted food to agriculture's total carbon footprint.

When you make a cup of instant coffee, you do just that – you make a cup, not a pot. The smaller the quantity of coffee that you waste, the smaller the carbon footprint. But there again – in GHG emission terms – there is no point in making a cup of instant coffee if you boil enough water to make a pot. Similarly, don't drink instant coffee to save the planet and then add cow's milk to make a latte.

If you pick up a takeaway on your way to work, it will likely come in a single-use cup; an estimated 16 billion disposable coffee cups are used each year. These single-use cups (along with their lids, sleeves and stir sticks) are often made with hard-to-recycle materials like Styrofoam, polyethene or polypropylene that are sent straight to the landfill.

Single-use coffee cups were traditionally made from Styrofoam; it is cheap and retains heat well. The problem is that Styrofoam, like all polystyrene products, is made from synthetic resins, polyesters and plastics that decompose exceptionally slowly in a landfill. Most coffee shop chains have now replaced Styrofoam with double-walled paper cups lined with polyethene.

This polyethene lining has to be separated from the cup before you can recycle the paper portion; this rarely happens. Besides, most people (including me, until I researched this chapter) throw their empty coffee cups into recycling bins, contaminating the other plastics. The plastic cups used for iced drinks are also a problem. Most are made from polypropylene, which is more challenging than polyethene terephthalate (PET) to recycle. Their attached lids make recycling even more problematic; they are made from different materials that have to be separated before you can process them in separate recycling streams.

In his book, The Blue Bottle Craft of Coffee, James Freeman reserves 'a special place in hell' for pod, or single-serve capsule, coffee. His first complaint - that the coffee in single servings is inferior in quality to freshly roasted coffee – is debatable. His second complaint – that capsule coffee is less environmentally friendly than ground coffee – is almost certainly incorrect. If you recycle them, capsule-coffee can be more ecologically friendly than fresh brew.

Coffee is more of a victim than a culprit of climate change. The arabica coffee plant is highly sensitive to climate, and it is grown in areas where climate change could make production unsustainable. Coffee production is already moving northwards and southwards, as well as to higher elevations.

According to the Jeffrey Sachs report, if global warming continues at its current rate, with an average increase of 0.2 °C per decade, coffee production will need to shift an average of 58 km toward the poles, or 37 metres higher, per decade. By mid-century, the minimum altitude suitable for coffee production in Central America and Kenya is expected to increase by around 400 metres.

Coffee growing areas are already experiencing the effects of climate change. Temperatures have increased at a rate of about 0.2 °C per decade since 1970, and the pace is increasing. Although all times of the year are getting warmer, the range of temperatures throughout the year is growing wider as hot months get even hotter. Similarly, wet months are getting wetter, and dry months are getting drier.

Different parts of the coffee belt are warming at different rates. Many of the coffee regions in southern Brazil and Guatemala have already warmed 2°C above pre-industrial temperatures. Colombia has seen less warming, as have Africa's coffee regions. Temperatures in the coffee regions of India and Vietnam are about 1°C warmer now than they were in the pre-industrial age.

By 2050, few places in the tropics will have experienced less than 1 °C of warming, and the average warming over the coffee belt will be 2.8 °C. Almost 20 per cent of the coffee belt will have warmed by more than 4 °C, which represents the limit of warming that can be offset by shade-grown cultivation.

As production migrates to colder regions, it could leave smallholder families behind. It could lead to a further consolidation of output, as well as a reduction in the variety of different coffee terroirs available on the market.

The solution is to stop and reverse the rate of increase in global temperatures. Unfortunately, that seems too challenging politically (understatement), so the only alternative is to develop new varieties of coffee that can thrive in higher and more volatile temperature ranges.

The Tropical Agricultural Research and Higher Education Centre (CATIE) in Costa Rica has been doing just that; it has developed one candidate that they call 'Centroamericano'. They combined the best local varieties with genetically diverse Ethiopian strains from CATIE's collection, manually taking pollen from one plant and pollinating flowers from another. As such, the resulting variety is not considered as genetically modified.

Researchers at CATIE had initially been looking for a coffee variety that was higher-yielding and more resistant to rust disease. When a frost hit their trial beds in 2017, they were surprised to see that the Centroamericano plants were the only ones to survive. They subsequently discovered that the hybrid was not only more resistant to disease but also better able to cope with broader temperature.

Hybrids are more expensive and, because their genes aren't stable, you can't take their seeds and plant them. Instead, you have to clone them in a laboratory. Even so, new varieties are being developed. It is good news that makes the recent alarming forecasts of the adverse effects of climate change on coffee production too pessimistic.

Coffee has environmental concerns other than global warming: deforestation, the loss of biodiversity, land pollution (through the chemicals used to produce the crop), water use and water pollution. These issues are inter-related.

A study conducted in 2003 by the Water Footprint Network estimated that it takes 140 litres of water to produce a cup of coffee. However, that depends on how the coffee is grown and processed. Shade-grown coffee needs less water than full-sun grown coffee; wet-milled coffee uses more water and produces more effluent than sundried coffee.

In 2016, the SCAA published a white paper entitled *A Blueprint for Water Security in the Coffeelands*. They estimated that a traditional wet mill uses over 75 litres of water to produce one kilo of parchment coffee. Modern mills can reduce water use to less than 6 litres per kilo. Naturally processed or pulp-natural coffees use even less water, often less than one litre per kilo of parchment coffee.

Wet milling is one of the leading sources of water pollution in coffee-growing areas. The wastewater from coffee mills is often released untreated into streams and rivers. Bacteria can break down the sugars and pectin in these honey waters, but they need oxygen to do it effectively. If there isn't enough oxygen, the result can be dead zones similar to raw sewage in terms of their impact on water quality. The pollution load in the wastewater from wet milling can be 30 to 40 times greater than from urban sewage!

The solution is to treat the wastewaters before discharging them back into the rivers. The technology is proven, and the solid waste matter produced is a nutrient-rich ingredient in organic compost. Even so, the SCAA estimated that in 2016 only 5 per cent of the world's mills had adequate water treatment facilities.

Most wet mills in the world are too small to invest in the necessary equipment. There are approximately 500,000 farmers in Colombia, each with their wet mill. There are 40,000 farmers with wet mills in Nicaragua. There are 120,000 farmers in Honduras; many own their mills.

Most producing countries have legislation in place to limit water pollution, but the legislation is often not strong enough or not enforced. As a result, sustainability certification agencies have increasingly replaced governments in terms of monitoring and implementing environmental safeguards regarding water pollution.

Arabica coffee has historically been grown under a forest canopy that provides shade for the coffee trees and a natural habitat for the fauna and flora. Of all crops, shade-grown coffee comes out number one as the crop that best supports biodiversity.

The environmental benefits of shade-grown coffee are many. It provides a habitat for native and migratory birds and, as the birds eat many of the insects that attack coffee plants, farmers can use less pesticide.

The forest cover helps to reduce soil erosion and stabilise the steep slopes on which coffee often grows. The leaf litter and other plant material from these shade trees contribute to increased soil nutrients such as carbon and nitrogen. The soil in shade-grown coffee acts as a carbon sink, as organic matter accumulates on the ground and gets broken down over time. There is less runoff of surface water in shaded plantations compared to unshaded farms, reducing both water and fertiliser use.

Sun-grown coffee is less environmentally friendly than shade-grown coffee. It requires more chemical fertilisers, insecticides, herbicides, fungicides, and pesticides to promote growth. These chemicals contribute to toxic water runoff and reduce biodiversity; some residues may find their way into your morning cup. As Steve Wateridge mentioned, some of the conilon coffees currently being held in European warehouses may have higher-than-permitted levels of glyphosate contamination.

Overall, this should not be enough to stop you enjoying your morning cup of coffee – nor should you feel guilty about the environmental impact it is having on the planet. But, please, only boil just the quantity of water that you need!

A conversation with Bridget Carrington

Good morning, Bridget. Could you please tell me a little bit about yourself?

I graduated in the early 80s in the middle of an economic downturn when jobs for graduates were hard to come by. I ended up doing a bilingual secretarial course for a year. I wasn't cut out to be a secretary. I wasn't very good at typing. I couldn't do shorthand, but I could speak French, German and Spanish. It was enough to get me a job as a bilingual French secretary with ED&F Man. I started doing bits and pieces of secretarial work for the directors and over the years moved into coffee trading admin and contracts.

I became increasingly involved in the coffee trading side of the business, helping to look after the company's East African trading book, particularly the relationship that ED&F Man had with Dormans in Kenya. In 1992, ED&F Man sent me on a business trip to Kenya for three weeks. I liked it so much. I stayed in Kenya with Dormans for 27 years!

I never intended to stay for 27 years. I planned to stay for three years to get some experience at the origin, but after three months in Kenya, I met my future husband.

Could you tell me a little bit about the different East African coffees?

If you were to 'basket' East African coffees, you would put Kenyan and Ethiopian in the same basket. And if you were to ask coffee connoisseurs – particularly third- and fourth-wave coffee roasters – to choose their favourite coffees, eight out of ten would say Kenya and Ethiopia. The two countries grow the best coffee in the world, and that's not a biased opinion!

It's the balance of acidity and flavour. Ethiopian coffee has more floral notes, while Kenyan is more berry or citrus based. They are refined, with a pure, clear, bright taste. You don't buy them for their body, certainly not their washed coffees. But then I'm talking about the washed coffee; I'm not talking about the unwashed Djimma or Mbuni coffees.

Rwanda closely follows Ethiopia and Tanzania. It took Rwanda a little bit of time after the civil war to get to where they are today. They still sometimes have a potato taint which you don't get in Ethiopian or Kenya coffee, but that's improved over the years.

Even though Burundi is situated next to Rwanda, their coffee is more comparable to Tanzanian coffee. Burundi and Tanzania are sometimes described as 'soft' arabica, with lower acidity and a heavier body – they have a sort of chocolatey velvety texture or mouthfeel. They do not have the refined, elegant quality of your best Kenya and Ethiopia coffees. However, I like Tanzania coffee as I prefer coffee with a little bit less acidity. In that sense, it is similar to Colombian coffee.

Uganda produces mainly robusta, but they do have some good arabica coffee. Their top-grade washed arabica comes from around Mount Elgon and from Bugisu. The quality has improved over the years.

The trend now is for unwashed, pulped natural, and honey processed coffees. They are trending on the consuming end, and coffee buyers are increasingly demanding coffees that have undergone different processing methods. Buyers will pay a premium for these coffees.

If you go to a coffee shop these days, you will get a lot of naturals. I don't like them. They taste fermented to me; I only like washed coffees.

How do marketing regimes differ between countries?

Ethiopia is the largest producer in East Africa, with a total volume of more than 7.5 million bags split between washed and unwashed arabica. Coffee is principally sold through the ECX Exchange in Addis Ababa to local exporters; they, in turn, sell to international trading companies and roasters.

The government set up the ECX Exchange in 2008. Although co-operatives could sell their coffee directly, much of the production lost its identity and fell back into the 'commodity' category. Some modifications have been made to the system since 2017 to allow for traceability.

Uganda is the second-largest producer in the region, with more than 1.5 million families dependent on coffee for their livelihoods. Farmers sell to intermediaries and exporters through a network of buying stations and aggregators dotted around the countryside. They then sell it to the larger exporting companies based in and around Kampala.

Kenya is the third-largest producer. Marketing agents bring the coffee to the marketplace for which they earn a commission. They sell the coffee through the weekly auction or directly to an overseas buyer. The marketing agents provide a critical role as extension service providers to farmers.

About 65 per cent of Kenyan coffee comes from cooperatives and about 35 per cent from estates. When I first arrived, it was the other way around, but the estates have slowly been lost to urbanisation or have moved into other crops, such as pineapples or avocados.

Tanzania is the fourth-largest producer in East Africa. They changed the way they sold their coffee in 2019. Instead of one centralised weekly auction, they now have multiple auctions to sell coffee in the different growing zones. The coffee is channelled through cooperatives and farmer groups in the hope that farmers can retain more of the value of their crop. The government hopes that rebuilding the cooperatives will also allow for better economies of scale, training and capacity building for farmers. The biggest challenge to this has been the cooperatives' limited access to finance.

Although the civil war practically wiped out the Rwandan coffee industry in the early 1990s, the country is now the next most significant producer in the region. The government has liberalised the coffee business in the sense that exporters can buy cherry directly from the farmers, but it still regulates it in terms of price setting, export quality controls etc

Burundi has also suffered many years of political and civil turbulence, but it has made some progress in re-establishing itself as a differentiated coffee origin. The government privatised coffee marketing in 2008.

Coffee is Kenya's third-largest export in terms of revenue, but acreage has fallen by 35 per cent in the past 30 years. Why – and what can be done about it?

The coffee sector has lost acreage to urbanisation and alternative crops.

Some of that shift to other crops was due to the corruption and mismanagement under a previous regime. Farmers weren't being paid for their coffee, and the money was disappearing. At one point, Kenya had a fantastic coffee research facility that provided extension services to farmers, but the funding dried up and the facility all but disappeared. Mismanagement and corruption led to disillusionment among farmers, and they went into other crops.

However, the main reason for diversification has been low prices.

Can anything be done to reverse this fall in acreage?

There are certain outlying areas where you could bring new acreage under coffee. Still, to expand production, you would have to increase yields by introducing new higher-yielding varieties. It is happening. There is also a lot of work being done to improve agricultural practices. The average cooperative yield in Kenya is probably 2-300 kilos per hectare; in a well-run estate it would be about 1,500-2,000 kilos per hectare; in Brazil, it's 2-3,000 kilos per hectare.

Tanzania is different. The country is vast and new planting is happening, bringing more land under coffee. The same in Rwanda; the planted area is increasing.

I wouldn't necessarily say that the coffee sector in East Africa is in decline, but apart from Ethiopia and Uganda, it's pretty stagnant. That is despite a lot of investment and a lot of initiatives to try and boost production.

What are the solutions?

Of the $3 that you might spend on a cup of coffee in a coffee shop, maybe one per cent goes to the men and women who cultivated the crop. Almost all the value is created after the farm gate. We have to find a way to allow farmers a more significant share of the global earnings.

One way might be through the development of local demand. Kenya needs to grow its domestic market, which is very small at the moment. Only Ethiopia and Uganda have a robust domestic market for coffee. Kenya is a tea-drinking nation because of its British colonial history, while Ethiopia has more of an Italian influence. If you visit a coffee farm or coffee cooperative in Kenya, they often give you tea to drink; they won't provide you with coffee.

Brazil has led the way in terms of developing a domestic market. They launched a big campaign in the late 1980s to boost domestic consumption from 6.5 million bags in 1985 to 22 million bags in 2018.

Indonesia has had similar success, where the two leading domestic roasters are each turning over a million 60 kg bags, primarily selling three-in-one products of coffee, sugar and milk. The coffee shop there has become the preferred hangout place in this predominantly Muslim country.

For the coffee farmer, the most significant benefit of stable domestic consumption is the guarantee of an outlet and reduced exposure to global price volatility.

Are coffee farmers in Kenya better off now than they were when you first went there 27 years ago?

Unfortunately, they are probably not better off now than 27 years ago, mainly because coffee prices have not kept pace with inflation over that period. It's tough for coffee farmers anywhere in the world to survive on coffee alone, which is why one of the things everyone is looking at diversification. It might mean that coffee farming is no longer sustainable in some countries.

The more marginalised East Africa becomes - because people are buying all their coffee requirements from Brazil, Colombia and Vietnam - the less reliance buyers put on it.

Brazil is a price setter while Kenya is a price taker.

When coffee prices are low, the underperforming origins suffer the most. The saving grace for much of East African production is its quality. Kenya is a price setter in terms of its quality, but it would be a lot better off if it could have a reasonable price for three or four times the crop size. Kenya and East Africa have become more reliant on the single origin market.

Just two countries – Ethiopia and Uganda – produce more than 85 per cent of East Africa's coffee. Many international buyers have reduced their reliance on other origins. Many commercial roasters have all but stopped using Kenyan coffee in favour of cheaper alternatives.

Why is Ethiopia more of a success?

Ethiopia is a popular origin globally and better known than Kenya. Japan buys a considerable amount of unwashed Ethiopian coffee, whereas Kenyan single-origin coffee tends to be well known in England because of the colonial link. Kenya AA is well known around the world, but only in small single origin lots.

What challenges does East Africa face in terms of coffee?

I would put climate change at the top of the list; it hampers the ability to improve yields.

Coffee farmers are getting older, and this is also a challenge. Young people do not want to be coffee farmers; they prefer to live in the cities.

Meanwhile, urbanisation is leading to the fall in acreage that we mentioned earlier. There is also the problem of access to finance. Lack of value addition retention is a problem. As I mentioned earlier, farmers are often price takers, unable to dictate when and at what price they sell their coffee. Very little coffee is sold as roasted coffee – less than 0.5 per cent is exported as a finished roasted, ground product.

But all of these problems are not unique to East Africa. They are global problems.

Government interference is a problem in East Africa. Even now, the Kenyan government is trying to change the rules again. They want to resurrect a central depository payment system. If they do, it will mean that all the money will pass through a central system before being distributed to farmers. In contrast, under liberalisation, marketing agents paid farmers within two or three weeks.

Compared to most other locally produced crops, governments impose heavy regulations on coffee production in East Africa. Governments don't seem to be making any moves to deregulate; on the contrary. Coffee is political in East Africa.

Could producing countries add value by roasting and exporting roasted coffee?

It depends on how you're roasting and packing it, and how quickly you can get it to market. That's why coffees are not roasted and exported from the origin. The coffee needs to be roasted close to the consumer. Perhaps producers could set up service arrangements with roasters in importing countries, rather than investing in their own facilities.

Does certification work well in East Africa?

Yes, certification works.

Certification was fundamental 10 to 15 years ago in terms of training and helping farmers get better yields, implement better agricultural practices, improve business skills and keep better records.

When the government extension service disappeared, the local marketing agents helped to fill the gap. Still, it was the requirement to meet the certification standards that drove the development of the coffee industry.

You've recently retired from Dormans; what does the future hold for you now?

I wanted to stop working at Dormans before I passed my sell-by date. I was happy to hand over to a younger generation; they have their own ideas and want to do some things differently.

I've been in the industry for 36 years, and it's been very good to me in terms of personal development, career, remuneration and everything else. I would like now to be able to give something back. I would love for others to benefit from my experience in this wonderful industry, to share my passion and build the same kind of relationships and friendships that I had. I cannot imagine a world without some of the coffee professionals I have met along the way. Once coffee gets into your blood, it never leaves.

Farmers need our help to ensure a sustainable livelihood, so that is where I would most like to focus. For the past few months, I have been working on a report with the International Trade Council (IRC) on value addition for East Africa's smallholder coffee farmers. The paper has been published, and I am now working on a project to test some of its recommendations.

For the past ten years, I have been on the board of trustees of CQI – the Coffee Quality Institute – and I am now Vice-Chairperson of it.

Could you please tell me a little about the CQI?

The CQI concentrates on training and education all along the coffee supply chain. It runs the Q-programme which teaches people how to cup coffee and certifies them according to quite stringent standards.

We do a lot of training at the origin, teaching farmers and exporters how to cup coffee so that they can understand what their buyers require. Q is the international cupping language so that parties to a transaction understand the quality they are talking about; if you buy an 88 coffee, you get delivered an 88 coffee.

In consuming countries, we do have some baristas who want to learn more and want that extra qualification, but many of our students work for roasters, either in their buying departments or in their quality labs. Most roasters nowadays view the Q certification as the international standard, even though they might use different protocols internally.

We have also started processing programmes. We have designed Q-Processing for both producers and buyers; the aim is to teach techniques that will lead to better coffee processing. It is as relevant to producers as it is to roasters who want to learn more about how their coffee is grown. The new generation of coffee roasters wishes to know everything about where their coffee comes from, how it is grown and processed.

We have three different levels of courses in the processing programmes. Q1 is a generalist course. Q2 is more specialised; you have to do it during the harvest. Q3 is more like a degree course; it takes about a year through the whole harvest cycle.

In addition to training courses, CQI also does project work at the farm level. CQI's overriding mission is to improve the quality of coffee and the standard of living for farmers.

How does the CQI scoring system work?

Put very simply, you start with a baseline and then add points for the different merits– acidity, body, aroma and flavour – and then deduct points for defects. Speciality coffee has to score above 80 points on the CQI scale. It is the same scale that the SCA uses.

So last question: what is your favourite coffee?

I'm not sure I should, but I think I'm going to answer this truthfully. It's always been a little bit of a joke. I drink instant coffee. It's not necessarily my favourite, but it's the most convenient, especially in the morning and at home. I am a bit of an instant coffee snob! I only drink a one hundred per cent arabica blend of soluble coffee. Nestlé Gold Blend had a lot of Kenyan coffee in it for many years, but now I drink the Alta Rica blend, a 100 per cent Latin American blend.

I love Kenyan coffee, although it can be quite acidic. I love Costa Rican coffee. I love Rwanda coffee. I love Ethiopian coffee. I just love coffee!

I generally brew it in a French press. We do have an all-singing, all-dancing, LED espresso machine, but it's just too complicated for me.

Thank you, Bridget, for your time and comments!

Chapter 14:
Certification

Unfortunately, we're often quite willing to let the perfect get in the way of the good.

- Jason Clay – WWF

For the past half-century, Non-Government Organisations (NGOs) such as Greenpeace and Oxfam have played a significant and positive role in alerting public opinion to the damage that we are inflicting on our planet and our fellow human beings.

Within the food supply chain, the NGOs realised that they could have the most impact by focussing on the international food processing and agricultural commodity trading companies that act as the interface between the millions of farmers and the billions of consumers. The NGOs call this 'the egg timer' model: putting pressure on the one hundred or so biggest companies at the narrowest point of the food supply chain.

To further their aims, the NGOs launched a strategy of naming and shaming food companies into cleaning up their supply chains. This strategy reached a climax in 2010 with Greenpeace's campaign against Nestlé's use of palm oil in their Kit Kat chocolate bars: a video showed an office worker unwrapping a Kit Kat only to find the severed, bloody finger of an Orangutan.

Commodity trading houses and food processing firms were caught off-balance by the strength of the movement and the aggressivity of the NGOs; they were initially unsure as to how to react. Commodity trading houses have for years been efficient at what they did: allowing buyers to purchase a product that is interchangeable with any other tonne of the same product.

Agricultural commodities have historically been defined by physical properties: weights, moisture content, foreign matter, broken pieces and other physically verified attributes. Suddenly, consumers began to ask commodity traders to address the social and environmental issues in their supply chains. Buyers began asking traders to confirm traits that they had never verified in the past, something that they were ill-equipped to do.

Similarly, processed food companies had been good at providing safe, tasty products at reasonable prices. Suddenly, they found that consumers were asking them to verify their supply chains. Failure to do so put their valuable brands – and their businesses –at risk from NGO naming and shaming.

The food supply sector had long argued that it was the role of the governments to implement social and environmental standards within their countries: no child or slave labour; no deforestation; minimum pollution etc. It became apparent that most governments — especially in developing countries — were not able to do this effectively – or at least to the standard now being demanded by consumers and NGOs.

The food industry turned to outside participants for help. Gradually a range of voluntary sustainability standards and certification agencies emerged, stepping in to fill the role that governments, traders and food companies couldn't fill. The trade houses and the NGOs, most notably WWF, supported and encouraged these agencies.

In 2003, stakeholders across the coffee sector came together to launch the Common Code for the Coffee Community (4C) Association to address sustainability issues within the coffee supply chain. The industry established the Association in 2006 as a business-to-business standard. Its membership comprises coffee farmers, trade and industry, and civil society.

In 2016, the 4C Association separated its commercial certification-related activities from its pre-competitive activities, splitting into the Global Coffee Platform (GCP) and Coffee Assurance Services (CAS). MEO Carbon Solutions acquired CAS and the 4C Certification System in 2018. CAS, renamed 4C Services, is now responsible for operating and assuring compliance with the 4C Certification System.

According to its website, the Global Coffee Platform has '150 leading coffee companies and organisations from every corner of the coffee world'. Together, they coordinate the $350 million spent annually on sustainability. By working together, they can have a more positive 'impact on the livelihoods of coffee farming families and their communities than by doing it alone'.

Two other similar organisations were set up at around the time as 4C. UTZ Kapeh was founded in 2002 with support from the Dutch charity Solidaridad. (Utz Kapeh means 'Good Coffee' in the Mayan language Quiché.) In 2007, the foundation changed its name and logo to UTZ Certified, and in 2016 shortened it further to UTZ.

The competing Rainforest Alliance was founded in 1987 to help 'farmers and foresters to produce better crops, adapt to climate change, increase productivity, and reduce costs while protecting natural resources and the environment'.

In 2018, the Rainforest Alliance and UTZ merged and, in June 2020, they published a single certification programme that will come into effect in July 2021. The current Rainforest Alliance and UTZ programs will continue to run in parallel as the transition across to the new standard takes place. From 2021, the merged organisation will go under the name of the Rainforest Alliance.

In the United States and Canada, there is a market for bird-friendly, or shade-grown, coffee; the emphasis is put on the conservation of shade trees to preserve birdlife and biodiversity. The Smithsonian Migratory Bird Centre has developed a certification system for it. So far, the market for such coffees is small and mostly limited to North America.

In 1988, when the Dutch NGO Solidaridad was looking to set up a foundation to help farmers in the developing world receive a fair price for their production, they called it Max Havelaar. Coffee was the first Fairtrade product that they launched.

Fairtrade coffee now accounts for about 1 per cent of the world production of coffee: 1.7 million bags versus world production of 175 million bags.

The Fairtrade system sets the following minimum prices: $1.40/lb for washed arabica; $1.35/lb for natural arabica; $1.05/lb for washed robusta; and $1.01/lb for natural robusta. Buyers pay an additional premium of 20 cents/lb either over the minimum price or, if world prices are higher, the corresponding futures market price. Producers are paid an additional premium of 30 cents/lb if the coffee is organic.

The revenues generated by these premia do not go directly to the producers themselves. Instead, Fairtrade invests the money in projects in their producing areas. The farmers decide whether the funds go towards improvements in health, education or other social facilities, or to improve productivity or diversify into other crops.

The system is not without its critics. Some interviewees privately voiced concerns over a lack of transparency as to how Fairtrade spends the money generated from the premia. They suggested that this might be one reason why some roasters and retailers are reducing their commitment to the Fairtrade scheme in favour of their own programmes.

In her book Selling Sustainability Short, Dr Janina Grabs of the University of Münster argues that certification has failed to live up to its promise of higher prices and lower costs.

Along with her colleagues at the University of Münster, she surveyed over 1,900 coffee farmers in Costa Rica, Columbia, and Honduras. She found that introducing sustainable practices increased production costs, whether planting shade trees, paying fair wages, providing personal protection equipment or protecting farm ecosystems.

She also found that these costs were not always recuperated in higher prices, primarily because the supply of certified coffee exceeds its demand. Dr Grabs estimated that only 22 to 42 per cent of the certified coffee from those three countries is sold as such. The rest is sold without the certification label, leading to an erosion in the premia for certified coffee compared to uncertified coffee. She writes that premia for certified coffee in Honduras have halved over the past ten years. Producers in all three countries are abandoning certification due to its high costs and low returns.

Incidentally, Dr Grabs argues that speciality coffee is now replacing certified coffee in terms of producers trying to differentiate themselves and earn higher prices. She writes: 'Quality today is where certifications were in the early 2000s, with validated consumer interest in the niche, high hopes for its expansion and an almost singular focus on value aggregation at the producer level. I want to argue that lessons learned from the world of sustainability standards are highly applicable to the future of speciality coffee as well.'

However, as I will argue below, there is a big difference between certified coffee and speciality coffee. Consumers may not be willing to pay more for certified coffee, but they are willing to pay more for speciality coffee.

I am not at all sure that Dr Grabs' study reflects the effectiveness of certification standards globally. In 2020 Eva-Marie Meemken from the University of Copenhagen published a paper entitled 'Do smallholder farmers benefit from sustainability standards?' It was a meta-analysis that consolidated results from 97 original studies.

She found that although the effects of standards on production costs and yields were mixed and varied across standards, farmers certified under a sustainability standard received on average 20–30 per cent higher prices than their non-certified counterparts. On average, certified farmers also obtained higher profits, leading to an overall increase in household income by 16–22 per cent. (Of course, just because certified farmers received higher payments on average, it doesn't mean that they all did.)

Meanwhile, the Rainforest Alliance tells me that, in 2019, 59 per cent of Rainforest Alliance certified coffee was sold as such. For UTZ the figure was 55 per cent. The Rainforest Alliance sees these numbers increasing each year.

Still, some of the bigger roasters have set up their own environmental and social certification systems, sometimes in partnership with the existing agencies.

In 2003, Nespresso launched its AAA Sustainable Quality™ Program in partnership with the Rainforest Alliance and Fairtrade International. It focuses on quality as well as environmental and social sustainability, while at the same time offering farmers training, technical assistance and in some cases, direct investments to improve their performance. Nespresso reports that farmers in the programme have higher yields while earning top prices for their best quality beans.

According to their website, Starbucks' internal sustainability programme CAFE (Coffee and Farmer Equity) Practices also focuses on quality and economic sustainability, working to 'sustain and strengthen communities that grow coffee while maintaining Starbucks high-quality standards, now and into the future.'

Starbucks pays premia for quality coffee verified as ethically and sustainably sourced by CAFE Practice standards. They pay more if supply chains show continuous improvement across CAFE Practices. They also require economic transparency in all contracts.

The independent certification agencies are also rising to the challenge. In June 2020, the Rainforest Alliance published the new criteria which will replace existing Rainforest Alliance and UTZ certification programmes from mid-2021.

The first innovation is to redress what they call 'systemic imbalances in global supply chains' that put too much burden on producers alone to achieve more sustainable agricultural production.' Under the new criteria, buyers will have to reward producers for meeting sustainable agriculture standards by paying a mandatory sustainability differential, an additional cash payment over and above the market price for the sale of certified crops. Unlike the Fairtrade system, this sustainability differential will be paid to the individual farmer, rather than at the cooperative level. Buyers will also need to provide financial assistance to producers to help them achieve their sustainability objectives.

The second innovation is an Assess-and-Address approach to tackling human rights issues such as child labour, forced labour, discrimination, and workplace violence and harassment. The Rainforest Alliance argues that rather than imposing a simple ban that often drives the problem underground, the new approach focuses on assessing the risks and engaging local communities to work together to prevent and address the issues.

Despite the excellent work being done, many traders feel that farmers still receive too small a share of the value in the supply chain. One senior trader told me: 'Everyone is there for the farmer at that moment, but no one is there for the farmer when it comes to paying him a good price for his coffee.' Another said: 'Everybody wants sustainability, but hardly anybody wants to pay for it. There's a lot of talk but little walk.'

In 2019, the Boston Consulting Group (BCG) conducted a survey in the fashion sector that found that 75 per cent of consumers felt that sustainability was 'extremely or very important' in their purchasing decisions. However, on closer questioning, only 7 per cent said that sustainability influenced their purchase decisions. More critical factors included low prices, high quality, convenience and fashion.

BCG concluded that sustainability is a prerequisite rather than a driver of purchasing decisions. Consumers expect and demand that everything they buy is sustainable. It is not an add-on, a nice-to-have thing. It is a prerequisite. But because it is a prerequisite, consumers are not willing to pay more for it.

The priority for most consumers in developing countries is to feed their families. Food is a significant part of the family budget. In Nigeria, for example, consumers spend 64 per cent of their income on food. Compare that to the UK, where consumers spend 8.2 per cent of their income on food. In the US, the figure is 6.4 per cent. Nearly all of us in the developed world could all pay a little more for our food (and coffee) without it impacting our standard of living.

However, we are all products of our evolution. We may go to the supermarket to buy organic, certified coffee, but we end up purchasing the two-for-one special offer supermarket own-brand. After all, we have a family to feed, and the wellbeing of our family comes before the health of the planet or the safety and wellbeing of the workers who produced the coffee.

But there is hope in our selfishness. Our first responsibility may be the health and wellbeing of our families—the survival of our genes. However, we know that we have to provide farmers with a living if we want them to continue to provide us with food and coffee. We also know that our genes won't survive for long if we don't look after the planet.

There is a growing alignment of interests among farmers, governments, food companies, civil society and consumers to ensure that food is environmentally and socially sustainable. Farmers want to protect their land; food companies want to protect their brands; consumers and governments want to protect their health and the health of their environment. It makes for a powerful coalition for continual improvement. Things could be better, but the world is moving in the right direction.

A Conversation with Michelle Deugd

Good morning Michelle, could you please tell us a little about yourself and how you ended up in coffee with the Rainforest Alliance?

After graduating in 1995 from the Wageningen University with an M.Sc. in Tropical Agriculture, I started my career as a natural resource management specialist with the UN FAO in the coffee regions of Costa Rica and Honduras. I have always had a connection in one way or another with coffee. I wrote my theses in Tanzania on nutrient balancing on coffee production systems.

What did you do when your contract ended with the FAO?

I returned to Costa Rica to continue to work on coffee production, rural development and rural finance projects. I joined the Rainforest Alliance in 2009 as the manager of coffee projects in Latin America, and I remained based in Costa Rica, where most of the Rainforest Alliance's groundwork started. Throughout the years, I have managed a range of coffee projects in Latin America, Asia and Africa, focusing on the development of the Rainforest Alliance Certified coffee supply at the origin. I've also served as the director of agriculture globally.

I am now the organisation's sector lead for coffee. I provide strategic direction to the Rainforest Alliance's coffee work globally.

What are the biggest challenges that coffee growers currently face, and what is the Rainforest Alliance doing to help them deal with them?

Coffee growers are facing many challenges, but the two biggest broadly related challenges are climate change and low and unstable coffee net incomes.

With our projects on the ground, we work to mitigate the adverse effects of climate change through preventing deforestation, keeping soil cover, avoiding emissions from coffee processing etc. We have integrated these practices into our standard.

We also work with farmers to increase their incomes by improving their productivity through pruning, renovation, efficient fertilisation and use of organic and non-organic inputs. We also support farmers in improving the overall management of their farms, through better bookkeeping, registers, planning etc.

Also, under our 2020 certification programme, companies buying Rainforest Alliance Certified commodities will be held responsible for contributing to the investment needs identified by farmers in their supply chain, and for rewarding certified farmers with a Sustainability Differential over and above the market price of the commodity.

What about on a global level?

At a global level, we engage with other supply chain actors to positively influence the debate on climate change and coffee prices. It is a shared responsibility, and ultimately it is through the combination of all these activities that we can create a positive impact.

You have worked in both coffee and cocoa in your career. How do the two compare in terms of sustainability challenges?

They are both tropical agroforestry crops sensitive to climate change, and they have historically both been subject to low and volatile commodity prices. Besides, most producers of both crops are smallholders.

Although cocoa in Central America is still partially grown under forest cover, it is mainly sun grown in West Africa. The region accounts for 70 per cent of the world's cocoa production. West Africa's cocoa plantations were primarily established through the near-complete clear-cutting of native forests. Although this initially generated high productivity – albeit with high amounts of chemical inputs – the sector has become unsustainable, accelerating climate change and biodiversity loss, and resulting in an unproductive system generating meagre family incomes.

The Rainforest Alliance has recently merged with UTZ.

We merged because we believe that together we can have a more significant impact and be a better partner to our many stakeholders.

In June 2020, we published our new 2020 Rainforest Alliance certification programme, which will replace the existing Rainforest Alliance and UTZ certification programmes from mid-2021.

Having a single certification programme will simplify certification for farmers and help companies to build more responsible supply chains and drive innovation more efficiently. Creating a single auditing process and streaming the certification process will not only help the more than 400,000 coffee farmers currently certified under both standards, but it will also help new farmers to certify.

It will also help to expand our advocacy efforts to ensure the conservation of entire landscapes in priority regions from India to Indonesia, and Guatemala to Ghana.

The Rainforest Alliance has recently published a new strategy called 'Reimagining Certification'. What does that entail?

'Reimagining Certification' is our long-term vision for the future of certification. It is part of our broader strategy at the Rainforest Alliance to drive change through our areas of work.

Certification has had a significant impact, but it must continue to evolve to drive further improvement for people and nature and provide more value for farmers and companies. The merger of the Rainforest Alliance and UTZ in 2018 was a good time for us to take a step back and look at the future of certification.

We are moving away from the idea that certification is a series of pass/fail requirements. Instead, we are adopting a continuous improvement approach that drives change from a set of core criteria.

What does this mean in practice? It means first ensuring that all workers are paid a minimum wage – but continuing to drive improvements towards a living wage. It means working to stop deforestation–and then going beyond that, towards reforestation or regenerative agriculture.

Could you please explain the economic elements in the new criteria?

Our 2020 Sustainable Agriculture Standard outlines two financial requirements for the buyers of Rainforest Alliance Certified commodities: The Sustainability Differential (SD) and Sustainability Investments (SI).

The Sustainability Differential is a mandatory additional cash payment made to certified producers over and above the market price of the commodity. We don't set the Sustainability Differential in the coffee sector. Whenever possible, it should be negotiated between the farm group or farmer and the market actor responsible for making the payment, which, in most instances, is the first buyer.

The Sustainability Investments are mandatory cash or in-kind investments from buyers of Rainforest Alliance certified products to certified producers for the specific purpose of helping them meet the farm requirements of the Sustainable Agriculture Standard. The investments must go towards the needs identified by producers in their investment plans, and buyers must report the investments they make.

Besides these new criteria related to shared responsibility, our 2020 Sustainable Agriculture Standard also enhances practices which promote improved efficiency and farm-based profitability as the basis for an improved farm income.

Additionally, post-harvest practices support crop profitability, where farms and groups achieve improved crop quality.

There was no economic element under your old criteria, but many social and environmental problems result from economic ones. In hindsight, weren't you putting the cart in front of the horse by concentrating on social and environmental issues before dealing with economic ones?

The Rainforest Alliance 2017 Sustainable Agriculture Standard and the UTZ standard both have an extensive set of criteria related to farm management and crop.

The Rainforest Alliance and UTZ have always recognised that the three dimensions of sustainability - the economic, social and environmental pillars - are all interrelated. We can only achieve true sustainability by tackling them all in an integrated manner.

Recent independent research has shown that certification has a positive environmental, social, and economic impact. In many cases, Rainforest Alliance certified farms have higher yields and profits than non-certified farms, and they often – but not always – receive higher prices.

Nevertheless, as a result of continued low prices since 2018, we realise that these practices simply are not enough anymore. The industry as a whole realises that a more significant proportion of the value has to return to the producers, for the industry to continue to be more sustainable.

It is important to note that the Rainforest Alliance works toward improving the overall situation of farmers not just through our certification programme guidelines, but also through our landscape and community work, tailored supply chain services, and advocacy.

We believe that certification is a crucial tool, but it is not the only way to support more sustainable agriculture and improve the situation of farmers. Certification is effective when you combine it with support targeted to meet farmers' needs with long-term commitments from all actors in the supply chain.

How has the Rainforest Alliance changed its approach to child and forced labour?

Child labour, forced labour, discrimination, and workplace violence and harassment have never been – and will never be – tolerated by the Rainforest Alliance. However, what we have learned through many years of experience is that merely prohibiting these human rights violations in our standard is insufficient. Automatic decertification as the response to any incident of child labour is more likely to drive the problem underground, making it harder to detect and address. That's why our new certification programme promotes an 'Assess-and-Address' approach to tackling these human rights issues.

The Assess-and-Address approach puts the interest of children and workers at its centre. Without solving the root causes of child labour, forced labour, discrimination, and workplace violence or harassment, the problems will not go away. That's why the Rainforest Alliance promotes collaboration between certified farms, governments, civil society and supply chain partners to solve these issues together.

Beyond certification, the Rainforest Alliance also promotes human rights through other strategic interventions, for example, in Côte d'Ivoire, Ghana, and Uganda. These programmes set up community and district committees that support farming communities with access to education and village saving and loan schemes. The committees also raise awareness about child labour and motivate communities to send their children to school.

What we see is that the more integrated supply chain programmes are within the community or broader landscape, the more sustainable the system to tackle child labour. We are currently looking at expanding these programmes to Asia and Central America as well.

One complaint often levelled against certification is that audits are announced in advance, and child labour 'disappears' ahead of the visit.

Agricultural systems are complex, and we know that there are different levels of risk for various issues. We also understand that no system can monitor a farm 24 hours a day, 365 days a year.

That's why we want to give auditors the ability to focus on the more high-risk areas. Rather than merely checking what they see on the day of the audit, auditors will check that the systems are in place to support more sustainable practices all year round. They will also use new technology, like satellite imagery, to capture data that they cannot easily detect in a single visit. Also, we are increasing investment in audit oversight and training for auditors. Together, these changes will make auditing and assurance processes more effective.

Another complaint is that certification is a standard model for all countries.

We want to move away from a one-size-fits-all model. There are many different realities in producing countries and across sectors, and we want to provide standards and assurance systems that are flexible enough to adapt to these contexts.

An example of this in action would be with practices like child labour and forced labour. In areas where there is a medium or high risk of these practices occurring, our standard would require farmers to put in place robust systems to assess and address them. It goes hand-in-hand with auditors using risk maps to help them focus more on the most pressing issues where the audit is taking place.

The supply of certified coffee exceeds its demand. Isn't the only solution to increase demand – and to work with roasters to change consumer behaviour and to get them to pay more?

Our market team continually works with brands, roasters and retailers to develop demand, and they have been successful in their work in the sense that both of our certification programmes have continued to grow since the merger. It has even been the case in 2020 in the context of the COVID-19 pandemic.

Besides that, you need to look beyond the data of one single certification system to get to the full understanding of supply-demand data. Many farms are double- or sometimes triple-certified. If they sell their coffee through one certification system, it is not available to sell through another certification system.

I believe that roasters and retailers can put the Rainforest Alliance logo on their packs even if as little as 30 per cent of the coffee is certified.

According to our 2016 labelling guidelines, products were eligible to bear the Rainforest Alliance certified seal when the percentage of certified content reached a minimum of 30 per cent, with the obligation to increase this to 90 per cent over time. As of 2019, more than 80 per cent of Rainforest Alliance Certified products contained or sourced 90-100 per cent certified ingredients. From 2020, coffee packs with the Rainforest Alliance seal must contain at least 90 per cent of the certified element.

How do the economic elements in your new criteria differ from Fairtrade's?

Both the Rainforest Alliance and Fairtrade International are non-profit organisations that share similar missions and goals but differ in their approach to implementation.

Our approach is a holistic one; it focuses on helping farmers grow their businesses and become more profitable and resilient through training in farm management, financial literacy, and market access. We are also promoting a shared responsibility approach that encourages companies to do their part as well.

The Rainforest Alliance approach to additional payments includes two criteria: the sustainability differential – a cash payment to producers, and sustainable investments, cash or in-kind, to certificate holders based on their needs identified in their investment plans.

To what extent does shade play a part in your new criteria?

Our 2020 Sustainable Agriculture Standard requires that there is natural vegetation cover on at least 15 per cent of the total area for farms growing shade-tolerant crops, such as coffee and cocoa.

Last question: what is your favourite coffee, and how do you prepare it?

My favourite coffee comes from a sustainably managed small farm in the Tarrazú mountains of Costa Rica, at 1,700 meters above sea level. A young family manage the whole process from cherry to roasted bean, selling the coffee at the local market of the village where I live. I prepare it with a Chemex coffee maker to obtain the full flavour!

Thank you, Michelle, for your time and input!

You are welcome. Thank you, for your interest in Rainforest Alliance!

Chapter 15:
Coffee & Health

It is inhumane, in my opinion, to force people who have a genuine medical need for coffee to wait in line behind people who view it as some kind of recreational activity.

- Dave Barry - Journalist

In 2018, a Los Angeles judge ruled that anyone selling coffee in California had to post cancer warnings at their place of sale. The decision followed a lengthy legal battle by a small non-profit group, the Council for Education and Research on Toxics, which argued that the chemical acrylamide, produced during roasting, was carcinogenic. The suit had been brought against Starbucks and 90 other companies under Proposition 65, the Safe Drinking Water and Toxic Enforcement Act, passed by California voters in 1986.

The NGO had previously sued potato chip companies over the same issue; the potato chip manufacturers settled the case by agreeing to change the way they produced the chips and remove the acrylamide. Coffee companies, on the other hand, argued that it wasn't possible to remove acrylamide from coffee without ruining the flavour.

The coffee sector also argued that NGO was exaggerating the dangers of acrylamide. The chemical increases the risk of cancer in mice and rats when it is placed in the animals' drinking water at doses 1,000 to 10,000 times higher than the levels people might be exposed to in foods.

The case was an important one: the judge had the right to set another phase to the trial to consider potential civil penalties up to

$2,500 per person exposed to coffee each day over eight years. That could have been an astronomical sum in a state with close to 40 million residents. The case was repeatedly appealed until 2020 when the California Superior Court ruled that the state's coffee shops and retailers could take down the warning signs.

This long-running legal issue is an excellent example of the way that the public, legal and scientific opinion on coffee drinking has swung back and forth over the decades.

When coffee first made its appearance in Europe in the 17th century, medical professionals weren't quite sure what to make of it. Doctors at that time believed that the secret to good health lay in balancing the body's (disgusting-sounding) 'humours': blood, phlegm, black bile and yellow bile. Doctors classified all food and drinks within one of four categories: hot, cold, wet and dry. Coffee, along with tea and chocolate, didn't fit into any of those categories. It was hot and stimulating but also cooling and diuretic, a mystery.

William Ukers wrote in All About Coffee that the first advertisement for coffee appeared in England in 1657. It claimed the drink had 'many excellent qualities, closes the orifice of the stomach, fortifies the heat within, helps digestion, quickens the spirits…is good against eye-sores, coughs, or colds, consumptions, headache, dropsy, gout, scurvy, and King's Evil.'

Losing business to the coffee shops, London's publicans got together in 1674 and published the Women's Petition against Coffee. It claimed that coffee made men impotent: 'As unfruitful as the deserts where that unhappy berry is said to be bought.'

The health debate wasn't just limited to England. In 1679, eight years after France's first coffee shop opened in Marseilles, local physicians attempted to have coffee banned on health grounds. They argued that coffee was 'a vile worthless foreign novelty, that it was hot and not cold as alleged, that it burned up the blood, and so induced palsies, impotence, and leanness.'

The debate raged throughout Europe. The Swedish historian Victoria Martinez wrote that Carolus Linnaeus, the country's most famous naturalist, believed coffee caused everything from haemorrhoids and constipation to senility and sudden death. On the other hand, he thought that tobacco could prevent and treat a variety of diseases.

Sweden's King Gustav III also believed that coffee was bad for health. To prove it, he conducted what Ms Martinez called Sweden's first clinical trial. The King took two identical twin brothers, prisoners in one of his jails, and forced one to drink large amounts of coffee every day, while the other had to drink equal amounts of tea. As it turned out, the King died first, by assassination, in 1792, followed by the two doctors appointed to oversee the experiment. The tea-drinking prisoner died at the ripe old age of 83. The last to go – nobody quite knows when – was the prisoner who was supposed to experience an early death by coffee.

Caffeine was first chemically isolated in a German laboratory in 1819. It is an alkaloid, as is cocaine, that occurs naturally in some 60 tropical plant species, of which cocoa beans, tea leaves and coffee beans are the most well-known.

When coffee leaves die and fall to the ground, they contaminate the soil with caffeine, which makes it difficult for other plants to germinate; it acts as a natural herbicide. But coffee plants mainly use caffeine as an insecticide. It can be toxic to insects, and they tend to avoid it. But coffee plants also lace their nectar with low doses of caffeine. When insects feed on the nectar, they get a buzz that makes them more likely to revisit the flower and spread its pollen.

It's not just bees that get a buzz from caffeine. Ukers wrote that the French writer Balzac was a big fan, drinking a reported (but scarcely credible) 50 cups of coffee per day. In his Treatise on Modern Stimulants, Balzac describes the effect that caffeine had on him:

'This coffee falls into your stomach, and straight away, there is a general commotion. Ideas begin to move like the battalions of the Grand Army on the battlefield, and the battle takes place. Things remembered arrive at full gallop, ensign to the wind. The light cavalry of comparisons deliver a magnificent deploying charge, the artillery of logic hurry up with their train and ammunition, the shafts of wit start up like sharpshooters. Similes arise, the paper is covered with ink; for the struggle commences and is included with torrents of black water, just as a battle with powder.'

The author Mathew Walker is less of a fan. In his book Why We Sleep: The New Science of Sleep and Dreams, he describes caffeine as 'the most widely used (and abused) psychoactive stimulant in the world. It represents one of the longest and largest unsupervised drug studies ever conducted on the human race, perhaps rivalled only by alcohol, and it continues to this day.'

When caffeine hits your brain, it adheres to your brain's adenosine receptors. Adenosine is what makes us feel sleepy. When caffeine binds to your adenosine receptors, it inactivates them and stops you from feeling tired. Caffeine tricks us into feeling alert and awake despite the high levels of adenosine that would otherwise make us sleepy.

Caffeine is removed from our system by an enzyme in our liver that gradually degrades it over time. Caffeine has an average half-life of five to seven hours: after five to seven hours, about 50 per cent of the caffeine you have drunk is still circulating in the body. So, if you enjoy an espresso at 10 pm after dinner, as I used to do when I was younger, then half of the caffeine will still be in your brain at 3 am.

Some people have a more efficient version of this enzyme than others, allowing them to clear the caffeine quicker. Others have a slower, less efficient version. Unfortunately, ageing affects the enzyme's efficiency: the older we get, the longer it takes to clear our brains of caffeine.

Just because the caffeine is stopping our brain from processing the adenosine, it doesn't mean the brain stops producing it. When the caffeine inevitably wears off, it leaves you with an adenosine build-up which makes you feel even more tired - the 'caffeine crash'.

Coffee is a diuretic. Drinking too much coffee can lead to dehydration which, if combined with caffeine withdrawal and the adenosine build-up, can make you feel more tired than you would otherwise feel.

The good news is that roasted coffee does not just contain caffeine; it is full of biologically active compounds that reduce inflammation, serve as potential anticancer mechanisms, and improve insulin sensitivity.

In the 70s, researchers found that drinking coffee could increase the risk of various types of cancer. Scientists have since discredited these studies. In the 1970s, most coffee drinkers also smoked tobacco; it was the tobacco that caused cancer, not coffee.

But, incidentally, there was a reason why smoking and drinking coffee often went well together: the nicotine in tobacco changes the way that your body deals with caffeine, reducing the time it takes to clear it from your body. The two drugs are complementary: you will sleep better if you smoke a cigar with your after-dinner espresso. (But don't try it at home!)

In 2015, the US Department of Health and Human Services (HHS) issued dietary guidelines that, for the first time, recommended moderate coffee drinking as part of a healthy diet. At around the same time, the World Health Organisation (WHO) removed coffee from its list of possible carcinogens.

In 2017, the British Medical Journal published a review on coffee consumption and human health that examined more than 200 previous studies. It found that moderate coffee drinkers had less cardiovascular disease and less premature death from all causes, including heart attacks and stroke, than those who didn't drink coffee.

The latest scientific view, as published in the World Cancer Report 2020, confirms that coffee is full of antioxidants that reduce the risk of certain cancers. The report, published by the International Agency for Research on Cancer (IARC), part of the WHO, is considered an authoritative source on cancer-related disease.

The National Institutes of Health (NIH) – part of the US Department of Health and Human Services – has conducted a study of 400,000 people that confirmed that moderate coffee drinking lowers the risk of death overall. The study found that relative to men and women who did not drink coffee, those who consumed three or more cups of coffee per day had approximately a 10 per cent lower risk of death. The leader of the research team wrote:

'We found coffee consumption to be associated with a lower risk of death overall, and of death from a number of different causes. Although we cannot infer a causal relationship between coffee drinking and lower risk of death, we believe these results do provide some reassurance that coffee drinking does not adversely affect health.'

In 2020, the American Cancer Society (ACS) updated its guidelines for diet and physical activity, sharing evidence that coffee may help people reduce the chance of developing certain types of cancer. The ACS wrote:

'The potential mechanisms by which coffee may exert beneficial effects on the risk of some cancers are not completely understood. Hundreds of biologically active compounds, including caffeine, flavonoids, lignans, and other polyphenols, are found in roasted coffee. Research shows they can increase energy expenditure, inhibit cellular damage, regulate genes involved in DNA repair, have anti-inflammatory properties, and inhibit metastasis. Coffee also influences intestinal transit time and liver metabolism of carcinogens, and therefore these factors may also contribute to a lower risk for some digestive cancers.'

The scientific evidence is clear: in moderation, coffee is good for you. Moderate coffee consumption means 3 to 5 cups daily, or up to 400 milligrams of caffeine. There isn't much research on how higher doses might affect a person's health. However, too much caffeine can lead to shakiness, nervousness, and an irregular heartbeat.

The European Food Safety Authority (EFSA) agrees, saying it is safe for healthy adults, including pregnant women, to drink single doses of up to 200 milligrams of caffeine. They add that drinking up to 400mg of caffeine through the day does not raise safety concerns in the general population.

In 2020, the British Medical Journal (BMJ) reported a case of caffeine poisoning at the Queen Elizabeth Hospital in London when a 26-year-old patient ingested two heaped teaspoons of powdered caffeine (approximately 20 grams), equivalent to 50 or 60 cups of coffee. When she arrived at the hospital, she was experiencing palpitations, sweating, anxiety, and difficulty breathing; she also had an abnormally rapid heart rate and low blood pressure and was experiencing both hyperventilation and vomiting. The patient survived, discharged after seven days.

In a 2018 review of scientific journal articles, researchers in Rome identified only 92 reported deaths from caffeine overdose in the previous ten years. In general, caffeine will begin to affect the body if there are more than 15 milligrams per litre (mg/L) in the blood. A concentration of 80 to 100 mg/L can be fatal. The woman in the above case had 147 mg/l.

You are unlikely to get a caffeine overdose from drinking coffee; it usually results from taking a dietary supplement or caffeine tablets. Meanwhile, purified caffeine powder is highly dangerous and much more likely to cause an overdose.

But what about the way you prepare your coffee – does it make a difference?

A study published in JAMA Internal Medicine found that drinking filtered coffee is better for you than drinking boiled coffee – and that includes the French press (my favourite way of preparing my favourite drink). The oil in boiled coffee contains compounds called diterpenes, which are known to raise LDL, the bad cholesterol, and lower HDL, the good cholesterol. You can usually remove these compounds by filtering the coffee.

Switching to filter coffee may be better for your health. Still, the clinical significance of such small increases in cholesterol may be questionable, given that they are not associated with an increase in cardiovascular deaths.

In 2019, researchers at the Chalmers University of Technology in Sweden affirmed that coffee could help reduce the risk of Type 2 diabetes, but only if it is filtered. The study showed that people who drank two to three cups of filtered coffee per day had a 60 per cent lower risk of developing type 2 diabetes than people who drank less than one cup of filtered coffee a day. Consumption of boiled coffee showed no effect on the incidence of type 2 diabetes among study participants.

And what about the temperature at which you drink your coffee?

In 2016 the IARC classified 'very hot' or 'scalding hot' drinks as 'probably carcinogenic.' They wrote, 'Studies in places such as China, the Islamic Republic of Iran, Turkey, and South America, where people traditionally drink tea or mate very hot (at about 70 °C), found that the risk of oesophageal cancer increased with the temperature at which the beverage was drunk.'

That classification deemed 'very hot' to be 65°C (149°F) or higher. The Speciality Coffee Association's Certified Home Brewer requirements state that 'the container that receives the coffee must contain a coffee temperature of no less than 176°F and no more than 185°F.'

Although that sounds alarming, the temperature of the coffee by the time it reaches your mouth will almost certainly be lower than those temperatures. In a Q&A amended to the IARC's 2016 classification, the group wrote: 'The typical drinking temperature for tea and coffee in most parts of the world is below 65°C (149°F).'

What about if you are pregnant: Is it safe for you and for your baby to drink coffee?

Until recently, the consensus was that expectant mothers could continue to enjoy coffee in moderation, limiting daily caffeine intake equivalent to two cups of medium-strength cups of coffee (200mg of caffeine).

However, in 2020, a study published in the British Medical Journal (BMJ) analysed more than 1,200 reviews of caffeine's effect on pregnancy and found: 'Persuasive confirmation of increased risk ... for at least five major negative pregnancy outcomes: miscarriage, stillbirth, lower birth weight and/or small for gestational age, acute childhood leukaemia, and childhood overweight and obesity.'

The report's authors recommended that pregnant women should cut out coffee completely to help avoid miscarriage, low birth weight and stillbirth. The study made headlines around the world, but, in response, the British Coffee Association argued that it had failed to establish cause and effect; it urged pregnant women to stick to existing guidelines. It wrote:

'This new study is an observational study, so importantly does not show any direct cause-and-effect link and also is subject to confounding factors such as cigarette smoking and wider dietary issues, which may limit its ability to draw clear conclusions.'

So, if you are pregnant, I will leave you to make your own decisions. For the rest of us, there is no reason why anyone should give up coffee. But what happens if you do?

Caffeine causes blood vessels in the brain to constrict, which slows blood flow. Reducing or stopping your coffee intake allows blood vessels to open up and increases blood flow to the brain. This change in blood flow can cause withdrawal headaches that can vary in length and severity as the brain adapts to the increase in blood. Headaches will eventually subside as the brain adjusts to this increase in blood flow.

Strangely enough, although caffeine withdrawal can cause headaches, caffeine can be used to treat certain types of headaches such as migraines. A work colleague of mine suffered from terrible migraines, and the only thing that would stop them was a double espresso! Caffeine can also enhance the power of pain-relieving medications.

Caffeine is a stimulant that increases heart rate, blood pressure and the stress hormones cortisol and epinephrine. In people who are sensitive to caffeine, just one cup of coffee can cause them to feel jittery and anxious. While caffeine can cause feelings of anxiousness, cutting it out can have the same effect. In the short term, you may become more anxious and jittery from giving up coffee than from continuing to drink it.

We all know that coffee helps us to concentrate – and I have a cup on my desk as I write. It increases levels of adrenaline, as well as the neurotransmitters dopamine and norepinephrine, which raise your heart rate and blood pressure and stimulates your brain, resulting in increased alertness and improved focus. Phasing out caffeine can negatively impact your concentration.

Phasing out coffee may also leave you feeling depressed. Coffee's ability to block adenosine not only increases alertness, but it also improves your mood. A 2011 study of over 50,000 women found that women who drank four or more cups of coffee per day had a 20 per cent lower risk of depression than women who drank little or no coffee.

As well as getting depressed, you may also get irritable if you give up coffee. Coffee lovers are used to the mood-enhancing effects of caffeine and can miss it when they stop drinking it.

What about weight: Will you lose or gain weight if you give up coffee?

It depends on how you take your coffee. A Starbucks' Salted Caramel Mocha complete with mocha sauce, toffee nut syrup, steamed milk, sweetened whipped cream, caramel drizzle, and turbinado sugar, weighs in at 470 calories. Although it sounds delicious (I suppose), you are likely to lose weight if you cut it out from your daily routine.

Even if you avoid the sugars and fats in a latte, just adding cream and sugar to your homebrewed coffee could quickly push it to over 200 calories per serving. Giving up sweetened milky coffee could help you lose weight. However, if you drink your coffee black and unsweetened, you could gain weight if you give it up. Because coffee can temporarily suppress your appetite, you might find yourself eating more without it.

Common coffee withdrawal symptoms include headaches, tiredness, low energy, irritability, anxiety, poor concentration, depressed mood and tremors. There are ways to reduce these symptoms, including cutting back on caffeine gradually, staying hydrated and getting plenty of sleep. In any case, the symptoms do not last long, usually between two and nine days.

But given the short-term adverse effects of giving up coffee compared to the long-term health benefits of moderate coffee drinking, well, why would you give it up?

A Conversation with David Griswold

Good morning, David. First question: what coffee are you drinking?

I'm drinking an estate coffee from Guatemala called 'Finca El Valle'. It is from Antigua, Guatemala. Finca El Valle was the first direct trade estate partner I worked with, going back more than 25 years now, and it is a coffee I still buy for the same roaster. It was from a small speciality farm nestled at the foot of three volcanoes, owned by a determined woman, Christina Gonzales. Her husband and three sons supported her. It is a delicious coffee, with intense sweetness, with notes of brown sugar, nougat, and molasses.

There seems to quite a high percentage of women growing coffee.

Finca El Valle was the first farm where I worked with a woman-owned farm. It was an estate. Later, we began working with women-grown coffee from coops in the Las Hermanas project in 2003 in Nicaragua. While far from perfect, some of the economic reforms following the Sandinista Revolution provided women with the ability to seek joint ownership rights to the land they worked with their husbands. Many women have since been able to grow their coffee separately from their spouses. A group of about 140 women growers came together to form a cooperative, and we found that their coffees scored consistently high in cup quality.

Women-owned collectives score higher across the board than mixed-coffee collectives, and this data point is valid in most origins. When I asked the women leaders why this was, they told me it was because they take better care of growing, picking and processing their coffee than the men.

In addition to quality, our buyers prefer women-grown coffees because of the higher impact of their purchases. The purchase premiums go directly to the women's groups. World Bank studies have shown that, on average, 90 per cent of their increased income stays in the household. If you want to impact families and lives, supporting entrepreneurial women coffee growers is an excellent way to do it.

You were somewhat of a pioneer in sustainability when you started Sustainable Harvest in 1996.

That's true. It was an unusual approach to business at the time. When I tried to share my sustainable business concept three decades ago, I would typically have first to define the concept of sustainability. People were sceptical, as though I was trying to cover up a poorly produced coffee with a lovely story.

But then buyers would call me a week after I had left them samples and say: 'Wow, that coffee tastes incredible! Please tell me the story behind it!'

The coffee speaks for itself. I always thought that if I found the right places to grow coffee, and found the right people to manage it, then we could produce coffee to the level that meets the demands of the speciality coffee market—and all of it done sustainably.

How did you get into the coffee business?

It wasn't something I planned on. I'm from Colorado; my dad was a history professor, and my mom ran the university's international students' programme. I grew up in a household with guests from all over the world, with everyone speaking different languages. I spent a year abroad in Spain, where I learned Spanish.

After college, I worked at various non-profits and NGOs, eventually becoming the Director of Communications for a group called 'Ashoka' in Washington DC; it was there that I got a sense of the meaning of 'social entrepreneurship'.

In 1989, around the time coffee prices collapsed following the end of the ISA, Ashoka was supporting a national coffee farmer organiser in Mexico. I volunteered to go to Mexico City to help him figure out a way for producer cooperatives to combat the severe drop in farmer income.

One day, a farmer named Pedro came into our office with a bag of coffee that he had brought from northern Mexico, where he lived – a seven-hour bus ride away. He told me that 300 families were waiting for him to come home with an answer to how they were going to sell their coffee crop. It was the only cash crop they had, and they desperately needed to sell it.

He showed me his crop sample, this plastic bag filled with unhusked coffee still in parchment. I knew little about coffee at the time, but I knew enough to tell him that if he wanted to send a sample to a foreign buyer, he had to have the coffee hulled and sent green, not in parchment. But he didn't know this, nor have access to a machine to hull his coffee.

Even though I couldn't help Pedro sell his beans, I thought that maybe I could teach him how to sell his beans for himself—but that meant that I first had to figure out how commodity coffee worked. And that's what I've been doing for the past three decades.

That was when you started your own company?

Yes, in 1990. I first started Aztec Harvest; a company focused on the needs of Mexican farmers. In 1997, I wanted to bring in other origins and founded Sustainable Harvest. With the help of leading environmental and social groups, we developed a set of standards for coffee, and I wanted to introduce coffees to the US market that met those standards.

I had almost no trading knowledge, but I've learned a few lessons over the last 30 years. I have made every mistake a coffee trader can make. Those lessons are what now form the core principles of Relationship Coffee.

Some of those principles include investing profits back into farmer training, which includes things like teaching better coffee-processing methods or showing leaders of coffee farmer communities how to evaluate their coffee through taste. Another is prioritising transparency in critical aspects of the business—from sharing operating margins to direct trade relationships.

I came close several times to quitting coffee because I didn't fully understand how to play the game of commodity coffee. Still, each time I came close, I was lucky enough to catch a business break or have friends who encouraged me to press on.

How do you define your Relationship Coffee business model?

When I got into the coffee business, I decided that my role as a trader would be to bring buyers and sellers together in a transparent conversation, rather than keeping them from getting to know each other. I called this approach 'Relationship Coffee'. The coffee can be speciality or commodity, Fairtrade or organic. Still, the fundamental way I would conduct business would be in a direct and transparent relationship between buyer and seller.

Relationship Coffee is a business model that is about stakeholders working collaboratively toward a common good that benefits all of the many actors in the supply chain. The core values in Relationship Coffee are empathy, communication, transparency, and trust. It considers the needs of all the stakeholders, rather than just maximising the profits of one party. It puts people ahead of profits and takes into account both sides of the coffee equation.

I believed early on that business can be a force of social good, and I set out to build a company to serve that vision. Sometimes we need to remind our partners why the investments we make toward bringing the supply chain together are so critical. At the same time, I recognise that we need to make money. Sustainability necessitates economic viability.

Do you put buyers and sellers together for a commission?

No, we buy from the growers and operate just like the other commodity trading companies. We find coffees, and then we finance, ship, warehouse, and market them. I found that when you work on commission, you need to keep the parties from knowing each other; you don't want them to be cut you out of future deals. Instead, we focus on the value that we add to each of our customers.

Do you buy your coffee on a fixed price or basis the futures markets?

We do both, according to the right circumstances. But regardless of the chosen pricing mechanism, the goal is to achieve a sustainable price for all actors in the value chain.

Fixed price contracts can be tricky in volatile markets. We need our suppliers to understand how futures markets work, so we've been a pioneer in teaching our cooperatives financial tools like price risk management. We need them to know how to use the futures markets.

The key is to help the groups reach an agreement where quality, price, and value meet the needs of both sides while ensuring that farmers are making a living from coffee. We always seek prices for coffee growers that are above their cost of production. No matter what the 'C' market price, we need to be sure the farmer meets their basic needs, or we aren't fulfilling our brand promise.

Isn't this just stakeholder, rather than shareholder, capitalism?

We are a big proponent of stakeholder capitalism, and we were the first coffee company certified as a 'B Corporation'. We are not just concerned with shareholder value, but also the needs of other stakeholders, suppliers, employees, the community, and the environment.

The Stanford Graduate School has conducted case studies analysing our Relationship Coffee model. They noted that whereas a traditional model focuses on a buyer-seller approach, the collaborative model of Relationship Coffee brings more actors to the table. If more actors have a vested interest in how a business decision may impact the community, they can then bring in other resources. We must find new and innovative ways to get a wider group of diversified stakeholders to the table.

The first step is to ask: 'Who else needs to be in this circle of influence?' When the Relationship Coffee model reaches out beyond the traditional coffee supply chain, the benefits of stakeholder capitalism works.

Do you buy only certified coffee?

We source both certified and non-certified coffee. We also support third-party verification of our claims; it is more expensive, but it is more rigorous. By having experts in the field verifying the claims, we can focus on building relationships that go beyond certifications.

We want to know every farmer group that we buy from, and every farmer behind the beans we sell. We think that level of traceability is what many buyers will require in the coming years.

Are coffee farmers better off now than when you started 30 years ago?

I want to say we've made progress, but we're nowhere near declaring 'Mission Accomplished'. Recent data shows that the current generation of coffee farmers makes less than half of what their parents made.

As I look back on my career, I focus on our efforts to innovate and influence the industry and to educate producers. I hope we have helped thousands of producer leaders to play the game better. I hope we have built some long-term relationships that will stand the test of time.

If farmers are worse off, doesn't it mean that only the coffee quality has increased and that all your efforts have benefited the consumer and not the producer?

Producers have not received their fair share of the benefits that the speciality coffee market has generated. The most recent data shows that the producer nations' slice of the pie is a mere 10 per cent of the total coffee market value. That is not sustainable for a global market. The coffee market is not serving all its members. We're putting our supply chain at risk if we don't take serious action as individual companies to reverse this trend.

We've also had to help farmers look beyond just producing coffee. We're trying to develop internal markets. We are also exploring crop diversification and food security programs to create a multi-income model.

Domestic markets seem to play a role in improving farmer incomes.

Domestic markets are critical, and we see them as the next frontier when it comes to finding more ways to increase farmer incomes.

It challenges the traditional model of sourcing low-priced commodity coffee in the Southern Hemisphere which only serves to add value to buyers further up the value chain, generally those in the North. If Southern Hemisphere farmers can sell their coffee locally, they will often earn higher prices.

Brazil has had the most success in expanding its domestic market, and we're now seeing progress in other producing countries like India, Mexico, and Colombia.

What does the future hold for Sustainable Harvest?

There is so much more to do! I am excited about exploring the ways that coffee agriculture can slow—or even reverse—some of the impacts of climate change. I'm hopeful about the Next Generation of coffee producer leaders, and the new level of energy and innovation they are bringing to the industry.

We've learned a lot from our recent work with women's coffee programmes in Rwanda. We now want to help cooperatives in other coffee-producing countries explore retail and roasting operations for their domestic markets.

We're continuing to invest in technology, like our cup tasting app, Tastify®, to develop tools that allow people to communicate about coffee remotely. We're expanding and improving our online farmer training and are finding ways to expand innovative programs for women's entrepreneurship in rural coffee communities.

The impacts of COVID-19 will be long-lasting. Travel to coffee farms was a significant part of my coffee career, especially when working with clients who wanted to have more direct trade relationships. We'll have to work extra hard to build relationships using digital tools.

As technology continues to advance, I think we'll see an overall reduction in the amount of travel that buyers have to do.

We all will need more human connectivity. We will have to develop collaborative models to meet the immense challenges we face across the planet. The coffee farmer needs to be connected to the coffee consumer through an equitable supply chain.

To move forward as an industry, we need to connect at a basic human level, so I don't think innovations like blockchain alone can create meaningful relationships.

We need to bring the model to scale if we want to help our industry sustain itself. It starts with a liveable income for all actors in the supply chain.

That's an exciting world for us.

Do you think you could build a brand in roasted coffee?

I'd instead help farmers do it. On the one hand, I don't want to compete with my roaster clients. On the other, we have learned some vital lessons in our work, building roasted brands for domestic markets as we did with Question Coffee in Rwanda.

Okay, the last question. What's your favourite coffee? And how do you brew?

That's a dangerous one to answer—I would be upsetting farmers from the producing countries I don't mention! I can only say that I love many different coffees. My approach is to try all the coffees we import and have them expertly roasted by our incredible Quality Control team. I also buy online from one of our Sustainable Harvest roaster customers.

I brew using a La Marzocco G3 espresso machine.

Thank you, David, for your time and input!

Chapter 16: Take-aways

I believe humans get a lot done, not because we're smart, but because we have thumbs so we can make coffee.

— Flash Rosenberg

As you and I both come to the end of this book, I hope you have enjoyed reading it as much as I enjoyed writing it. Coffee is the most complex and exciting commodity that I have ever studied.

I have learned a lot on this journey of discovery, and I have been surprised by what I learned. Here are my ten top takeaways:

1. Coffee is good for you

I started drinking coffee in the 1970s when many people smoked a cigarette at the same time as they drank a cup of coffee. The newspapers of that period were full of articles about the cancer risks associated with coffee, and I can remember reducing my coffee consumption as a result.

Somehow, that negative view of coffee and health stayed with me over the years. They say that bad news sells newspapers; the good news that coffee doesn't cause cancer - and that it can help prevent it - never seems to have made it onto the front pages. I was delighted to discover that my lifelong coffee habit is actually good for my health – and that it will hopefully lead to a longer life, with many more cups of coffee on the way!

2. Coffee is environmentally friendly

Talking about good news never making a headline, I was also delighted to learn that coffee production is a victim rather than a culprit of global warming. There are, of course, nuances to this: shade-grown coffee is better for biodiversity and carbon emissions than sun-grown coffee and millers need to put more effort into treating wastewater from washed coffee. But overall, coffee is a lot more environmentally friendly than many other agricultural commodities.

My biggest surprise during my research was when I discovered that capsule coffee is not as bad as I had thought for the environment – and that it might even be more environmentally friendly than fresh brew. (I am going to have another capsule coffee to celebrate!)

3. Alfred Peet preferred tea

Alfred Peet is the hero of the coffee world, credited with increasing the consumption and quality of speciality coffee. Because of the renewed interest in coffee worldwide, he has also helped increase the consumption of commodity coffee. Coffee producers around the world are in his debt.

Imagine my surprise when I read that Alfred Peet preferred tea. In his book, The Coffee Visionary, Jasper Houtman quotes Alfred Peet as saying: 'In essence, tea is a more interesting product than coffee. Tea you can really compare to wine; there are as many teas as there are wines, with as many different flavours, colours and bouquets. In contrast with tea, coffee is a rather coarse product; the subtle difference that you see in tea, you can't find in coffee. Also, it is much more difficult to become a tea taster. I can teach anyone to become a great coffee taster in a few months, but with tea that takes much longer.'

However, given all that Alfred Peet did for the coffee business during his lifetime, we can probably forgive him this temporary lapse of judgement.

4. Coffee is cool

I was surprised when I learned that JAB paid about $1 billion for Peet's Coffee in 2012. At that time, Peet's had a roasting plant and 300 coffee shops in rented properties. To put that in perspective, Alfred Peet received about $2 million for the company when he sold it in 1979, the equivalent to $7.5 million today. Admittedly the company only had two outlets at the time.

I was also surprised when Nestlé paid about $425 million for a 68 per cent stake in Blue Bottle Coffee. At the time of the purchase, Blue Bottle operated 40 (leased) shops in the US and Japan, as well as selling direct to customers.

I was bewildered by the $7.15 billion that Nestlé paid Starbucks for the right to distribute Starbucks coffee through retail outlets outside Starbucks stores. Nestlé didn't buy anything - no shops, factories, or other infrastructure - other than the right to sell Starbucks products. If you ever wondered where the money is in coffee, then there is the answer.

Coffee companies now have valuations that approach those that the market puts on the stars of the tech world, such as Google, Microsoft or Facebook.

So yes, I have learned that coffee is now as cool as software.

5. Coffee is like beer

Many industries have seen consolidation over the past half-century with companies changing hands quicker than cards in a game of Snap. Famous and familiar brands have ended up in the hands of hedge funds or private family offices. However, both beer and coffee have arguably seen more frenzied M&A activity than many other sectors.

There have seen similar drivers in both industries; consolidators have reached out for economies of scale in marketing and distribution (rather than in production), more significant market (negotiating) power, and better financial management. The result has been a greater industry concentration along with a corresponding increase in the value of roasters and retailers compared to merchants and producers.

6. Coffee is like wine

It did not come as a surprise to me to learn that small coffee farmers are an endangered species; they are in every sector. In 1840, for example, agriculture employed 70 per cent of the American workforce; the figure today is 1.3 per cent. In 1935, there were 7 million farms in the US; today, there are less than 2 million.

Smallholder farmers are being squeezed out across the food chain. Compared to large farms, smallholders are inefficient and uneconomic. As societies develop and become more prosperous, these smallholders are better off doing something other than farming. Well-meaning consumers and activists who want to maintain smallholders are maintaining poverty.

This argument doesn't necessarily apply to the world of speciality coffee where each origin, altitude and farm have their terroir and their characteristics. Corn is the same, whether it is grown in the US or Brazil. Coffee is not. Speciality coffee is like wine.

There are industrial-sized wine estates which produce a perfectly drinkable wine year after year, just as the big coffee estates in Brazil and Vietnam make a perfectly drinkable coffee that is the same each year. Some outstanding small vineyards produce a small amount of wine that varies from year to year depending on the weather (among other factors). Consumers are willing to pay the price that is necessary to keep these small wineries in business; they are also willing to pay what is required to keep the smaller coffee estates in business.

Many coffee drinkers are like many wine drinkers: they develop a strong relationship with their favourite coffee and feel a connection with the farmer that grows it.

If we as consumers want to maintain choice, along with our favourite coffees, we will pay enough to provide a living wage for the farmers to keep on growing it. If we do not value a particular farmer's coffee enough to pay him a price that allows him a living wage, then he - or his children – will have to grow, or do, something else. We must not maintain coffee farmers in poverty just because we want cheap coffee.

I do not share the pessimism expressed by some of the people I have interviewed. If producers grow coffee that consumers want to drink, then consumers will pay for it. And consumers want to drink a lot of good coffee.

What's more, coffee has an advantage over wine: it is much cheaper.

7. Roasters are good guys

I began this book with the preconceived idea that companies such and Nespresso and Starbucks sold coffee that was just good enough (but no more) to keep consumers drinking it and that they paid their farmers just enough (but no more) to keep producing it. I also imagined that big company sustainability programmes were centred more on PR and marketing than on the welfare of their farmers and the planet.

I was wrong on all counts. Roasters put enormous effort into continually improving both the quality and the variety of their coffee (look at Nespresso's Reviving Origins and Starbucks Reserve coffees). These big roasters know that if they want to continue to source good coffee, they have to pay farmers a good enough price that farmers and their children continue to produce it.

The roasters also know that if they want to keep selling their coffee to the new generation of coffee drinkers, they have to put sustainability right up there – at the same level, if not higher – with price and quality. As we have seen, consumers may not pay extra for certified coffee, but they may not buy it if it isn't.

And thank goodness that roasters are stepping up to the mark. As Dave Berhends, the founder of FarmerConnect and head trader at Sucafina told me: 'We would say that the raw green coffee spend is about $20 billion a year, while consumers spend $200 billion a year. It doesn't make sense to me that it should be left to the $20 billion industry to try to solve the problems of farmers. We have to get the consumer involved. It makes a lot more sense.'

Consumers and roasters have the market power - and the responsibility that goes with it - to effectuate positive change all along the supply chain. And they are doing it.

8. Traders have a role to play

Most people don't understand that commodity traders are efficient at what they do. They are less efficient when it comes to certifying that their commodities have not negatively impacted on social and environmental welfare.

But one thing that I am fascinated by – and which I only picked up on when writing this book – is that trade houses are in the best place in the supply chain to implement the changes that roasters and consumers want to see. The trade houses can use their supply chains in one direction to source and market the coffee that consumers want to buy, and in the other direction to implement the social and environmental projects that consumers want to see implemented.

Traders have a role to play in managing and coordinating this two-way traffic along the coffee supply chain. In one direction, they merchandise coffee from farmer to roaster. In the other direction, they act as a conduit for social and environmental sustainability programmes.

Managing these programmes on behalf of civil society (the NGOs) and governments has become a revenue stream for the traders; in some cases, they may earn more money moving these programmes upstream than they do moving coffee downstream.

You might not like to hear that traders are being paid to implement these programmes but remember the rule is that if something is not profitable, it is not sustainable.

Which brings me on to an old theme of mine: trade houses must improve their public image. Physical commodity merchants, rather than being seen for the good that they do, are often perceived as evil speculators, accused of pushing food prices higher, creating shortages and hunger.

As a sector, we have to explain to the world what we do, to show the public that we are under the same pressures and constraints—and have the same challenges—as everyone else. And we must also explain that we are not perfect, that there is progress to be made, but that we are trying to make that progress.

9. You can't fix the world's problems with the price of coffee

The role of price is to balance supply and demand. It doesn't always do an excellent job at it, but as Winston Churchill once famously said about democracy: 'It is the worst system apart from all the others.'

Price is there to balance supply and demand; it is not there to make everyone happy. Price does its job by making people unhappy: if the price is high then consumers are unhappy because they have to cut back on consumption; if it is low, producers are unhappy – so much so that they reduce production.

And as Jan Lühmann so rightly said earlier in this book, merchants and roasters are not the poor farmers' enemy; the greatest enemy of a poor farmer is a wealthy farmer (in another country).

One of the worst flaws of market pricing is that it does not correctly price the externalities – the indirect costs of pollution or environmental degradation. It is the role of government to fill this gap – to price in these externalities and recover the costs through taxation.

It sounds harsh, but if the coffee price is so low that growers can no longer afford to send their children to school, the answer is not to make coffee more expensive, but to make the school free.

Although that sounds simple, it isn't.

When I asked an old coffee hand what he would like to read in a book about coffee, he told me that I should make sure that I get the message across that coffee is complicated, and that there are no simple solutions. 'For every complicated problem,' he told me, 'there is a simple solution that won't work.'

10. Everyone loves coffee

Having spent my working life in the commodities business, I am used to the look my friends give me when I start to talk about the markets that I know best: sugar, grains and oilseeds. I have found that when I talk about coffee, everyone listens. People want to know All About Coffee: where it comes from, the best origins, the best varieties, and the best way to make it. People have a connection with coffee that they don't have with other foodstuffs – not even with coffee's most comparable commodity, cocoa.

Talk about sugar, and the conversation soon turns to the obesity epidemic. Talk about palm oil, and the conversation soon turns to orangutans. Talk about wheat, and people will tell you about their gluten allergy. Talk about soy, and you get blamed for deforestation in the Amazon. Talk about corn, and you get into an argument about the merits of ethanol. But talk about coffee, and everyone wants to know more.

In the public eye, sugar traders can go to hell, but coffee traders will go to heaven.

When my children were younger, when they asked me for advice, my answer was always the same: 'Follow your heart.' If they were to ask me now, I would reply: 'Follow your heart, but take coffee with you!'

Bibliography

In 1905, William H. Ukers, the founder and, at that time, editor of the Tea and Coffee Trade Journal, began research for his book All About Coffee. It took him 17 years to complete, personally visiting many of the countries where coffee is grown, as well as libraries around the world where he researched coffee's history. He drew on a network of agents around the world to help him, as well as on medical professionals, botanists and engineers to help him with all aspects of his favourite drink.

The final work, running at over 700 pages, was published in 1922. Since then, it has become the definitive reference work for most of the books that have since been written about coffee. I have also drawn heavily on All About Coffee for this book, especially for my chapters on the history of our favourite beverage.

The full, original, version of All About Coffee can be downloaded for free from the Guttenberg Project website. In 2012, Adams Media published an abridged version of the book, still called All About Coffee, which can be obtained at all the usual outlets.

For more recent history – especially for the chapter on market intervention – I have drawn on the following two works:

Uncommon Grounds: The History of Coffee and How It Transformed Our World, by Mark Pendergast

Coffee: A Global History, by Jonathan Morris.

I recommend both books to anyone interested in learning more of the history of our favourite beverage. Other books that have helped me in my research include:

The Blue Bottle Craft of Coffee: Growing, Roasting, and Drinking, with Recipes, by James Freeman, Caitlin Freeman, Tara Duggan

The World Atlas of Coffee: From beans to brewing – coffees explored, explained and enjoyed, by James Hoffmann

Coffeeland: A History, by Augustine Sedgewick

The Devil's Cup: Coffee, the Driving Force in History, by Stewart Allen

The Coffee Visionary: The Life and Legacy of Alfred Peet, by Jasper Houtman

The Monk of Mokha, by Dave Eggers

A Coffee Dream, by Andrea Illy

The Coffee Trader, (a novel) by David Liss

God in a Cup: The Obsessive Quest for the Perfect Coffee, by Michaele Weissman

A Rich and Tantalizing Brew: A History of How Coffee Connected the World, by Jeanette M. Fregulia

The Coffee Paradox: Global Markets, Commodity Trade and the Elusive Promise of Development, by Benoit Daviron and Stefano Ponte

Selling Sustainability Short: The Private Governance of Labor and the Environment in the Coffee Sector (Organizations and the Natural Environment), by Janina Grabs

Food Citizenship: Food System Advocates in an Era of Distrust, by Ray Goldberg

Innovation and Its Enemies – Why People Resist New Technologies, by Calestous Juma

Why We Sleep: The New Science of Sleep and Dreams, by Matthew Walker

Food of the Gods: The Search for the Original Tree of Knowledge - A Radical History of Plants, Drugs, and Human Evolution, by Terence McKenna

Where the Wild Coffee Grows: The Untold Story of Coffee from the Cloud Forests of Ethiopia to Your Cup, by Jeff Koehler

The Craft and Science of Coffee, by Britta Folmer

How Bad Are Bananas? The Carbon Footprint of Everything, by Mike Berners-Lee

Silent Spring, by Rachel Carson

The Scent of a Dream: Travels in the World of Coffee, by Sebastiao Salgado and Marion Brenner

Greed is Dead: Politics After Individualism, by Paul Collier and John Kay

I have also drawn on the following published papers:

The Coffee Exporter's Guide, published by the International Trade Centre

Ensuring Economic Viability and Sustainability of Coffee Consumption, by Jeffrey Sachs, Kaitlin Y. Cordes, James Rising, Perrine Toledano, and Nicolas Maennling from the Colombia Centre on Sustainable Investment

A Blueprint for Water Security in the Coffeelands – SCAA

Do smallholder farmers benefit from sustainability standards? A systematic review and meta-analysis - Eva-Marie Meemken, University of Copenhagen, Denmark

The International Coffee Organisation 1963-2013: 50 years serving the world coffee community.

Acknowledgements

I would like to thank Nicolas Tamari for encouraging me to write this book and for introducing to many of his contacts.

I would also like to thank all the people whom I interviewed and published - as well as the people whom I interviewed, but who preferred not to be named.

I would also like to thank my 'Readers Committee' for reading innumerable drafts of this book, for their advice, their kindness and their patience: Ivo Sarjanovic; Gert ter Voorde, Swithun Still; Jan Lühmann; and Chris von Zastrow.

I also thank Daim Hall, our graphic designer, for another brilliant book cover.

Finally, I would like to give huge thanks to Shirin Moayyad for introducing me to her coffees. Throughout my research, I repeatedly asked people which coffee they preferred. No one has yet asked me that question but if they did, I would without any doubt reply: 'Anything from Sweet Bean Coffee in Etoy, Switzerland.'

About the Author

Jonathan Kingsman has spent over 40 years in agricultural commodities. After obtaining a master's in economics from Cambridge University, he began his career with Cargill, working in their sugar-trading department in both Minneapolis and London. He then moved on to the brokerage side of the business, first on futures and then on physicals.

In 1990, he founded Kingsman SA, which he developed into a leading analytical research company in sugar and biofuels. In 2012, the company was acquired by what is now S&P Global Platts.

Jonathan retired from the markets in 2015 and has since become a blogger and author. He has previously published Sugar Casino, Commodity Conversations – An Introduction to trading Agricultural Commodities, and The New Merchants of Grain – Out of the Shadows.

Jonathan is married with four children, three of whom have followed him into the world of commodities. He lives in Lausanne, Switzerland.

You can find Jonathan's blog posts on
www.commodityconversations.com